THE HAPPY HACK

Mike Molloy was born during an air raid on 22 December 1940. He began art school at the age of thirteen, but at fifteen ran away to join the *Sunday Pictorial* as a messenger boy. The editor, Colin Valdar, took a shine to him and sent him back to art school whilst employing him part time in the art department.

Later, after two years on the *Daily Sketch*, Molloy was hired by the *Daily Mirror*, which was then the best-selling newspaper in the world with a daily circulation of over five million copies. He held various roles on the *Mirror*: including associate editor of 'Mirrorscope', and editor of *Mirror Magazine*. Finally, he was appointed editor of the *Daily Mirror*. After ten tumultuous years, simultaneously fighting Rupert Murdoch's *Sun* and the militant press unions, Robert Maxwell bought the Mirror Group, but instead of firing him, as Molloy expected, Maxwell made him editor-in-chief.

When he and Maxwell reached a parting of the ways, Molloy began to write and published several novels and children's books. He also returned to painting and has exhibited twice at the Galerie Aalders in the South of France and four times in London. His work has also been accepted by the Royal Academy Summer Exhibition.

Mike Molloy

THE HAPPY HACK

A Memoir of Fleet Street in Its Heyday

Foreword by Michael Parkinson and Anne Robinson

JOHN BLAKE

Published in Great Britain by
John Blake Publishing Limited
3 Bramber Court, 2 Bramber Road
London W14 9PB

www.johnblakebooks.com

www.facebook.com/johnblakebooks 📘
twitter.com/jblakebooks 📧

First published in paperback in 2016

ISBN: 978-1-78418-651-7

British Library Cataloguing-in-Publication Data:

A catalogue record for this book is available from the British Library.

Design by www.envydesign.co.uk

Printed in Great Britain by CPI Group (UK) Ltd

1 3 5 7 9 10 8 6 4 2

Papers used by John Blake Publishing are natural, recyclable products made
from wood grown in sustainable forests. The manufacturing processes conform
to the environmental regulations of the country of origin.

Every attempt has been made to contact the relevant copyright-holders,
but some were unobtainable. We would be grateful if the appropriate
people could contact us.

Whenever Lord Northcliffe, the greatest of the Edwardian press barons, was asked a difficult question by a reporter he would wag an admonishing finger and say, 'Don't think you can trick me like that, young man, I'm like the boy in the jam factory: I know how it's made.'

CONTENTS

PART II: THE SPECTRE OF MAXWELL

FOREWORD BY
MICHAEL PARKINSON

I was twenty-five when I came to Fleet Street and a job
as a features writer on the *Daily Express*. After two
years on the *Manchester Guardian* (as it then was) it felt
a bit like exchanging the groves of academia for a period
in Bedlam. The *Daily Express* in the early sixties sold 4.3
million copies a day; if you travelled abroad you went first
class, the features department had more than thirty writers
on staff, competing for a couple of spaces on the features
page. One of my colleagues, tired of going into the office
and not being given a job, started working from home. In
three years he had one article published but no one noticed
and no one cared. Those were the daft carefree days.
Television loomed but we were told it wouldn't last. I was
asked to do a screen test for ITN but was told if the bosses
found out I'd be sacked. I did it anyway under an assumed
name. It was dreadful. The boss, Geoffrey Cox, was kind.

'Television is not for you,' he said. Later he was knighted for his significant contribution to the industry.

We drank a lot, stayed out all hours and thought life was a cabaret. Into this world came a remarkable young man whom I didn't meet until much later, in which time he – a young art student who was hired as a part-time 'dogsbody' by the *Daily Mirror* – became editor from 1974 to 1984 and editor-in-chief until 1989, creating a reputation for popular serious journalism as well as fun and frolic which caused the publisher of this book to describe him as 'the first Fleet Street rock 'n' roll editor.' He has his own significant place on the Honours Board of Grub Street. He summed up thus: 'It all had to come to an end, we all knew that. Only a former Fleet Street employee can really know the surreal world in which we ended up. When I was made editor of the *Daily Mirror* in 1974 my staff was looked on by management as a beacon of rectitude, compared to the bizarre excesses of the print unions. But I had a motoring correspondent who was banned from driving, a gardening correspondent with no garden, a slimming editor who was a stone overweight; a travel editor who was barred from flying British Airways, and a delightful feature writer who hadn't written an article in five years. Six years later we gave him a farewell dinner at the Ritz Hotel – and he still hadn't written anything.'

Looking back at what he calls 'those hilarious years,' he concludes: 'We were sure Fleet Street would be there for ever. Then one day the accountants told the owners it made sense to move, and suddenly it was all gone with the wind.'

Foreword

Every few weeks or so a half-dozen of those who worked alongside him or simply admired him both as a man and an editor meet, yarn, eat and drink and generally feel a lot better for it. During one of our meetings the subject of the book came up. The publisher was looking for a suitable title – I looked at my friend who, as usual seemed to be having a marvellous time, and said, without having to think, '*The Happy Hack*'. It summed up not just the life of Mike Molloy, but the joy we all felt about being in Fleet Street before the world changed.

MICHAEL PARKINSON

FOREWORD BY ANNE ROBINSON

I joined the *Daily Mirror* as a bright, eager, thirty-something whose previous experience was a decade at the *Sunday Times*. I should have arrived with body armour. From the quiet, polite, collegiate atmosphere of a senior common room, I entered a Wild West saloon.

Discussions at morning conference ranged from politics, philosophy and events of the day to who had shagged whom and who was worth shagging.

By one in the afternoon the newsroom had emptied for the start of a three- or four-hour lunch. The evenings were no less indulgent. Yet we produced some great newspapers.

Not least because Mike Molloy was one of the most talented of twentieth-century editors; handsome, erudite and mischievous. For a decade he ruled with tolerance and humour and allowed his executives, even green ones like me, to operate without interference. I owe him a great debt.

Fleet Street might have been heading for an almighty crash. But the *Daily Mirror*, with an economy equivalent of a small country rich in oil, was the most fabulously exciting place to work. 'There are no budgets, Blossom,' Mike explained, when once I was naïve enough to ask how much I could spend.

The Happy Hack is a jaw-dropping, page-turning, account of the fun we had.

ANNE ROBINSON

PART I
BEFORE MAXWELL

Chapter 1

PUBLISH AND BE DAMNED

In the early summer of 1956, I began work as a Fleet Street messenger boy, the job I'd applied for five months after my fifteenth birthday. It proved to be the luckiest decision of my life. Recently, I'd been idling away my time at Ealing Junior School of Art, a type of establishment, now long abolished, that prepared pupils for entry to the senior art school. Once there, students could prepare for a teaching diploma.

My parents hoped that a teaching career would provide me with a respectable living, but the idea filled me with foreboding. The man who'd encouraged me to go to art school was a dark, melancholy figure known as 'Pop' Reed. Although of average height, he seemed bigger because of his thick body. His head was on the large side, too, with bold, fleshy features and hooded eyes.

Pop Reed had been a brilliant student at the Royal College of Art, but somewhere along the way he'd abandoned his plans to be a painter and drifted into teaching youths like me, who, for the most part, displayed the higher feelings of farmyard animals.

Despite Pop Reed's encouragement, I had no desire to devote myself to art. Drawing was just something I could do a bit, like riding a bike or whistling; still, it proved enough to pass the examination.

Once I was there, it was clear that we junior art students were simply an unwanted appendage to the rest of the school, which was studying conventional academic subjects. But the headmaster, a wintry character called Faukes, suffered from the delusion that he was running a much grander Establishment school, and we, the art section, let the side down.

After a few days, at the morning assembly, Faukes directed his remarks to us members of the new intake. Grasping the collar of his gown, he began to speak in a curiously growling manner, as if he were chewing his words.

'In previous years this school took its students from the cream of Middlesex,' he began. We glanced about us incredulously. It was obvious this hotchpotch of boys and girls were of average merit. How had Faukes transformed them in into his fantasy of gilded youth?

He continued: 'This year's intake is the first ever to be granted places without interviews.' He paused significantly. 'It is an experiment that is never going to be repeated. From Monday, the new intake will commence instruction from our newly appointed elocution teacher.'

This announcement presented no problem for me. My mother had a pleasant voice, with a slight trace of her Durham upbringing as a publican's daughter. My father had been born and brought up in Paddington's Lisson Grove, a place Eliza Doolittle claimed 'weren't fit for pigs', but a lifetime of reading three library books a week had given him a fair command of the mother tongue.

Although I'd attended state schools, the staff and pupils tended to use what we might term BBC English. However, my own tones were occasionally influenced by the longish periods I'd spent in rural Durham.

In the years, after my grandparents had given up keeping pubs, they'd lived as tenants on a grand estate, in a mews cottage festooned with honeysuckle. It was across a stable yard from a Georgian house occupied by a solicitor, his wife and their two young children, Emily and Thomas. As I was the same age as Emily, I was invited to share her days in the nursery under the supervision of the nanny. There, my accent was gentled, and the nanny even taught me to read from a set of children's books that had been in Emily's family for generations.

When I returned home to the suburb of Alperton, I sounded pretty much like Little Lord Fauntleroy. Upper-class accents were far more polished and precise in those days; consequently, I was mocked by my friends, who spoke with more slovenly vowels. So I learned to speak with two tongues: the accent of west London and the smarter tones of a BBC newsreader. Also, my best friend, Clive Bowler, had, since he was a small boy, wanted to be an actor. Because of his influence we'd been going to the theatre since we were able to see over the ticket counter.

Elocution lessons were nothing: I was undaunted by a few instructions in rolling my R's, articulating my vowels and speaking from the diaphragm. The rest of the time, apart from lessons in English grammar and literature, mathematics, geography and history, was spent drawing plants, lettering in the Roman style, mastering perspective, understanding the composition of pictures, and the theory of colour.

After the first year I was bored to distraction. Eventually, for relief, I would stay away from the classrooms for longer and longer periods and read in the library. I was never challenged – who would expect to find someone playing truant *inside* the school?

It was in the school library that I came upon a book that changed my life. *Publish and Be Damned*, by Hugh Cudlipp, tells the story of the men who, in the early years of the twentieth century, had fashioned the *Daily Mirror* from its failed beginning as a newspaper for gentlewomen into the most popular and politically influential publication in Britain.

Cudlipp told the story with such engaging gusto I was fired with a desire to see what life was like on a newspaper: particularly one of the *Mirror*'s political persuasions. Cudlipp had applied for a job on the *Mirror* after seeing a small ad in London's *Evening Standard*. When I'd finished the book, there then occurred one of those Dickensian coincidences that can sometimes happen in real life.

I looked at the classified pages of my father's copy of the *Evening Standard,* something I had never done before. And there were a few lines announcing that the *Daily Mirror* was offering a single year's employment for messenger boys.

I knew immediately what I would do. My plan was to apply for one of these temporary jobs on the *Mirror* and then, after a year's employment in the big city, return to art school as a man of the world. I was confident that I could re-enrol with a plausible excuse for my year-long absence.

I didn't for a moment expect to make a career in journalism. The idea of working with the written word seemed out of the question, as I was aware that I had a problem in that department: I was dyslexic. This condition – the inability to spell because of word blindness – was hardly understood in my childhood. Reading presented no problem because I see words as overall shapes, but spelling can sometimes prove impossible.

By good fortune, my part-time nanny in the North had taught me to read by recognising whole words rather than breaking them down into individual characters. Had I been taught in the conventional way I might have had trouble reading for the rest of my life.

But, even so, my most influential teacher, Mr Fowler, was puzzled by the gulf between my grasp of subjects during discussions in the classroom and my inability to write an essay that was not pockmarked with infantile spelling errors. 'If you could manage to take more care with your written work you could be quite good at this,' he said with a sad shake of his head.

Now, however, the *Mirror*'s advertisement acted like a clarion call. My father was not happy about my decision, but, reluctantly, he agreed, probably because, at the age of sixteen, he'd lied about his age and, against his own parents' wishes, had enlisted in the army. A year later he'd found himself on India's Northwest Frontier as a trooper in the 11th Hussars, where he'd wake up each morning to find his downy chin being lathered by a servant before being shaved in bed.

We took two newspapers at home, the *Daily Express* and the *Mirror,* but the *Mirror* was closer to our way of thinking: its politics were our politics.

I was born into the Labour Party; the only member of my family who didn't vote for Clem Attlee was Uncle Howard, who was a communist. But, still, the attitudes of my family were hardly revolutionary. They thought if people were ambitious enough to work their way up in life, or were prepared to face the stress and worry of self-employment, then they deserved what they earned.

By the age of fourteen I'd already become hooked on politics, and, looking back, I realise I was a bit of a prig when I railed against my father's relative contentment compared with my own dissatisfaction with the injustice of the world.

My father, whose views on life were shaped by his long experience as a soldier, held a more pragmatic view of human nature. 'I've known decent people in every walk of life,' he told me, 'and some nasty bastards from all classes.'

I would discover just how true his words were as I continued along the journey I was about to begin.

Chapter 2

THE JOURNEY BEGINS

Having abandoned school, I set out on the half-hour journey to Fetter Lane, a turning off High Holborn. This byway, leading to Fleet Street, was still gapped with bomb sites, like missing teeth in an ancient smile. At the head of the lane overlooking Holborn Circus, was a vast building site, designated to be the Mirror Group's new headquarters.

At the centre of the Circus was an equestrian statue of Prince Albert. Never would I have imagined that one day I would have an animated conversation with the Queen about that statue.

At the Fleet Street end of Fetter Lane was a scattering of shops – all that remained of a little high street that had once served the working-class inhabitants who had been bombed out in the winter of 1940. Later, I discovered that I'd been born during that air raid – but in the safety of a nursing home in Hertfordshire. My father, who was on leave, said that when he'd left the hospital before dawn the sky over London glowed red with the fires.

Fetter Lane contained four public houses, but the most imposing building was the churchlike Public Records Office, which overlooked the three-storeyed *Mirror* building. The floors of this building were piled on top of one another in diminishing tiers, like those of a wedding cake. It was set back beyond a wide asphalt yard crammed with motorcars and lorries, where the gigantic rolls of newsprint were discharged.

It turned out the jobs on the *Daily Mirror* were filled, so I had been assigned to its sister paper, the *Sunday Pictorial*, whose offices were located in Geraldine House, a more conventional Edwardian building across from the Public Record Office (now known as the National Archives), its façade forming the third boundary of the *Mirror*'s publishing yard. I presented myself at the doorman's cubicle and told the uniformed figure – who, I would learn, was called Horace – that I was reporting for duty. He handed me a door key, an armful of post and a large bundle of newspapers rolled in brown paper.

'Third floor, the door opposite the lift gates,' he said sharply. 'It's your job to open up.'

Next to the staircase was an old-fashioned caged lift. I struggled with the concertina gate and my pile of post. Before I pressed the button, a tall, rather shambling figure wearing a heavy, dark-blue overcoat and a homburg hat also entered. He looked at me without expression and I said, 'Good morning, sir.' 'Good morning,' he replied, in rather a high-pitched voice. We were not to speak again for another seven years.

The door I unlocked revealed a room about thirty feet wide

and fifty long. This space was filled with metal desks, some standing alone, others pushed together, each desk equipped with a telephone, the lead dangling from the ceiling, and a typewriter. Wire baskets were piled high with books and papers. The linoleum floor was scarred with cigarette burns and the ceiling stained brown from rising smoke. Banks of filing cabinets stood against the walls piled with telephone directories, and there were a few smaller offices with half-metal walls topped with reeded glass. A battered wooden desk was placed just inside the door, where I deposited my load.

I looked about me and tried to guess the function of each area. The wall opposite the entrance had large windows overlooking a glazed-brick light well. An art table rigged with an Anglepoise lamp stood next to a large plan chest piled with art equipment. Another pair of desks pushed together had a bank of telephones. At the far end of the room was a long wooded desk surrounded by chairs. The tops of the filing cabinets in that area were heaped with boxes of flashbulbs. In all, the room contained seating for thirty-five people.

With nothing yet to do I began sorting the post. By the time I'd finished I was joined by a new arrival. He was a neat, hunched figure with suspicious eyes fringed by a lock of dark hair falling over his forehead. He hung up a gabardine raincoat and looked me over.

I'm Tap,' he said. 'Arthur Tapping. I'm in charge of the *Sunday Pictorial* tape room. What's your name?'

'Michael Molloy, sir,' I answered.

'What do they call you? Michael? Mick? Mike?' he asked. Here was an interesting decision. My mother insisted my family call me Michael. But, to friends, I'd always been Mick. Suddenly I had a chance to break with the past and start making myself a new man-of-the-world identity.

'Mike,' I decided.

'Right, Mike, I'll take you around with the post,' he said. 'From tomorrow you do it on your own. You call me Tap.'

We began a tour of the paper's other satellite offices in Geraldine House. The sports department stood, self-contained, away from the rest of the paper. Down a long corridor was Rex North's office. Rex was the *Sunday Pictorial* diary writer. Newspaper diaries didn't bother much with show business in the fifties. 'Café society' still dominated the columns. It was a world where a ragtag of debutantes, Guards officers, fading aristocrats and slightly shady 'businessmen' went to nightclubs togged up in dinner jackets and long frocks.

Like the rest of the journalists, Rex had not yet arrived, but his secretary had. I was introduced to Annie Bishop, a great-looking, red-headed girl who had a smile to lighten anyone's day. We have remained friends for the whole of our lives.

Another office was shared by Bernard McElwaine, a feature writer, and Paul Boyle, the television critic. It also served as an anteroom on the route to the offices of the editor and his secretary. Bernard and Paul's secretary, Trixie Newburgh, was at her desk. And so was Sadie Zussman, the editor's secretary. These two rather grand ladies smiled on me in a kindly fashion.

'I've got one rule,' said Tap, as we returned to the newsroom. 'When in doubt, shout out.'

Tap further explained my duties and I was surprised to learn I would never handle reporters' copy. That was a man's job.

Messenger boys fetched tea, brought cigarettes and delivered packages about London. Only union membership entitled men to carry the copy. When a journalist shouted, 'Boy,' his call was answered by a man. But often the slowness of their response bordered on that wonderful army charge: 'dumb insolence'.

These men tended to see themselves as members of their union rather than employees of the newspaper and often looked upon the journalists as class enemies. In those postwar years the them-and-us attitude had gradually replaced the wartime all-in-it-together type of cooperation that I could still actually remember.

When I was a toddler, for instance, my mother was taking me home from a brutal session at the dentist. My mouth was bleeding and I was crying with the pain. As we passed Alperton Bus Garage a driver standing on the opposite side of the road called out, 'What's the matter with him, missus?'

'He's had a bad time at the dentist,' she replied.

'Have you got far to go, love?' he asked.

'About twenty minutes,' said my mother.

'Hang on,' said the driver.

To my mother's astonishment he went into the garage and re-emerged driving a double-decker bus. 'Hop in,' he called out.

The estate where we lived was a long walk from a bus stop and the sight of a gigantic double-decker stopping on our tranquil street is a memory that has stayed with me through life.

Arthur Tapping was an exception to the hostile attitude. Tap's integrity was granite-like. He'd seen a lot of action in the North Atlantic and he regarded the *Sunday Pictorial* as his ship. He considered his work an honourable job and never concealed his contempt for those who didn't.

By 10.30 that first day the newsroom was bustling. I was enchanted to see how the staff matched the characters portrayed in films. Men wore trilby hats, some bowties. The two women reporters also wore hats, and elegantly tailored two-piece suits.

But it was the conversation that impressed me most. Sharp, funny banter flashed between them, typewriters clattered and the air filled with cigarette smoke.

'They work hard,' I ventured to Tap. He smiled ironically. 'Tuesdays are the first day of the week on a Sunday newspaper. They're doing their expenses.'

The deputy news editor, Peter Hawkins, a tall, languid man, called out to the reporters in general, 'Has anyone seen Ray Wilson? I thought he was coming in for a freelance shift this morning.'

A reporter called Comer Clark answered in a drawling voice, 'He's lying low. He broke up with Jack Murray's wife last Friday.'

'What's this I've missed?' asked Madeleine McLaughlin, one of the two women reporters.

'You've been on holiday,' answered Comer.

'So, has Ray been with Gloria Murray?' she asked.

'It was a lightning romance,' Comer said. 'Jack Murray walked out on Gloria and the kids the day after you went on holiday. Gloria went mad. She called up the news editor to say she'd been left flat broke and she'd sell her story to the *News of the World* if she wasn't given enough money to feed the kids.'

'So?'

'They sent Ray Wilson to her flat with twenty quid.'

'And?'

'Well, Ray had always fancied Gloria, so he stayed.'

'How romantic,' said Audrey Whiting, the other female reporter.

'Well it was for ten days,' said Barbara Marks, the newsdesk secretary. 'Then Ray left her as well. Jack was furious. He was going around saying, "That bastard Ray Wilson's left my wife and kids destitute."'

I was sent on a cigarette run and returned with twelve packets of twenty, from which I earned an amazing five shillings (25p) in tips. Then to the canteen to buy jugs of tea, and then to the post office in Fleet Street to wire £25 to Victor Sims, a reporter who was stuck on a job in Norwich. It was the largest amount of money I'd ever held in my hand.

Because over the years the company had acquired several buildings that lay cheek by jowl, they had been interconnected by a mixture of sloping corridors, and unexpected flights of steps. The shortest route to the canteen was by way of the roof over a set of narrow metal walkways and staircases that connected Geraldine House to the *Mirror* building. The canteen was a charmless place staffed by rough-tongued women who exchanged insults with the constant queue of men in blue overalls buying mugs of tea and bacon sandwiches. It didn't attract me as a place to eat.

Later, when I was going out to find somewhere for lunch, Horace, the doorman, stopped me as I passed. 'Hey,' he said. 'Messenger boys aren't allowed in the lifts.' I paused, and

Horace added, 'You're lucky you've still got a job. You know who that was you went up in the lift with this morning?'

'No,' I answered.

'Only the chairman, Cecil King,' he replied in a reverent voice.

I recognised the name from *Publish and Be Damned*. My first day, and already I had met someone mentioned in a book. It was all turning out to be as exciting as I'd expected.

Chapter 3

GETTING TO KNOW LONDON

In 1956, the part of London where Fleet Street was located still contained acres of bombsites. Scrub bushes, weeds and stunted trees had taken root, and feral cats roamed. The surviving buildings were blackened with soot and the air was polluted by millions of coal fires.

It was also a city of messenger boys. We were everywhere: riding delivery bikes; carting armfuls of post; guarding important packages. Every office employed a 'smart lad' with an eye open for future promotion. But we didn't all look the same. In the past few years the youth of England had divided along new sartorial lines.

The toughest youths wore drainpipe trousers, suede shoes with thick crêpe soles, and heavily oiled Tony Curtis hair styles. To the universal outrage of the adult population, the cult of the Teddy boy had arrived. The style was more than a fashion preference: it was a way of life. The wrong sort of eye contact with certain Teddy boys was to invite instant violence, with the chance that it might be delivered with a broken bottle, a flick knife or an open razor.

Not every youth followed the craze. There were still plenty of teenage boys who remained faithful to the fashions of their fathers. They went about their business unarmed.

There was also a subdivision of the Edwardian fashion adopted by male art students to which I subscribed. We also wore drainpipe trousers, but with baggy sweaters and duffle coats. Hair was grown long but no grease applied.

The Beatles were still several years away, and the music that suddenly enflamed the youth of Britain was brought to our shores by a chubby, kiss-curled, middle-aged guitarist: rock 'n' roll was born, and nothing was the same again. Suddenly, Teddy boys and those who dressed like their fathers were united in their love for a music that all their parents detested.

We of the art-school persuasion were unimpressed. We had our own brand of music: the traditional jazz of New Orleans. Art-school girls took their inspiration from the existentialist fans of Jean-Paul Sartre: long hair, heavily outlined eyes, baggy sweaters and obligatory black stockings.

At first these divisions between the young tribes of Britain were of no interest to newspapers. As far as Fleet Street was concerned market research was mumbo jumbo. No scientific investigation was ever conducted into the likes and dislikes of the readers. It was taken for granted that those who controlled the industry knew what they were doing. The popularity of individual writers was judged by the number of readers' letters they received.

Getting to Know London

By the time I'd joined the *Sunday Pic* a sense of unease was setting in about the unpredictability of the young. Suddenly, the youth of Britain seemed to be evolving into two or three new species that bore no resemblance to their parents at all. Because I was still a teenager, I began to be consulted about what appeal stories would have for the young.

I mentioned that I went to a jazz club on Eel Pie Island in Twickenham and the following week the paper ran a story: 'Mothers – do you know what your daughters get up to?' It was illustrated by photographs of people I actually knew. The girls, sipping halves of cider, their eyes heavily outlined with mascara, looked particularly depraved.

I wasn't sure about how my friends might react to being displayed in a Sunday newspaper, but I needn't have worried. As far as egomaniacs and art students were concerned there was no such thing as bad publicity.

During my early months on the paper I got to know London. Previously I'd always travelled by tube. Now I saw the city as it truly was. Vast flights of shops, parks, crescents, squares, circuses, streets and avenues. I recognised places by their look now, rather than as names on a Tube map or a Monopoly board.

I was tipped off by the other messengers that, when I was told to take a taxi, I should use the Underground and keep the cab fare. But I loved taking taxis. Rattling around the streets reclining on their padded leather seats seemed to me to be the height of luxury.

But there was also a lot of walking involved in the job, and my old school blazer and raincoat seemed to become sodden after even the lightest of showers. So I bought a tweed suit and a rubberised, riding coat from Leonard Lyle's, the gentlemen's outfitters, in High Holborn. It was a combination in which I could have faced violent storms at sea. The tweed suit was certainly hardwearing. It felt as if it had been woven from barbed wire and eventually wore all the hair from my legs.

In those early days I saw things that I wouldn't have experienced on my quiet home streets. One night I went to Paddington Station to pick up a package from the luggage office. The station then was filled with atmosphere: wet cobbles; dramatic shafts of light cutting through the deep shadows; the pervading smell of sulphurous steam trains. Waiting on the concourse was a large group of elderly men. Something about the way they held themselves marked them as old soldiers. As I passed among them, I saw what they had in common. Each wore the small purple-ribboned medal of the Victoria Cross. I've remembered the time I walked among those heroes the whole of my life.

Chapter 4

THE GOOD, THE BAD AND THE GRUMPY

M y job as a messenger boy often required more than merely carrying messages. To save the cost of hiring models I took part in the photographic reconstructions of blood-curdling crimes; rowed a swimsuited girl across the Serpentine; and had tea with a group of chimps. This last picture was stuck on the wall in the office with the caption, 'Spot the Mike competition'. I was proud of the recognition.

One day I was assigned the job of assisting one of the older photographers, Bill Turner, in taking pictures of a wild-eyed individual who'd sold his story to the paper. The staff writer ghosting the articles was Victor Sims, a kindly man with a mellifluous voice and an almost supernatural charm. He specialised in exposing the most appalling villains to the wrath of the *Sunday Pic* readers.

It was Vic's habit to read his story over the telephone to the criminals he'd persuaded to confess their deplorable transgressions. The whole office would fall silent as we listened in awe to a master craftsman going about his trade. The conversations would go something like this:

'Lionel, Vic Sims here . . . Wasn't that a splendid evening . . . I do hope you and your wife got home safely . . . She wasn't your wife? . . . I see, well who am I to condemn the way a man earns his living? . . . She brings in that much each week, does she? Lucky you . . . Now, Lionel, let me read you what we're printing about you this Sunday.

'"Can there be a lower swine in London than the man known to the Vice Squad as Lionel Baker? Like a bloodsucking vampire, Baker preys on innocent young girls, promising them a life of luxury until they find themselves set up as sex slaves in the chain of squalid bedsitters he owns in the seedy Paddington area . . .

'"This man, who even fellow criminals consider to be lower than the belly of a poisonous snake . . ."'

At the conclusion of the call the recipient would always thank Victor and they would part the best of friends.

For the present task, I was instructed by Bill Turner to first find a cardboard box that had contained tins of baked beans and then stuff a rolled-up carpet with pillows. We set to work in the photographic studio, and Bill's first pictures were to be of the man to be exposed holding an SS officer's ceremonial dagger in a menacing fashion.

It was a Saturday afternoon and the FA Cup final was showing on the studio television set, so we took a break to watch the match. The wild-eyed man became transported into a frenzy of excitement by the game. At half-time he went to find a lavatory and Bill said, 'What's the baked-bean box for, Vic?'

'Oh, I forgot to tell you: he kept Setty's head in a baked-bean box after cutting up the body with an SS dagger. He only had the torso tied up in the rolled-up carpet.'

'Well, he's enjoying the football now,' said Bill.

'I should think so,' said Victor. 'He hasn't seen a Cup final for nearly ten years.'

It transpired that the wild-eyed man was Donald Hume, who had served eight years for his part in disposing the body of a used-car dealer called Stanley Setty. Hume had cut the body up and dumped it from a light aircraft over East Anglia. The prosecution had never been able to prove he'd actually committed the murder. So he escaped hanging, and, under the law, he couldn't face trial twice for the same crime. Even when he'd confessed the murder in the *Sunday Pictorial* he remained free.

Some years later, Donald Hume killed again. He murdered a taxi driver in Switzerland. This time Victor Sims interviewed him in a Swiss jail. Later, Vic said he was plagued by a recurring nightmare. In his dream he would visit Hume in jail and Hume would find a way of changing places, leaving Vic to plead his innocence to unresponsive prison guards who would not release him.

As a reward for his long years of service, Vic was finally awarded a plum job. He finished his career as a staff man in Germany, even though he didn't know a word of the language.

Another job I found myself doing was something of a spirited affair. When I was a boy, my best friend's mother was a devotee of spiritualism. In the school holidays we would accompany her to tin-roofed halls and sit before mediums, who would give out reassuring messages from the dead. It was easy to see how simple the deceptions were, but occasionally the odd performer would impress.

However, any lingering beliefs were dissipated when, as part of an exposure, I was cast as a medium's assistant and photographed producing ectoplasm, speaking through ghostly trumpets, and demonstrating manifestations in full-length mirrors. One of my aunts, who believed in all matters concerning the 'beyond', deeply disapproved of my taking part in such a cynical exercise.

'Can't Michael get a job on a *respectable* newspaper?' she asked my mother.

Looking back, I suppose I was a pleasant enough lad, but not everyone was friendly, and a few were quite nasty pieces of work. To study human nature there's no better vantage point than the bottom of the heap. The secretaries were delightful and even those from ordinary backgrounds sounded as if they'd been educated at Cheltenham Ladies' College. The men were more of a mixed bag.

I learned that authority produces different sorts of behaviour in those with power. Natural leaders issue orders easily with charm and grace, but they convey their wishes with a steely determination. These are the sorts of people who get things done, and change the way the world goes about its business.

Others, with responsibility are filled with secret dread. Their lack of confidence makes them bullies. For messenger boys there was no one lower in the chain of command. But it is an unwise individual who bullies the serf. I have seen sharp-witted boys fake stupidity and fail in simple tasks just to frustrate their ill-mannered masters. And it is always a wise precaution to be civil to anyone who brings you food and drink.

The deputy editor, Reg Payne, had an abrasive tongue and fearsome reputation among journalists, but the messenger boys loved him because his orders were always accompanied by a handsome tip.

In later years, when he edited the paper, he fell from grace because he implicated the bisexual Lord Boothby in a relationship with Ronnie Kray. Kray was supposed to procure young men for Boothby in return for personal favours. At the time Hugh Cudlipp, who was editorial director, was away on holiday, painting his boat in Honfleur, and Payne was encouraged to print the story by the chairman, Cecil King.

The relationship between Cudlipp and Cecil Harmsworth King was an interesting one. King had been born into the royal family of Fleet Street. His mother was a sister of Lord Northcliffe, whom King revered. His father was Sir Lucas King, a member of the Anglo-Irish ascendancy. The only people he held in affection were the Irish servants in his parents' home and the Nigerians who worked on the company's West African papers. He claimed that Africans were just like the Irish.

Cudlipp, the son of a Welsh commercial traveller, left school at fourteen. However, there must have been something amazing in the genes of the Cudlipp family, as Hugh's two brothers, Percy and Reg, also became Fleet Street editors.

King was a Machiavellian businessman, painfully shy and

completely without editorial judgement. He did, though, have a mischievous sense of humour. He returned late one night to the bedroom in his suite of rooms and found a cleaner taking a nap in his bed.

The cleaner claimed he'd been taken ill. King ordered him to stay where he was and sent for an ambulance to have him taken to St Bart's Hospital.

Cudlipp was brilliant, mercurial, gregarious and able to excel at any job on a newspaper; a natural leader, who pretended to be ruthless but was far more soft-hearted than his icy master.

King encouraged Reg Payne to print the story about Boothby. When Boothby threatened to sue, the paper settled out of court for £20,000, a vast sum in those days. King insisted Reg Payne be fired.

Cudlipp did not want to see his old friend suffer too much. Mirror Group Newspapers owned an empire of magazines and publishing concerns dotted all over London. So Cudlipp removed Payne from the *Sunday Mirror* and hid him safely on *Tit-Bits* magazine in Covent Garden, far away from King's vengeance.

I really liked the *Sunday Pic*'s assistant editor, Michael Christiansen. He had a dry sense of humour and a rich vocabulary of curses, my favourite being 'God's trousers!' Son of Arthur Christiansen, a famous editor of the *Daily Express*, Mike was a bespectacled, gangling figure, with a booming voice. One day I brought tea and cakes to his wife and his young son and daughter, who were visiting. Later, he left this family to marry his secretary.

Fifty years passed and the little boy, Rupert, by now a columnist on the *Daily Telegraph*, was writing a book about his family. He contacted me. It was a melancholy business to tell his son how much I'd liked his father, a man he hadn't really known at all.

Mike had mastered all the various skills of journalism, but he suffered from a particular drawback. Occasionally some short-circuit would take place in his reasoning process, and he would display a bizarre lapse of judgement.

Memorably, he decided that it was time for upside-down week. This entailed the columnists swapping places: Felicity Green, the women's editor, would write the motoring column; Patrick Mennem, the motoring writer, would review the week's movies; and so on. All reluctantly agreed, until he came to Bill Connor, known as the columnist Cassandra.

Connor was a peaceful enough figure, until anyone tried to interfere with his column, when he became as dangerous as a phial of nitroglycerine.

Mike Christiansen entered Connor's office and informed him that for one day he would write the gardening article and the 'Cassandra' column would be written by Xenia Field.

Connor physically threw Mike out of his office, announcing to the startled newsroom, 'This man is a doughnut masquerading as a ping-pong ball.'

Pat Brangwyn, the *Pic*'s features editor, was a sardonic character. He was an Oxford graduate, and I think what I liked about him was the fee he paid to his friend, Christopher Logue, the impoverished poet. When challenged why the *Sunday Pictorial* needed the services of a poet, Brangwyn said it was good for the soul of the newspaper.

The *Pic*'s news editor, Fred Redman, had the avuncular

charm of a country doctor. His personal assistant was Barbara Marks, who knew more about the news operation than anyone else on the paper and acted as confidante and matron to the reporting staff. Later, she became a reporter herself.

An aspect of the newspaper I found impressive was the pragmatism with which it indulged the shortcomings of the staff. As long as the paper rattled along, discipline was as flexible as a rubber band. Thus, George Casey, the sports editor, a fat, blustering cockney, refused to have a telephone installed as it would encourage people to ring him up.

'The bastards get enough out of me while I'm at work,' he always claimed.

Ross 'Dickie' Richards, one of the reporters, was always late, and the newsdesk just made allowances. One transgression that earned forgiveness for everyone was the excuse that would be unthinkable in any other sort of job. 'He was pissed' was always greeted with an understanding nod of the head.

The picture editor, Jack Crawshaw, was a David Niven lookalike and something of a dandy who seemed to be constantly in a foul temper. He, too, had started as a messenger boy, but he didn't like me much, and once told me he'd make sure I'd never get a job in his department. I gained a certain amount of pleasure some years later, when I was an assistant editor on the *Mirror*, in noting that he had by then passed lower down the pecking order.

The men I admired most were those who'd seen action in the war years. It was as if by risking their lives they saw peacetime as an unexpected bonus. They were a friendly crowd, and generous with tips for the slightest service. They were also impossible to bully.

The Good, the Bad and the Grumpy

The photographers were different: the older ones, whose hands were still scarred from the magnesium flash powder used in their youth, were a grumpy charmless lot; and they all seemed to be consumed with ancient grievances. An exception among the team was the young Carl Bruin.

Most were cockneys, though not Percy Bosher, who had been an officer in the Great War and drove a silver Jaguar sports car. On cold days they went about their business swaddled in vast tweed overcoats carrying bags of heavy equipment, moaning like the wind passing through a forest.

The *Pic*'s circulation had recently gone over 6 million with the publication of a series about a child who was claimed to have been conceived as a 'virgin' birth. The story died sometime later when it was discovered an American Air Force sergeant may have also been involved.

But stories concerning nuns fleeing from their convents, pools winners who spent recklessly, hellhole holiday camps and daughters who ran away from home to lead a life of vice in the big city still fascinated the public, as did stories about the pioneers of sex-change operations.

In my first few weeks, one of these pioneers caused me a perplexing problem. I had arrived, as always, half an hour before the rest of the staff and I entered the newsroom to hear a phone ringing. It was Horace the doorman. 'I've got someone down here who says they've got an important meeting with Mr Sims,' he said.

'You'd better send them up,' I answered. 'I'll meet them at the lift door.'

The lift gates opened and I was confronted by a daunting sight. A figure over six feet tall, with the face and body of a powerful man, wearing an orange dress, high heels, and topped with golden tresses.

'Hello, dear,' he said in a Liverpool accent. 'I'm Doreen Reilly. I've come to see Vic Sims about my sex-change operation, but I must dash to the lavvy first. Can you show me the way?'

Here was a testing dilemma and there was no one to whom I could pass the buck. Had Doreen had the operation already, or was she still technically a man? To which gender's lavatory should I escort Doreen?

For a few seconds I was paralysed, but suddenly making a swift choice I led the Liverpudlian down a corridor to the editor's exclusive lavatory. Then I waited outside with bated breath until Doreen had finished. From that moment on I might not have always made the right decision but I'd learned to make up my mind quickly.

Chapter 5

PIECING THINGS TOGETHER

I t was a few weeks before I had my first encounter with the editor, Colin Valdar, because he was rarely seen in the newsroom. He was a dashing figure, who always wore a dark-blue suit and polka-dot bowtie. He was of average height with chiselled, Anglo-Saxon features, and a scar on his chin that gave him the air of a thirties matinée idol. In a profession that seemed to be powered by prodigious amounts of alcohol, it was well known that he was a nondrinker.

It was also known that when he'd been production editor of the *Daily Express*, he was the only man who didn't fear Carl Giles, the cartoonist. Giles was a personal favourite of Lord Beaverbrook, and was paid more than the editor. Giles sent his cartoon by train, but it was often late. Valdar would leave a shallow space on the page, and when the cartoon finally arrived it would be too deep. Valdar would order that a large lump of the sky be chopped off. When I became friends with

Giles in later years, he would still recall 'Slasher' Valdar with a shudder.

One afternoon I was given an urgent proof for the editor. His secretary Sadie was away from her desk so I knocked on his door and entered. Valdar was drawing on a layout pad with a very thick pencil. He had a pipe clamped between his jaws and was so completely absorbed in his task that his ferocious concentration seemed to fill the room with his energy.

He glanced up and I said, 'I was told this was urgent, sir,' as I handed him the proof.

'Who are you?' he asked, in a staccato voice.

'Mike, sir, Mike Molloy,' I answered.

He stared, unsmiling, at me for a few seconds, and then said, 'Where did you go to school?'

'Ealing Junior Art School.'

'Art school – do you have any examples of your work?'

'Yes, sir.'

'Bring them in next Tuesday,' he said, dismissing me. Beyond the door, in Sadie's still-empty office, I stood for a moment. It was as if I could feel the world turning beneath my feet.

The Fleet Street that I had come to work in had existed for only about sixty years. Lord Northcliffe started the *Daily Mail* in 1896. Before that, newspapers were produced for the ruling classes and were small businesses. But Northcliffe was convinced there was a vast untapped market.

A river of money began to pour into Northcliffe's coffers. Although nothing could be more decorous than the early copies of the *Daily Mail*, then it was considered shockingly vulgar. Even Northcliffe's mother disapproved of the *Mail* because it published drawings of ladies' corsets in the advertisements.

In Northcliffe's day, England's sense of morality was as ironclad as her dreadnoughts, and those standards were to prevail until they were blown away in the 1960s. Before that, the Church of England still held power and influence in the land.

From Victorian times the Royal Family had set a standard of rectitude that was slavishly followed by the middle classes and respectable working people. The Lord Chamberlain had the power to ban books, theatrical productions and films he deemed damaging to the moral fibre of the country, and it was a power he frequently exercised.

In 1956, newspapers could only by innuendo report sexual matters. Court cases were different: anything said in court was fair game. Hungry for salacious stories, on Sunday mornings, virtually the whole population read the *News of the World.*

In the 1950s, popular papers tiptoed through the minefield of the law in a ceaseless quest to titillate the readers, but raw sex was definitely out of the question. Nonetheless, the *Sunday Pictorial* did its best to hint at the unmentionable, and girls in two-piece swimsuits were printed.

But British readers enjoyed one delight unknown to the readers in the Catholic countries of Europe. For that market, we had to produce a special edition, known as 'The Malta Slip', where the navels were painted out of pinup pictures – lest the sight of a bellybutton in their *Sunday Pictorial* aroused the sun-drenched recipients to acts of depravity. Editors were also careful not to offend the club of press lords and their families, who had an unwritten code of not throwing stones at each other's glass house.

So Fleet Street remained a haunted house where the past was present everywhere; the very building containing the *Sunday Pictorial* offices was called Geraldine House, after Northcliffe's mother, who had disapproved of the *Mail*'s corsets.

This was the world into which I was about to be recruited when, the following Tuesday morning, Colin Valdar examined the portfolio of drawings and paintings I brought for a few minutes, and then, to my astonishment, told me I was to be trained in page design. It didn't seem possible that I would be given such an opportunity after a few minutes' acquaintance with the editor. I actually felt dizzy as I walked from his office.

For my new line of work I was seconded to the care of Peter Mills, the deputy picture editor. Peter drew up the news pages, and cropped the photographs for the block makers. The work was simpler than the complicated features layouts. It was also quite stressful.

Now I began to learn how newspapers were put together. The composing floor was an impressive place: noisy, and harshly disciplined, a place where ink got on your hands and clothes. In those days, the printers and block makers served a seven-year apprenticeship. They were overseen by the printer, a martinet of enormous authority. Some were bloody-minded and uncooperative; others dazzled you with the expertise. My newfound responsibilities meant I worked at night. So, during the day the *Sunday Pictorial* paid my fees and I returned to art school.

Now, I began also to appreciate the joys of art student life. Some years later I met the author, director and broadcaster Ned Sherrin and I asked him if he'd enjoyed his time at Oxford.

'I loved it,' he replied. 'Wouldn't you have liked to have gone too?'

I lied, and said yes. The truth was that art students in my day considered all other types of education inferior, and the students who pursued them lesser human beings. But my short-lived days as an office boy were among the happiest of my life

It wasn't all roses though. I had one difficult episode concerning a woman in Swansea who wrote to the paper saying her husband bore a remarkable resemblance to Adolf Hitler and enclosed a snapshot as proof.

'Perfect letter,' said the deputy features editor. He handed me the snap and told me to match it with a photograph of Hitler from the library. I set about the task with fanatical thoroughness.

At 1.30 in the morning I left the library, my clothes impregnated with dust, and caught the night bus home. Images from the last five hours filled my mind. Hundreds of faces of Hitler floated past, but none of them resembled the man from Swansea.

The next morning, sore at heart, I presented myself to the deputy features editor and confessed my failure.

'Show me what you've got,' he demanded briskly.

Miserably, I produced a selection of Hitler portraits. He studied them for a few moments, then spoke: 'Tell you what,' he said brightly. 'Get the retouchers to make Hitler look more like this Welsh berk.'

Then, once again, I felt the world turn beneath my feet. Mike

Christiansen emerged from the editor's office and instructed me to follow him. Baffled, I hurried after him and he led me to the empty art bench usually occupied by Lewis Morland-Abrahams, who was the art and production editor, a very important role. It seemed Lewis had fallen deeply in love with the family's Spanish maid, and decided to elope with her to the Middle East. To this day, I am grateful for the power love has to change lives.

'This is your desk now,' Mike declared airily. 'Lewis has resigned; you've got the job.'

Now I was sitting in the vacated seat, life couldn't have worked out better for me. I even got a new girlfriend. Because of my tender years, the editor instructed that I should take a car home when my work was done. Minicabs didn't exist then, so I was chauffeured by a driver in a peaked cap in a limousine hired from Victoria Cars. It was an extraordinary experience to sink into the soft leather seats of a limousine and be wafted through the night, almost as much fun as taking taxis when I was a messenger boy.

I was now leading two lives: one at art school and the other in a newspaper office. On the paper I was considered something of a boy wonder because I could draw a bit. Among my fellow art students my talents were considered only fair to middling; but I was envied because I could afford cigarettes and bacon sandwiches.

Although still underage, I was taking my breaks in pubs, and every conversation was the equivalent of a quiz show. I soon came to realise that my fellow youths tended to have a narrow focus of knowledge. As even the youngest of my newspaper companions was at least a decade older than I was, and a few of the older ones had actually fought in World War One, I had some catching up to do.

I liked all the staff reporters, but my favourite was Dickie Richards, a true Bohemian. He lived in a tiny basement flat in Earl's Court with his fiery French mistress and their lovechild. One warm evening he took off his jacket in the office and Barbara Marks said, 'Jesus Christ, Dickie, your back is covered in blood.'

'Is it?' he answered matter-of-factly. 'Jeanette attacked me with a piece of firewood this morning and it still had a nail in it.'

The holes and the blood didn't worry Dickie. His shirts never reached the laundry: Jeanette considered housework bourgeois. So, every couple of days, he would but a new one and throw away the old.

One night Dickie told us of his real fear that Jeanette would attack him unexpectedly and he would react as he had been trained too in the army. He'd been a major in the commandos and had won the MC in the Normandy campaign.

Jeanette devised a punishment for Dickie that would go some way to encouraging the possibility of her sudden death. She would wait until he was in bed asleep and then place the coal scuttle over his head and beat it with the coal hammer. Still, they did seem to love each other.

Although Fleet Street was known for the bitter divisions, virtually everyone did like a drink. Compared with this age of government health warnings, the consumption I saw in my youth seemed to match the carousing of Vikings. Part of the reason people spent so much time in the office pubs, apart from the obvious pleasures, was that the hot-metal process involved long periods of waiting. It was a waiting game for everyone, and the pubs seemed the natural place to kill time. But, in truth, no one really needed an excuse.

Each newspaper had a few dedicated pubs near its office, and it was a custom to sometimes go and see the opposition on their own territory. The bars attracted secretaries, girlfriends, groupies and sometimes even wives. People were hired, given credit, counselling and a great deal of friendship. For journalists, life in the office pubs was conducted as a perpetual party – and I had just been invited.

Chapter 6

OF DOGS' EYES AND SUEDE SHOES

The *Sunday Pictorial*'s main newsroom was a pleasant enough place to work, but the great newsroom of the *Daily Mirror* and its satellite offices had a different atmosphere. Even in the morning before the day staff arrived you could sense the tension – and the fear. Hugh Cudlipp was seldom seen about the building, but the *Mirror* editor, Jack Nener, a gravel-voiced Welshman, was a familiar figure on the floor.

Leaving the later editions to the attention of the night editor, Dick Dinsdale, he would spend an hour or so in Barney Finnegan's before departing for his home in Wimbledon.

He and his wife, Audrey Whiting, would always go to bed early and the first edition would be delivered to their home. Then Jack would begin searching through the paper for errors that he would telephone to the back bench, where the night editor commanded the men who brought out the news pages.

Nener's nightly tongue lashings were legendary. His threats

could reach awe-inspiring levels of invention, but he saved his most devastating rage for anyone who forgot his standing instructions about the retouching of dogs' eyes. It was a phenomenon of photography that a picture taken of a dog using a flash would produce an effect that gave the impression the dog had cataracts. This was easily corrected by a retoucher painting a dot of white in each eye.

Curiously, this firm instruction from Nener would sometimes be overlooked. Maybe it was something to do with fear, and all would flee from the responsibility of getting it right.

Finally, Nener declared that next time he would fire the whole of the back bench if they failed to correct a dog's eyes. Of course, the next time the picture of a dog was published no retouching had been done to the eyes and it gave the customary impression of blindness.

The editor's rage was awesome when the following exchange took place:

'Who am I talking to?' Nener roared.

'Dick Dinsdale, Jack.'

'No, I'm not. You can't be Dinsdale – Dinsdale is a newspaperman. I'm talking to some fucking imposter; some whoreson sewer rat who's crawled onto the staff in order to sabotage the *Mirror*. Let me speak to Joe Grizzard.'

'Grizzard here, Jack.'

'Don't "Jack" me, you fucking useless bag of human ordure. How many times have I told you about dogs' eyes? And still you—'

'But, Jack—'

'Don't interrupt me, you fucking incompetent. I'm going—'

But, Jack—'

'Don't interrupt me. Tomorrow, I'm going to trawl the gutters of Fleet Street and recruit a better team of men.'

'But, Jack—'

'What are you trying to say you half-baked excuse for an arsehole?'

'You haven't read the caption to the picture, Jack, the dog *really* is blind.'

One person who actually got the better of Jack Nener was Xenia Field, the gardening editor. Xenia, a quivering, wrinkled, sticklike figure, was held in wary respect by the staff because she was known to be a friend of Cecil King.

Xenia had been a successful playwright in the thirties, but her major concern was her tireless work as a prison visitor. She became dissatisfied with her rate of freelance pay and approached Nener in the corridor to ask for more money.

Xenia's column, tucked away at the bottom of the page at the back, was the only part of the paper he never read, but he decided to compromise.

'Do you get many letters, Xenia?' he asked.

'Yes, I have a few correspondents,' she answered.

'I'll pay you a shilling for every letter you answer.'

Xenia accepted and allowed him to pass on his way.

A few weeks later Nener arrived at the office, where his secretary said, 'The post room's been on in a bit of a panic, sir. There are thousands and thousands of letters addressed to Xenia Field.'

The editor's antenna for disaster came into play. 'Get me a copy of Saturday's paper,' growled Nener.

There it was: one short paragraph at the end of the gardening notes, it read:

> I have a few cuttings from the Rose of Christ, a bush
> that was reputed to have grown at the feet of the True
> Cross and was nurtured by the blood of Our Lord. If
> anyone would care for a cutting, please write to me
> at the following address . . .

Jack rang her and said, 'You win this one, Xenia. Send a stock reply to all the requests and after that I'll pay you an extra tenner a week.'

Few men at the top of popular journalism had enjoyed the civilising experience of universities. Most had started work as boys on provincial newspapers. Homosexuals in Fleet Street were still concealed in the deepest recesses of the closet.

Having few experiences of anyone who was actually gay, Jack Nener and his henchmen devised and declared a list of slipups gays made that revealed their secret sexual preferences. Drinking white wine was declared homosexual; so were beards and waistcoats and coloured handkerchiefs; and a dead giveaway: suede shoes!

I was once talking with Simon Clyne, the *Mirror*'s long-serving picture editor, who remembered Nener with some dread: 'Oh, he was a coarse man,' said Simon, shaking his head. 'I was on the telephone to our rabbi one day when he shouted in my ear, "Clyne, I need a tit picture to take the sting out of the train crash."'

Matt Coady told me of his experience when he was a subeditor (or 'sub') during Nener's editorship. 'They were primitive men in charge in those days,' Matt recalled. 'Jack Nener had only a couple of years at school and had read nothing but popular newspapers since those days. When Reg Payne came to the *Mirror* as assistant editor, Jack found a soulmate who was as rough-hewn as himself.

'They became almost inseparable and took to walking about the newsroom together. Both of them were flatfooted and, with their barking smokers' coughs and their habit of jangling the change in their pockets, the sound of their approach was known as "The Devil's Jazz Band".

'Many of the subs, on the other hand, were well-read men and in the habit of bringing books to work so they could entertain themselves while waiting to be given assignments. One day, Sandy Smith had a novel open and Gough Cotsford asked him, "What are you reading, Smith?"

'"*Tom Brown's Schooldays*," he replied.

'"That's a children's book, isn't it?"

'"On the contrary," said Smith, "it's splendid stuff. Listen to this passage of Dr Arnold expelling Flashman: 'Flashman, you are a bully and a coward and there is no place for you here.'"

'The whole subs' table heard the exchange and the quote caught the imagination of everyone. For the next few months, whenever someone committed a misdemeanour the transgressor would be told, "Flashman, you are a bully and a coward, and there is no place for you here."

'At the height of the craze,' Matt continued, 'I was in a lavatory cubicle and I heard the sound of two pairs of slapping flat feet as Nener and Payne entered the room. After much coughing Nener said irritably, "Who is this bastard Flashman everyone's talking about?"

"'I don't know, Jack," answered Payne darkly. "But I hear he's a bully and a coward."

"'Well, fire the fucker, then," said Nener.'

Chapter 7

NEW BOSS, NEW GIRL, NEW JOB

I was still finding it hard to believe how fortunate I was. The work on the *Sunday Pictorial* features pages came easily to me and I was also encouraged to provide comic drawings. I was paid the princely sum of £13 a week.

At art school during the day, I fell among two boon companions: Derek Pryce and Paddy O'Gara. We remained friends throughout our lives. In later years Paddy came to the *Mirror* via advertising and Derek followed, having worked on magazines.

A pleasant couple of years passed, then Colin Valdar was fired. He'd committed an offence against the Royal Family by breaching the agreement that no servant would reveal any secrets of their private lives. The stories Valdar printed had come from Marion Crawford, the Queen's nanny. Crawfie's memoirs were completely obsequious but even these bland and flattering stories were enough for the Royal Family to complain.

This caused Cecil King to react in his usual paradoxical fashion. Although he always claimed he cared nothing for the opinion of others, he nursed a deep and secret ambition, later admitted in his diaries, that someday he would be called upon to perform a great service for his country. Valdar had offended the greatest in the land, so Valdar must go.

Cudlipp was ordered to do the job. Valdar understood the rules of the game and invited Cudlipp to his champagne farewell in appreciation of the generous severance payoff he'd received. It was at this party that I was first introduced to Hugh Cudlipp.

Cudlipp looked at me curiously and said, 'How old are you?'

'Eighteen, sir,' I replied.

He saw the glass in my hand, removed the Havana cigar from his mouth and gave a wolfish grin. 'Eighteen and drinking champagne, eh? They don't teach that at the poly.'

I wasn't to speak to him again for four years.

I was deeply saddened by the departure of Colin Valdar, and it was compounded by the fact that I had just been given the elbow by a girl who happened to be a couple of years older than I.

'You're going to be quite attractive when you're thirty, Michael,' she'd said, 'but I can't wait that long.'

Both events depressed me; but my reporter colleague Madeleine McLaughlin, gave me some brisk words of advice about losing Valdar's patronage. 'Always beware of hitching your bandwagon to a star, Mike,' she said kindly. She had no advice about the departing girl.

The whole staff of the *Sunday Pictorial* waited in apprehension for the coming of Lee Howard, the new editor. Over six feet tall and twenty-two stone in weight, he had a clean-shaven face that had all the stonelike qualities of the Sphinx. Invariably, he spent the day in shirtsleeves, revealing the broad red braces he wore with his blue Savile Row suits. Unlike Colin Valdar, he consumed astonishing amounts of whisky and smoked a hundred Player's cigarettes each day.

He also brought with him a women's editor, Felicity Green, a tiny, fashionable figure with a stainless-steel resolve. Felicity and Lee were to play major parts in my future life and I can best describe my relationship to her as something similar to the bond that existed between Wodehouse's Bertie Wooster and his Aunt Agatha.

Lee Howard was an easy man to admire. He'd never gone to school, having been privately educated by tutors. He'd written three bestselling novels before he had become an editor, but he'd decided that Fleet Street was more fun than staying alone in Earl's Court with his typewriter.

When I'd brought a piece of work that required his approval, I would be invited to linger in his office and have a drink with other revellers. On one such occasion he offered a piece of common sense about page design that stayed with me always.

Someone was pontificating on what were the best techniques for a layout in a popular paper. Lee listened for a while and then said, 'I'll show you what the greatest layout can ever be, old dear.'

He took a fresh sheet of paper on which he drew an oblong, saying, 'This is a picture of the Archbishop of Canterbury fucking Elizabeth Taylor.' Above the oblong he wrote the headline, ARCHBISHOP OF CANTERBURY FUCKS LIZ TAYLOR.

Down the side he scribbled an indication of the copy. 'This is the caption telling how, why, when and where the deed was done.'

I looked at the scheme he'd drawn in a sudden epiphany. Of course, I realised: the simpler the better.

I was happy at the *Pictorial*, and I'd fallen in love with Sandy Foley, a girl I'd met at art school, who was as beautiful as she was sweet-natured. It was flattering for me to take out a girl whom other men turned to look at in the street, but the day I knew I was in love was when I accompanied her on a sketching expedition to Osterley Park. I'd brought no drawing material as I was supposed to be at a lecture on the history of art, so I borrowed a pencil and paper from her sketchbook.

My pencil broke and I asked if I could use her knife.

'I don't have a knife,' she said, her green eyes looking suddenly sad.

'What happens when your pencil's worn down?' I asked.

'Then I know it's time to go home,' she answered simply.

With a girl who was so beautiful, sweet-natured and with a gift for wisecracks, life was looking up.

Then I got a telephone call. Would I like to join Colin Valdar at the *Daily Sketch*, where he'd recently been appointed editor? The job entailed doing the overnight feature pages, which would allow me to continue with art school during the day.

I accepted.

Chapter 8

THE *SKETCH* TEENAGE ARTIST

After an amicable parting from the *Pictorial*, I moved south of Fleet Street to an office that overlooked the Thames. The *Sketch* newsroom seemed familiar territory. All newsrooms were interchangeable in those days. Departments were scattered about a vast room and the same noise from shouting figures, clattering typewriters and constantly ringing telephones was comforting.

I saw a friend among the subs: Ted Simon. Then I was shown to an art desk in the features department. In 1960 the *Sketch* was vastly overshadowed by the might of the *Daily Mirror*. The paper had tended to recruit executives in the twilight of their careers and they often trailed a gaudy past with defiant splendour.

During wartime newsprint rationing, many regular features had been suspended, so, when peace came, there were jobs going that could earn an additional fee as a sweetener to the salary on offer.

On the *Sketch*, the gardening column was the perk of the features editor. In my early days that role was filled by Charlie Rowe. Legend had it that Charlie had been appointed under duress by the previous editor Bert Gunn. It was said that Charlie secured the job when it fell vacant by locking himself in the features editor's office and refusing to come out until he was appointed. Everyone who tried to order him out was met with a barrage of abuse culminating in Charlie shouting, 'It's my turn.'

Bert Gunn, in the next office, was disturbed by the commotion and came to investigate. Informed what was happening he shouted, 'Rowe, I'm ordering you to come out.'

Charlie replied, 'Ah, Bert, do you remember the time we met those two girls in Berlin?'

Before he could go any further the editor shouted, 'All right, Charlie, you can be features editor.'

Late one evening, as the new boy, I was instructed by the chief sub to go and pester Charlie, who was in his office supposedly writing the gardening column. I entered the room to find him slumped over the desk. Before him was a large pile of gardening magazines from which he extracted his required column.

'Charlie,' I said deferentially, 'the chief sub needs your copy.'

He slowly raised his head with a groan and pushed over the pile of magazines. The whites of his yellowing eyes were also an interesting shade of red.

'Mike, dear boy,' he croaked, 'what we need is a bloody Mary. Have you ever had a bloody Mary, Mike?'

'No, Charlie.'

'Come with me to Auntie's,' Charlie insisted.

The chief sub looked up in resignation as the delinquent features editor, his arm now around my shoulder, led me past saying, 'I'm taking Mr Molloy for a drink. Take my gardening copy from the magazine on my desk.'

'I don't know anything about gardening, Charlie,' called the chief sub plaintively.

'Do you think *I* know anything about fucking gardening?' Charlie shouted back.

We entered Auntie's and Charlie leaned on the bar, saying in a confiding voice, 'I've brought my young friend Mike Molloy here for his first bloody Mary. Two large ones, please.'

'We don't have any tomato juice, Mr Rowe,' the barmaid answered.

Charlie would not be daunted. He waved imperiously to the section containing pub snacks and thundered, 'Then squeeze some of those fucking tomatoes.'

During the next week letters arrived from aggrieved readers complaining about his gardening column. It seems the chief sub had picked up a magazine for quite the wrong month and instructed the readers to severely prune their roses.

I began to draw more for the paper. I started writing features, and then produced a daily cartoon for young readers called 'The Ravers'. To the mocking delight of friends my byline read, 'Mike Molloy, the *Sketch* teenage artist'. It was a relief when I finally reached my twentieth birthday and I could drop the 'teenage' tag.

Terry O'Neil was also on the staff and being roughly the

same age we became friends, but Terry was much more a man of the world than I was in those days. True to form, he could boast that his current girlfriend was the astonishingly beautiful actress Shirley Anne Field.

In later years, Terry and I sometimes reminisced about our younger days. He'd known some of the most beautiful women in the world, but he never boasted about any of his conquests, though he did once mention a famous name. He began by saying, 'Don't you find it hard when you're talking to old mates and you can't mention the famous people you know in case it sounds like showing off?'

'How do you mean?'

'Well, one night a friend I'd been at school with rang the bell of my flat.'

'Go on.'

'I'd only got a tiny place, not much more than a bedsitter, even though it was in a smart part of town, so I talked to him on the doorstep. Finally, he said, joking, "Aren't you going to let me in? What's up? Have you got Jean Shrimpton in there?"'

'Yes?' I prompted.

'Well that's the point: I *did* have Jean Shrimpton in there.' At that time, the model Jean Shrimpton was one of the most desired girls in Britain.

'How did you do it, Terry?' I asked. 'How did you have all those fabulous women fancying you?'

'It wasn't so hard, you know,' he answered. 'All actresses and models are crazy. No matter how beautiful they are, they always think there's something wrong with themselves: their legs are too thin, or their eyes are too close together, their mouths are too wide, or their breasts are too small. All I had to do was listen to them talk about themselves until about four in the morning, then they wanted to go to bed.'

Well, it worked for him.

At art school I had friends who considered themselves free spirits, but the most Bohemian behaviour I ever encountered was among the group of young subs and reporters I mixed with on the *Sketch*. They boarded in a wonderfully seedy hotel near Richmond Bridge but spent most of their leisure time in the bars around Fleet Street.

When the need came for a game of poker they would break into Tom Merrin's flat in Gray's Inn Road. Tom cared nothing for such liberties being taken with his property. If he returned early from his night beat around the West End as the *Sketch* show-business reporter, he would join the game.

Fergus Cashin was another friend on the *Sketch* who prowled Soho at night. He was also the *Sketch* film critic. Private showings for newly released films invariably took place in the morning. To the outrage of producers, on those occasions, Fergus would often catch up on his sleep.

One night he visited Ronnie Scott's jazz club, taking his seat just as the blind multi-instrumentalist Roland Kirk began his set. Ignoring the performance, Fergus began a loud conversation with friends at a nearby table. When Roland Kirk's performance ended, Ronnie, who knew Fergus well, said, 'For Christ's sake, Fergus, show some manners to Roland. After all he *is* blind.'

Fergus was mortified and replied, 'I'm sorry, Ronnie, I thought all saxophonists wore dark glasses. Bring him over so I can apologise.'

Ronnie brought Kirk to the table and Fergus said, 'Can I buy you a drink, Mr Kirk?'

'Sure,' relied Kirk. 'I'll have one of my specials.'

'What's that?' asked Fergus.

'A long glass filled with three shots of vodka, two of grenadine, and a triple brandy on ice.'

'Jesus Christ,' said Fergus, 'No wonder you're blind.'

Another star of the *Sketch* newsroom was Joyce Hopkirk, the prettiest reporter I ever saw. She glittered like a diamond among the men, which was appropriate, as she later married Bill Lear, a diamond merchant. Years later, Joyce and I again worked together on the *Daily Mirror*. That was some time after she'd made a spectacular success as editor of *Cosmopolitan* magazine's British edition.

When she'd been appointed to *Cosmo* she was flown to New York to meet the editor, Helen Gurley Brown, who'd found great fame with her book *Sex and the Single Girl*.

I asked Joyce if she'd found the transition from newspapers to magazine easy.

'Easy enough,' she answered, 'and Helen Gurley Brown taught me a couple of interesting lessons.'

'Tell me.'

'One Friday afternoon Helen called a staff meeting and said to them, "The publishers of *Cosmo* are looking for executives to launch a new magazine. It will be aimed at young ambitious women. I want your ideas on my desk by nine-thirty Monday morning."'

Joyce paused to give emphasis to her story.

'On Monday morning,' she continued, 'they all gathered

in her office while she read through the ideas. Then she said, "Ladies and gentleman, these ideas are brilliant. Now I must tell you there is no new magazine. Why the fuck aren't these ideas in *Cosmopolitan*?'"

Life on the *Sketch* was still on the up. I'd bought my first car, a second-hand Fiat 500, and I was still going to art school. This led me to boast in later years that, as I'd owned a car and a suit, I'd been the richest art student in England. This boast ended one Sunday morning when I was visiting Graham Benson, a friend who lives on the Isle of Wight. He took me for a drink at his local and we joined a group of his friends, one of whom looked vaguely familiar.

During our conversation I repeated the boast that I'd been the richest art student in England.

'No, you weren't,' said the familiar figure. '*I* was.'

'When I was at Ealing Art School I had a Fiat 500 and a tailored suit,' I claimed indignantly.

'When I was at the Royal College of Art I had a Rolls-Royce,' was his crushing answer. Then I finally recognised him: it was Cephus Howard of the jazz band Temperance Seven.

Newspaper offices are fertile ground for envy, and my relationship with the editor had caused more ill-feeling than I had realised, particularly the previous Christmas, on 22 December, my twenty-first birthday. Colin Valdar had announced that champagne would be served in his office to celebrate the occasion, *and* Christmas. I was asked by one or two disgruntled colleges what it felt like to be Jesus Christ.

Envy was compounded when Vere Harmsworth, the heir to the Rothermere empire, briefly attended the party and spent practically the entire time chatting to me.

Then Colin Valdar was fired, and I was experiencing a distinct cooling from some people who had been warmly friendly when I'd been the editor's blue-eyed boy. Then the old earth took a couple of whirls and life changed again. I was working late in the office when Tom Merrin returned from his late-night ramblings in the West End to collect his expenses.

'Come and have a drink in the Press Club,' he urged.

'I can't Tom,' I replied. 'I've got all this stuff to do.'

'Bollocks!' he answered. 'Leave it to those bastards on the day staff.'

To hell with it! I thought, and accompanied him to Wine Office Court, where the old Press Club was located.

Standing at the bar was Mike Christiansen. He'd recently moved to the *Daily Mirror* with Lee Howard, who had been appointed editor. Mike's greeting was among the most joyous I had ever heard. 'Ah! young Molloy,' he boomed. 'Why don't you come and join a decent newspaper again?'

Chapter 9

MIRROR, MIRROR...

In the time since I'd last worked for the Mirror Group the papers had moved to Holborn Circus. The new building was a garish, red-tiled monstrosity with the central nine storeys faced with a wall of plain white stone; but the main newsroom had quickly become almost as scruffy as any other in the world. With their customary behaviour, the editorial staff continued to throw newspapers and sheets of copy paper under desks and stamp out cigarettes on the floor; and abandoned tea mugs and half-eaten plates of canteen food lay scattered around the tops of filing cabinets.

Cecil King lived in quite a different atmosphere in his suite of offices on the ninth floor, which were reached by private lift. There, he enjoyed the services of his butler, Mr Lucas, who presided over a private dining room, kitchen and bathroom. The vast office looked east towards the City of London.

Recently, the Clean Air Act had been passed, but King

claimed, quite illegally, that as a member of the National Coal Board, he was entitled to burn the stuff in his splendid Adam fireplace. He sat at a priceless William Kent desk, with oriental rugs scattered on the floor, the Georgian bookcases filled with rare French first editions.

Hugh Cudlipp had a far less grandiose office on the fifth floor above the *Mirror* newsroom. Within a few months of my arrival, the circulation topped five and a quarter million copies a day and we all received a £25 tax-free bonus.

On my first morning in the features department I was directed to a large, bleak office constructed of grey metal and glass, made bright with neon strip lights. It was adjacent to the part of the newsroom where the reporters sat, and was deserted but for a single figure in shirtsleeves. He was hunched over a metal desk facing rows of empty metal desks, like a schoolteacher awaiting his pupils. Piled in front of him were towers of copy baskets, heaps of magazines and spiked copy proofs arranged like a barricade.

He looked up and, fixing me with a pair of glittering blue eyes, spoke in what seemed like a tortured voice: 'I was told to expect you. I'm Freddie Wills, the deputy features editor. I'll have some work for you in a moment.'

I sat at a desk he'd indicated and waited until he'd scrawled on a layout pad a small box, saying, 'This is the space for readers' letters. Lay it out.'

The job took me about four minutes. I presented it to him and he studied it intently, then altered it in more ways than I would have thought possible, but I carried out his corrections without comment.

Gradually, people began to trickle into the room, each of them saying, 'Morning, Freddie.' Then they would take a few more steps, spot me, retrace their steps to say in a low but audible voice, 'Who's that fucker?'

'Someone Mike Christiansen's hired.'

I furtively studied the new arrivals. A plump, sharp-featured young man with a plummy voice was Roy Blackman. He talked from time to time with an angry-looking companion called Tony Miles, who glared around him through heavily framed glasses.

Dixon Scott, a cheerful individual with a head of iron-grey hair sat with his hands interlaced behind his head, deep in thought. A beautiful, sad-looking woman, Sheila Duncan, talked quietly into the telephone. A rather imposing figure called Eric Wainwright, who was dressed in a tweed suit, greeted everyone warmly, shuffled some papers for a time and then left the office for the rest of the day.

The production of daily newspapers started slowly in the mornings. Half the staff came on duty after three o'clock, so the large, horseshoe-shaped news subs' table was deserted, but for a lone figure in a waistcoat who sat working diligently.

I later learned he was Auberon Waugh, who had been hired by Cudlipp and seated away from the features department. He was occasionally given special tasks. But for the greater part of his time he got on with writing his novels. We got to know each other in later years, but while he was on the *Daily Mirror* we never exchanged a word.

That morning an incident took place across the newsroom that caught my interest. A wastepaper basket the size of an oil drum caught fire. Not an unusual event in the days when most people smoked; but the method employed to put it out interested me.

Two picture desk assistants decided to tackle the blaze by piling large layout pads over the top of the basket. A common enough way of dealing with wastepaper-basket fires, as the resulting lack of oxygen usually stifled the flames. But this basket was made of open-weave metal. Subsequently, the two men gazed hopelessly as the conflagration grew even more intense. Finally, two tape room men strolled across the room and doused the flames with jugs of cold tea.

Until that moment I had imagined that the *Daily Mirror* would be staffed by journalists with razor-sharp minds, as they had achieved the greatest daily circulation in the world. Now I realised that they were made of the same stuff as the staff of the *Daily Sketch*.

No more work was given to me and a few hours later the room suddenly emptied. After a time I saw a familiar figure passing in the newsroom. It was Grenville Robinson, a diary writer I'd known on the *Sketch*.

'Hello, Mike,' he greeted me.' What are you doing here?'

'My first day,' I answered.

'Come for a drink,' he suggested.

'I'd better not, no one's here to give me permission.'

'They've all gone to the pub,' he said. 'It'll be all right.'

Rather hesitantly, I followed him to the White Hart, a pub that was always known in Fleet Street by the name Cassandra had christened it: the Stab in the Back.

It was filled with news reporters and photographers, but no one from the features staff. I returned to the office, four halves of bitter later, to a still-deserted features room. At 3.30 a new figure entered. He was tall, rangy and stylishly dressed. 'You're sitting at my desk,' he accused.

'I'm sorry,' I apologised, vacating the seat. 'Mr Wills put me here.'

'That's all right,' he said cheerfully. 'I'm Roy Foster, the other art man. Freddie's mad. Has he set fire to anything yet? You'll get used to him. Use that desk over there.'

Gradually the staff returned, but no one seemed to do any work. There were a couple of overnight pages to do, but Roy Foster quickly polished them off. Then, mysteriously, the staff disappeared once more.

At 6.30 I saw Grenville again.

'They've all vanished, Grenville,' I said.

'They've gone to the pub again,' he answered. 'You'll get used to it. Fancy a quick one?'

We returned to the Stab, where we now found most of the features staff. This time they were friendlier and I was invited into their circle.

'Where do you drink at lunchtime?' I asked.

'Always the Printer's Devil,' answered Dixon Scott.

'Why not here?' I asked.

'Tradition,' said Tony Miles forcefully. There was something dangerous about Miles. He had a personality like a hand grenade with the pin pulled out.

'How old is the tradition?'

'Nearly six months, now,' answered Roy Blackman airily.

I had taken one step forward, but the following day I went

backwards again when Felicity Green, by now the women's editor of the *Mirror*, greeted me affectionately. It seemed to startle several people. Then Mike Christiansen, who had been away from the office on my first day, greeted me with equal warmth. These encounters earned suspicious glances among my new colleagues. Mike boomed, 'Come and meet Harold Keeble. I gave him your cuttings book to look over.'

Keeble was a legend in Fleet Street. For some years he'd worked at the Express Group but in recent times Cudlipp had lured him to the *Mirror* to bring some fresh ideas to the presentation of the paper.

I was shown into a room where a tubby figure, shirt unbuttoned to the waist, stood at a lectern. He was wearing tight black gloves as he drew on a layout pad with a fat black pencil. There was a large oxygen cylinder in one corner and an English longbow with a quiver of arrows in the other. The desk was scattered with papers from which several five-pound notes peeped.

I was introduced and he picked up my cuttings book and slapped it. 'Great stuff in here,' he said with a slight Yorkshire accent. 'We'll do fine work together.' Then he turned to Christiansen. 'What time is it, dear boy?'

'Twelve thirty, Harold,' replied Mike.

'So late already,' he said anxiously. 'I'm meeting Orson Welles at the Savoy in ten minutes; do you think I'll make it?'

'What about the centre spread, Harold?' asked Mike.

'I'm having trouble with the headline,' he answered. 'I'll finish it this afternoon.'

'Don't be late, will you?' said Mike. 'I'd like to see it and I've got to go early.'

'Fear not,' said Keeble. 'I'll see Freddie Wills gets it in good time.'

Throughout the afternoon Freddie Wills prowled the office asking anxiously, 'Has any one seen Harold Keeble?'

Roy Foster took me on a tour of the new building. Showing me the location of the production departments, he explained the complex politics of the office.

'The main problem is Geoff Pinnington, the night editor. Hates the features department.'

'Why?' I asked.

'It's nothing personal, except for Keeble – he really hates Keeble. Pinnington just wants control of all the pages in the paper.'

'Why Keeble?'

'Everybody hates Keeble, except me, so now they all hate me too.'

'What about news and pictures?'

'Pinnington controls them so they're anti-features. The newsdesk hate feature writers because the feature writers think they're a cut above them. The photographers hate Felicity Green because she gets her fashion pictures taken by freelance fashion photographers. They hate Keeble, too, because he buys a lot of freelance pictures.'

'So the features department and Felicity Green stand together?'

'Oh, no: the features subs hate Felicity Green because they can't stand taking orders from a woman. Except for Marje Proops. Everybody loves Marje.'

'What about the sports department?'

'Cudlipp's not interested in sport, so nobody cares about the sports department.'

'Why do you and Keeble like each other?'

'When Keeble arrived he was contemptuous of everyone. I drew up his designs for pages and he liked the job I did, so I became his chosen boy. So now they all hate me too.'

'I wonder what they'll think of me.'

'They think you're related to someone important. When they saw Felicity Green and Mike Christiansen greet you they all became suspicious.'

'But I knew Mike and Felicity from the *Sunday Pictorial*. I started there as a messenger boy.'

'They still think you're related to someone important.'

'What exactly is Harold Keeble's title?'

'He refused to have one. If you haven't got a title no one is in charge of you. When he sees a part of the paper he wants to redesign he just goes ahead and does it. Pinnington can't stand that.'

'Don't you design anything?'

'Me? You and I are the lowest form of life in the features department. We don't even design the pages at the back of the paper. The chief sub makes sure the subs design those.'

'Why?'

'Laying out the pages is the basis of power on the *Mirror*. Cudlipp does all the big issues, Pinnington and Keeble do the rest, the subs do the scraps. You and I just copy what we're given; it's crap work. To think I used to be a designer on *Vogue*.'

'Who is Denis Futrell again?'

'He's the chief features sub. He's on holiday at the moment, but he's got a lot of power.'

'Why?'

'He plays boogie-woogie on the piano.'

'Boogie-woogie?'

'Cudlipp had to stop going into pubs around Fleet Street because drunks were telling him what he should do with the paper.'

'So?'

'So, he built a pub in his house on Strand on the Green. A couple of nights a week he used to have his mates around and Denis and Pat Doncaster were invited along to play the piano. It doesn't happen so much now, since Cudlipp's moved to Sonning'

'Pat Doncaster the music writer?'

'Yeah, he's back tomorrow, too.'

'Does he do layout, too?'

'Everyone who's ambitious on the *Mirror* does layouts, except the art department.'

'But you like Keeble?'

'I love him. He's such a mischievous bastard. A few weeks ago Pinnington was going to have dinner at the Savoy with Lee Howard. Pinnington made sure everyone on the staff knew about it. They were halfway through the meal when a waiter delivered a bloody great package addressed to Geoff. Inside was a handwritten note on layout paper. It read: "My dear Geoffrey, I do hope you're enjoying your meal. I envy you getting away from the office. I just thought you'd like to know, your pages for the first edition, seven and nine and the centre pages, were a disaster, but don't worry, I've done them again. I can recommend the cheese board. Yours ever, Harold."'

'How did everyone know what he'd written?'

'He made sure he'd left a draft of the letter lying about the office.'

When we returned to the features department I sat at my desk deep in thought, wondering if I'd made a good career move. By 6.45 Freddie Wills was still frantically searching for Keeble; eventually he returned at seven o'clock.

'Roy,' he called out, 'shall we wrap up the spread? Bring Mike into my office; he can see how we work together.'

I followed Roy Foster, intrigued. Keeble stood at his lectern, Freddie Wills at one elbow and Foster bearing a type book at the other. I hovered behind. There were two huge glossy photographs of Sophia Loren next to the incomplete layout. One was a full-length picture of her intended as the larger picture on the page, the other was a portrait. The pictures had red wax lines drawn on them showing how Keeble wanted them cropped.

Across the top of the page Keeble had scrawled, 'She's one of the most beautiful women in the world, but what makes her so special?'

Keeble and Freddie's attempts to finish the headline littered the floor.

'I just can't get it,' Keeble finally moaned. Then to Roy Foster, 'Roy, show me that type that looks as if it's got wellington boots on.'

Foster turned the *Mirror* type book to the page depicting the font called Ludlow, and held it up for Keeble's inspection.

'Cudlipp has banned us from using that typeface, Harold,' said Freddie Wills nervously.

'Banned it? Why?'

'He says it looks Jewish.'

'Jewish?' repeated Keeble, a sudden light of mischief in his eye. 'Dear, oh dear, I didn't know Cudlipp was anti-Semitic.'

'He's not,' said Freddie, hastily. 'Sydney Jacobson is his best friend and he's Jewish.'

'Ah!' said Keeble. 'Some of his best friends are Jewish, are they?'

'It's getting late,' said Freddie, made fearful by Keeble's innuendoes. 'This page is off stone at nine o'clock.'

'Roy,' instructed Keeble, 'send the pictures to the block makers. I'll write the main headline when I get back.'

'Where are you going?' wailed Freddie.

'To the theatre first, and then to supper.'

'But I've already told you the page is due off the stone at nine o'clock,' said Freddie, near to panic.

'Plenty of time, old boy,' soothed Keeble. 'I'm only going for the first act, and then for a boiled egg at the Savoy Grill.'

Freddie, overcome with nervous exhaustion, went home in despair and Roy Foster and I went to the Stab. At 8.30 we returned just as Keeble entered the office.

'I've got it. I've got it,' he shouted as he strolled towards us. 'Roy, reverse the pictures. Make the largest into a gigantic close-up of her mouth, and use the glamour shot as the small filler.'

'What about the headline?' called out Roy.

'Let it read: SHE'S ONE OF THE MOST BEAUTIFUL WOMEN IN THE WORLD . . . BUT JUST WHAT IS IT THAT MAKES HER SO SPECIAL?

'THE LIPS OF LOREN!'

Chapter 10

GNOMES, CRAZY PAVING AND SWINGING CATS

After the hurly-burly of the *Sketch,* life was very tranquil in the *Mirror* features department. A typical day saw us starting at 10.30, casually correcting the overnight proofs. At one o'clock, we would go to the public bar of the Printer's Devil, where we would argue while we played darts.

The arguments were never of an abstract nature, but always over factual matters. Were Shakespeare's plays originally performed in a Midlands accent? Was fire a more important discovery than the wheel? Did Lonnie Donegan write his own hit records? All human knowledge was grist to the mill. These days, such questions can be answered instantly by tapping an iPhone, but then research was a more demanding business.

The arguments would often continue after closing time, when we would repair to a workmen's café in Fetter Lane. Once, a debate on Einstein's theory of relativity became so noisy and the expletives so coarse that the proprietor asked us to moderate out language because we were upsetting some lorry drivers.

Afternoons tended to be a time of quiet contemplation. Towards five o'clock we would quickly dispatch the overnight pages and soon after six take up our regular position at the bar of the Stab.

However, I do recall a wave of excitement one afternoon. Roy Harris, the deputy chief sub, entered the slumbering room and shouted, 'There's a sale of galoshes in Gamage's!' The department rose as one and rushed for the door. It wasn't until I got to the lifts that I remembered I wouldn't be seen dead in galoshes.

Gamage's was a delightfully eccentric place in its declining years, staffed by grave gentlemen who, in their younger days, had served the gentry. Felicity Green once asked where the dog food was in the food department, to be told frostily, 'Madam, this is the food hall.'

'So where is the dog food?' she persisted.

'In the *luggage* department, madam,' was the withering answer.

Keith Waterhouse decided to buy a gnome for a friend he wanted to insult by giving it as a wedding present. He asked the overseer of the gardening department to see their selection of gnomes. Disappointed by what was on offer, he asked, 'Haven't you got anything bigger?'

The salesman drew himself up and said, 'Sir, gnomes are small.'

We were all moderately paid, but there was an upper level of stars on the paper who had been hand-picked by Cudlipp. It consisted of Cassandra, Marje Proops, Donald Zec, Peter

Wilson and Rex North, who by then wrote the *Mirror* 'Diary'. They were considered the writing aristocracy, and rewarded accordingly.

Roy Blackman had once been in the cashiers' department and saw Rex North collecting his expenses. 'They handed him a wad of money as thick as a ham sandwich,' he told his envious audience.

After I'd been there a couple of months, Mike Christiansen hired John Pilger as a subeditor because John convinced him he was a keen cricketer and Mike wanted to put together a team to beat the *Daily Express*. We didn't beat the *Express*. They smuggled a county player on to their side who bowled us all out for nine. John turned out to be about as good as I was.

About that time, Mike asked me if I knew of anyone who could join me on the art bench, as Roy Foster had resigned. I suggested Paddy O'Gara, who was working in advertising, and he was hired. For a time we were known as 'those two Irish fuckers'. Paddy, like me, has an aggressively Irish name, but the nearest we'd ever been to Ireland was the saloon bar of Barney Finnegan's. Bill Hagerty joined the Devil darts gang when he told a classic Fleet Street story. It concerned a sub on the *News of the World* who woke up in pitch darkness, fully dressed on a hard freezing floor; he also had a hangover of monumental proportions and no idea where he was. He lit a match and in the flaring light saw a vast film poster for *Ben-Hur* leaning against a wall.

He was in a cinema, but how did he get there? He stumbled from the room and made his way along a corridor, burst through a barred door and into a high road bright with sunlight as a bus bearing the destination DOVER roared by. Still baffled, he made for a nearby pub that was just opening and asked the barman. 'Where am I?'

'Dover,' answered the barman.

'What day is it?'

'Sunday, twelfth of July,'

Of course, he realised. I got married yesterday afternoon.

The marriage was annulled.

The tale was matched with the story of Franklin Woods, who swayed from the Liverpool press club after a nightlong session and into a shipping company. As an ex-officer in the Fleet Air Arm, he signed up for some kind of voyage.

A long sleep followed and when he awoke he'd quite forgotten that morning's contract. But two weeks later the police picked him up and took him to the docks, where he was put aboard a ship departing on a whaling voyage.

To his apprehension the captain had him unpack a large crate that contained a helicopter. Aided by the ship's engineer, he got the helicopter to fly and was then supposed to use it for spotting whales.

It seems he had some success at this venture, because the captain, with whom he had become bosom friends during the voyage, allowed him his freedom when they finally reached South Africa and put him ashore with a satchel full of cash, which was his share of the prize money.

John Edwards told of when he'd been put in charge of a defunct *Mirror* column called 'Beep beep', named after the sound the Russian satellite, *Sputnik*, made as it circled the earth. John, desperate for an item to fill the column, had invented a new German product, 'soon to be available in Britain', called 'Roll-Down Crazy Paving'. To his horror, the following day the paper was besieged by readers demanding the name of the fictitious German company.

John Edwards once came to Manchester with us on a trip that Denis Futrell and I made. On the second night Edwards urged that we visit Bill Marshall, the *Mirror* district man in Liverpool. When they'd worked together in Liverpool as freelancers they'd concocted the infamous tale of how Liverpool Infirmary had run out of surgical thread. But quick thinking surgeons had sterilised a pair of nurse's knickers and drawn out a strand of nylon long enough to stitch up the patient after an operation.

Inspired by this coup – which made the nationals – they cultivated an RSPCA man and told him of a dreadful sport that had been devised. Depraved youths were taking alley cats by the tail and seeing how far they could hurl them. The RSPCA man declared that he would 'not rest until this vile crime has been stamped out'.

Unfortunately, the bodies of dead cats began to turn up on the streets. John and Bill, who were animal lovers, were filled with a terrible remorse.

At one time Bill had taken to living under the snooker table in the Press Club and even had his meals served there, but John had checked that he was going through a phase of sanity for our visit. We met him at the Liverpool Press Club and he turned out to be a spare, bespectacled figure with a shock of hair. He looked more like the popular image of an eccentric scientist than a hard-bitten reporter. Bill had decided to adopt a mid-Atlantic accent that was half Barrow-in-Furness and half Los Angeles, but among Liverpudlians he sounded like Laurence Olivier.

He invited us to make his nightly rounds to call in on the clubs, pubs and bars. We climbed into his Ford Zephyr and after a few blocks we skidded to a halt in a dank side street. We walked away from the car, Bill having asked us to leave the doors open.

'Why did we do that?' asked Denis.

'The cops drive Zephyrs,' Bill explained. 'Only they have the nerve to leave their cars with all the doors open.'

Liverpool then was Beatle town. Someone in every bar or club would tell us of his schooldays with the immortal four, the girlfriends they'd shared, the time they'd beg him to join the group. The blackened old Victorian buildings seethed with atmosphere and the population seemed to be performing a comedy show. In later years the only place I ever found that could hold candle to it was the French Quarter of New Orleans.

When we said goodbye to Bill in the small hours, he quite unexpectedly, and quite sincerely, said to me, 'Take care of yourself, Mike. You're going to be a big shot on the *Mirror* one day.'

I laughed along with the others. Years later, when Bill was one of our prized feature writers, he asked me to take him to the Ritz because he'd heard it was a 'a fancy kinda place'. The dining room of the Ritz is one of the loveliest restaurants in the world with a view over Green Park. During the lunchtime I'd booked, there were few men at the tables, the restaurant being mostly filled with groups of elegant ladies.

Bill found this atmosphere somewhat daunting and he viewed

the battery of glasses, napkins and various knives, spoons and forks with disdain, but he set upon his steak with gusto and happily drank the wine. When he'd pushed his plate away he said in a voice that penetrated to the corners of the room, 'Hey, Mike, did I ever tell you about the time I fucked my niece?'

Around us a deep silence fell. I glanced about to notice that all the ladies within earshot had laid down their cutlery and were straining towards us in order not to miss a word. Bill smiled and raised his glass to the attentive ladies.

Chapter 11

ANDY CAPP AND A BEER-SWILLING CHIMP

John Edwards was part of another misadventure Mike Christiansen perpetrated. The *Mirror*'s most successful cartoon strip was 'Andy Capp'. Its creator was Reg Smyth from West Hartlepool. Reg was drawing regular cartoons when, in the late fifties, Cudlipp began a circulation drive in the North and asked for ideas.

Reg put forward 'Andy Capp' and the cartoon became a huge hit. Reg was paid a decent salary and was a happy man. Then, in the early sixties, Al Capp came to London.

Al Capp was the creator of one of America's favourite strip cartoons, 'Li'l Abner'. The strip was an institution in the United States. Mike Christiansen decided that Al Capp would meet Andy Capp and John Edwards would cover the event. Later, Mike received a call from John to say the lunch had taken an unexpected turn.

The pair had immediately hit it off and after a general

conversation Al Capp asked Reg how much he was earning. Reg smiled contentedly. 'I'm getting a hundred pounds a week.'

'What's that in dollars?' asked Al Capp.

John Edwards translated.

'So what do you get from the syndication?' asked Al Capp.

'Nothing,' said Reg.

'What kind of contract are you on?'

'I don't have a contract, Al.'

Al Capp paused and laid a hand on Reg's arm. 'Go back to the office and resign. I guarantee I'll get you a million dollars a year from King Syndication, the guys who handle my work.'

At that point, John Edwards rang Mike Christiansen.

Things moved fast at the office. Incredibly, Reg was still getting the salary he'd been given when 'Andy Capp' first started in the Northern editions. When Reg returned from lunch he was summoned to Cudlipp's office. Reg was rather apprehensive about this meeting, because Hugh was a remote, fearsome figure known to be capable of ferocious anger. But Hugh was in a benign mood when Reg was shown into his office.

'Reg,' he said, 'I'll come directly to the point. Your salary is going up from five thousand a year to twenty thousand. You will receive an office car, and generous expenses. You will become a member of the group top-hat pension scheme, and in addition you will receive fifty per cent of the syndication on "Andy Capp". What do you say about that?'

Overwhelmed by this sudden largesse, Reg could remember only one thing that puzzled him. 'What's the top-hat pension scheme, Mr Cudlipp?' he asked.

Cudlipp sighed and took the cigar from his mouth. 'Fuck off, Reg,' he said.

Reg became the highest earner in the Mirror Group. When he retired he chose to go home to West Hartlepool.

Harold Keeble caused a flurry of surprise when he resigned and took Roy Foster with him to the *Daily Sketch*. Geoff Pinnington was delighted, but it was short-lived. Keeble's role was taken by Mike Christiansen, who revealed an equal talent as a designer. My own status also went up when I was appointed to lay out Felicity Green's fashion pages.

Life on the *Mirror* was about everyone waiting for a call from Hugh Cudlipp that would raise them to stardom, but we on the editorial floor seldom even saw him, except in the distance.

The features room was dominated by the brooding presence of Freddie Wills. To keep his overheated mind busy, he had decided to teach himself Russian and consequently his desk was piled with Russian-language newspapers and magazines, as well as ancient heaps of spiked copy and proofs. One morning he returned from the editor's office to the Sargasso Sea on his desk. A few minutes later he gave a great shout of anguish: 'Aaaagh! I've lost something vital.'

We watched as he began to throw heaps of paper onto the floor. Then he shouted, 'For God's sake, will no one help me?'

A few of us gathered about the chaos. Finally, Denis Futrell asked, 'What have you lost, Freddie?'

'A vital sheet of paper,' he snarled.

'What does it say?'

A look of suspicion came to his face, 'I can't tell you that –

it's highly secret. If anyone finds it don't read it, hand it straight to me.'

Freddie's most heartfelt desire was to impose discipline on the feature writers. He had a blackboard installed on which he wrote the assignments, the names of the writers and the date when the copy was due. John Edwards and I returned to the deserted office late one night and John wrote the title MEAT BUBBLE in a vacant assignment slot. A few weeks passed before an angry Freddie assembled the features staff before the blackboard and demanded to know who had altered it.

'How was it altered?' asked Edwards.

'The person who was assigned "Meat bubble" has rubbed out their name,' he said angrily. 'When I find out who it is I guarantee they will be fired.'

One lunchtime the usual crowd were assembled in the Printer's Devil when someone noticed an absentee.

'Where's Pat Doncaster?' asked Blackman.

'He's having a early drink with an agent,' Futrell informed us.

'Where?' asked Dixie Scott.

'At the pub next to the Palladium.'

'Whose agent is it?' asked Miles. Pat frequently brought famous rock performers to the pub so he could play darts and interview them at the same time.

'It's a chimpanzee,' answered Futrell.

'A chimpanzee?'

'This chimp does an impression of Frank Sinatra,' it was explained.

Now we nodded understandingly. Pat reserved his greatest adulation for Frank Sinatra. The lure of a chimp that did an imitation of his idol had proved irresistible.

An hour later Pat Doncaster joined us. He was questioned on how the interview had gone. 'The chimp came in the bar with a raincoat over his shoulder and a little trilby, but apart from that he didn't look like Sinatra at all,' Pat said. 'I was all for packing it in, but the photographer wanted to get a picture.'

'Go on,' we urged.

'The photographer said, "Can he do any other tricks?"'

'The agent said, "He likes to drink a pint of bitter."'

'"Great," said the photographer, "I'll suggest the headline APING HIS BITTERS. Will you sit him on the bar next to the beer pumps?"'

'Go on,' urged Miles.

Doncaster shook his head. 'It's a funny thing about chimps,' he said. 'They don't have throats like us. They relax and just pour a drink down. Before the photographer could focus, the pint was straight down his gullet.

'The barman passed the chimp another pint. He seized the glass and repeated the performance; the photographer missed that shot too.

'"Please give him another one. I'll be ready this time," he pleaded.

'But the agent stepped forward and said, "You'll have to buy him a round of ham sandwiches first. He's got to ride his bike in the second act."'

Chapter 12

CALL ME HUGH

As 1963 ambled towards Christmas, the *Sunday Pictorial* changed its title to the *Sunday Mirror* but the paper remained pretty much the same. I began to have concerns about my progress. On the *Sketch* I'd produced a fair amount of stuff under my own byline; on the *Mirror* I was still low on the ladder.

Then, as December came to an end, Tony Miles and I were told to report to Hugh Cudlipp the Saturday morning before the New Year. Intrigued, we arrived and found Cudlipp surrounded by stacks of library photographs.

'This has been a hell of a year for news,' he announced briskly. 'We're going to do a review of the year and we'll take most of the paper to do it.'

Many extraordinary stories had broken in the past year: it started with the worst winter since 1947; then the spy Kim Philby defected; Hugh Gaitskell died; Charles De Gaulle vetoed Britain's entry into the Common Market; the Profumo affair broke; the Great Train Robbery took place; Harold Macmillan resigned; and President John F Kennedy was assassinated.

'First,' he said, 'I don't want any "sir" stuff: call me Hugh.'

'Yes, Hugh,' we answered.

Working with Cudlipp was a revelation. He made the job seem like a conspiracy; the three of us were going to steal the paper and turn it into our own playground. Occasionally, we would pause to light Havana cigars, drink champagne and chew handfuls of macadamia nuts. It was exhilarating.

Sometimes his phraseology made him sound like a politician trained by a Welsh preacher. He held up a picture of the Pope talking to Kwame Nkrumah, the president of Ghana.

'Here's a picture of a great man, a man who is a shining example to the troubled continent of Africa, where so many live in hope of a better future. Talking to him is the spiritual leader of billions of Catholics throughout the world.'

Inspired, I took the picture and in cropping it found it didn't fit quite as he'd indicated. 'It doesn't scale as you wanted, Hugh,' I told him. 'I'm going to have to cut off some of the Pope.'

He snatched back the photograph and said in quite a different voice, 'Fuck Nkrumah – keep in all of the Pope.'

The pages we produced were powerful. Cudlipp supplied the headlines, but he wanted the shortish copy on each page to be written by Tony Miles. Few people appreciate what a skill it is to produce terse, factual prose. Miles was brilliant at the task. My finished layouts were exactly as Hugh had stipulated, so he was delighted with them, too.

This day turned out to be a significant one in our lives. From then on Tony Miles and I became his blue-eyed boys. Tony was given the opportunity to devise 'Inside Page', a new diary for the *Mirror*, which he excelled at. I became Cudlipp's chosen layout man. He even gave us each a £50 bonus.

Both Tony and I got married in 1964: I to Sandy, who by this time was working as an artist on *Woman's Own*; Tony to Rosalie Macrae, a reporter on the *Daily Express*. Our friendship was cemented when Tony borrowed my wedding suit for his own ceremony, which gave a certain symmetry to our wedding pictures.

Tony was a complex man in those days. Mercurial and foul-tempered, he was one the best writers and judges of newspaper copy I ever knew, and probably one of the most difficult men I ever worked for in journalism.

Rosalie told me of an event that happened when she was posted to Paris. Although she spoke good French, she was nervous about the importance of her new job. But Peter Stephens, the head of the *Mirror* bureau, invited her to dinner at the Café de Paris by way of welcome. Because it was good public relations, the great couture houses would lend their creations to women members of the press corps for special occasions, and so Rosalie borrowed a stunning white Dior dress.

The Café de Paris was built with steep tiers rising from the dance floor, so you could be seated at a table where there was empty space behind your back and a five-foot drop to the tables of the tier below you.

Rosalie was introduced to Peter Stephens's other guests: an

Arab prince, a French general and a senior politician. Rosalie could feel the pressure building up in such exalted company, but she did her best to relax. After a couple of glasses of champagne she felt better, as everyone had complimented her on her command of French. The general told a joke and Rosalie, whooping with laughter, leaned back, forgetting there was only space behind her, and toppled in a back flip from her tier to crash down on the unoccupied table below.

Rosalie said later that she lay there, with the sound of breaking glass and the tinkle of falling cutlery, and time seemed to stand still. All she could do was wish she could die. But Peter Stephens, with his customary *sang-froid*, descended to the tier where she lay. Taking her by the hand to raise her from the table, he said, 'Now, we shall dance.'

The next year was eventful for Mirror Newspapers. Edward Pickering joined as editorial director. Pick, as we called him, was an owlish-looking figure who was probably the luckiest man in journalism. Every time his career seemed to be about to crash to earth a guardian angel would pluck him from disaster and gently place him in some even more splendid cockpit. Although he edited the *Daily Express* very successfully following Arthur Christiansen, Lord Beaverbrook never really cared for him.

'Mr Pickering is an old soldier,' he would grumble. 'Always ready with an excuse.' So he banished him to obscurity on *Farming Express*. But the guardian angel had other ideas.

When Reg Payne printed the notorious picture of Lord Boothby with the Kray twins, King instructed Cudlipp that from now on someone senior would have to be in the office on

Saturdays to keep an eye on the editors. Cudlipp had always kept the editorial reins in his own grasp, but he liked going out on his boat at the weekends. Knowing Pick would have no ambition to seize his position, he appointed him to the best-paid Saturday shift in the history of journalism – with the title editor-in-chief. During the week Cudlipp would be in charge, and on Saturdays Pick would contact Cudlipp ship-to-shore if there was a problem – he was also a fine piano player.

Pick was a kindly, man with a rare characteristic among newspapermen. He was quite unable to tell any sort of anecdote. During World War Two he'd served as a major on Eisenhower's staff, where he was highly prized for his ability to deal with the egos of the great commanders in the field. It was Pick's job to get up at dawn and gather the communiqués from the various generals and combine them into a statement that Eisenhower could release to the world's press each morning.

In this role he'd known every famous figure in the Allied armies. My hobby is military history, so I thought Pick's appointment would give me a chance to question someone who had known the major commanders.

'What was Eisenhower like, Pick?' I asked, hoping for a personal insight. He gazed into his glass and said with deep feeling, 'He was wonderful.'

That was it!

Vainly I went through the list: Patton. Montgomery, Tedder, Bradley, Alexander, Spaatz . . . After I'd named someone, Pick would again stare into his glass before offering the same verdict: 'He was wonderful.'

Pick continued through the years, becoming chairman of the

Mirror Group until his retirement. But, even then, the angel was watching. When Pick had been editor of the *Daily Express*, he'd taken under his wing an Oxford undergraduate who was doing a holiday internship. The student was Rupert Murdoch. When Pick retired from the Mirror Group, Murdoch brought him to News International, where he started a new career that lasted into his nineties.

Chapter 13

SUN RISE

Harold Wilson won the election in 1964 and I was invited to a celebratory cocktail party at 10 Downing Street. It is interesting to look back on Wilson, who is now almost forgotten, and remember the high expectations the country had of him. He was considered the most brilliant prime minister since Lord Salisbury; even my father-in-law, who called for his conservative postal vote on his deathbed, wished him well.

What was most evident when we arrived at Number 10 was how delighted Wilson was to be there. He'd already gleaned an extensive knowledge of the fixtures and fittings. He ushered us all to a small anteroom to see a portrait of a brooding James Fox, the Georgian grandee.

'Amazing, isn't it?' he said, gazing up at the long dead face. 'Even with that wig on he looks like George Brown having a sulk.'

We didn't see too much of Hugh Cudlipp in the early part of

1964 as he was busy planning the launch of the *Sun*. The head of the publicity department, Tommy Aitkins, a man of inspired sycophancy, had done his bit by confining a parrot to a dark room and playing it a tape recording of the words 'Read the *Sun*' until the bird was word-perfect and ready to be presented to Cudlipp.

There was an air of being abandoned at the *Mirror*. In our darts sessions, anticipation of the *Sun* caused old hands to recall 'the good old days' with bittersweet nostalgia. There was that occasion, for instance, when it was discovered in the first edition that there was a major mistake in the Coronation route map. There was the time Tony Grey, a features editor, was fired and he sat slumped drunk, in his chair as workmen removed the partitions around his office. And there was the occasion a photographer was instructed to think of a picture to illustrate the coming of spring, and he produced a tortoise looking at a daffodil. After the publication, Cudlipp asked him how he'd found a tortoise that had already woken up. He replied, 'Easy, I stuck it in the fucking oven.'

A new man named Derek Dale arrived from the City office to be features editor. He'd been a sergeant during the war years. This was unusual, as previous executives had all been officers. Almost his first words to me were, 'Time you got a haircut, son.'

It looked as if Derek Dale was going places, but eventually he failed the Cecil King test. If someone was marked for high promotion on the *Mirror*, Cecil King would take them as a companion on one of his frequent trips about the world.

Derek Dale accompanied him to the West Indies, where Mirror Group Newspapers owned newspapers. King arranged for Derek to join him in his suite for breakfast and he arrived at the arranged time.

'It's a lovely morning, Dale,' King observed. 'Shall we have breakfast on the balcony?'

Without thinking, Derek began a struggle to move the already laid table through the French windows until King said frostily, 'I think it would be better if you asked a servant to do that.'

It was the end of his advancement in the Mirror Group.

One man who frustrated all features editors was Eric Wainwright. Eric was rarely seen around the office. He'd decided sometime around 1959 not to work any more. Until then he'd actually been bylined as 'Go-anywhere-do-any-thing Wainwright'. Eric had tried life as a lion tamer, and there were pictures in the library of him having his trousers ripped off in the lion's cage. On another occasion he took up skydiving. No job was too dangerous or outlandish. And he wrote about his adventures with breezy humour. But then one day, for no known reason, he decided to quit.

Successive features editors tried getting him to work, all to no avail. Eric spent his days in a Soho club, of which he was rumoured to be part-owner. During the 1960s the only time he appeared in a newspaper was when he was fined for causing a disturbance in Southwark Cathedral, where he'd taken refuge. He was awakened from a deep sleep by dreadful moaning sounds coming from wind trapped in the organ. In terror he smashed his way out through a stained-glass window.

Most people on the paper drank a great deal and occasionally mishaps would happen. One of the reporters, Ed Vale, had served in a Scottish regiment and would regale us with a bar stool tucked under his arm while he performed his impression of bagpipes going into battle. One night Ed was stopped by a pair of City of London constables and asked to come with them to a cell at Snow Hill Police Station. Dan Ferrari, the night news editor, rushed to Snow Hill to confront the desk sergeant.

'I hear you have falsely arrested one of my reporters, I insist on his release,' demanded Dan.

The desk sergeant was unimpressed. 'He's pissed, chummy,' he answered.

'Nonsense!' thundered Dan. 'I know he's not drunk.'

'How do you know?' asked the sergeant.

'Because, when Ed Vale is drunk, *he sings!*' declaimed Dan.

There was a moment's silence, and then a voice rose from the cells: 'There was a soldier, a Scottish soldier . . .'

The night news editor shrugged in surrender.

Dan did have one notable triumph, though. One evening he came on duty and saw and odd-looking chap sitting in the waiting room clutching a large box.

As the news editor handed over the day schedule, Dan said, 'Who's the chappie in the waiting room?'

'Some nut we can't get rid of,' said the news editor. 'He's been in there all day.'

'What's his story?'

'He says he's invented a time machine.'

A glint of interest came to Dan's eye – machines fascinated him. 'I'll have a word with him,' he said.

He returned after a time and said, 'He's gone.'

The Happy Hack

'How did you do it?' asked the impressed newsdesk assistants.

Dan smiled. 'I told him to go home and come back yesterday!'

The *Mirror* waited with apprehension for the launch of the *Sun*, but probably the person who suffered most was Tony Miles. He was sent to Quebec to write about a gang of French Canadians who threatened violence towards the Queen on a forthcoming visit. Incredibly, this was the only idea that the *Mirror* put up to fight the launch of a new newspaper.

Of course, in business terms it made sense, but Tony Miles felt he'd been given an intolerable load of responsibility. For the first and only time, he froze at his typewriter. He said his mind just wouldn't work. He decided he would set his alarm clock for the middle of the night and, if he still couldn't write, he would send his resignation instead. The piece he sent was brilliant. It was the kind of stuff that in those days made us proud to work for the *Mirror* – but it took a lot out of Tony.

He was always a paradox. His writing was flawless: precise and sharp, yet the simplest of readers could understand his prose. When Cudlipp made him editor of 'Inside Page' the whole of Fleet Street admired the edge and wit of his copy. But Tony hated writing. When he was finally made an assistant editor he pushed his typewriter away, saying, 'Thank Christ I'll never have to touch you again.'

The *Sun* didn't come up to expectations. The circulation fell like a stone. Finally, at the urging of King, Cudlipp returned to give his full attention to the *Mirror*, a newspaper that still responded to his touch.

FRANCIS, LUCIAN AND A HORSE CALLED CHARLOTTOWN

In the *Mirror*'s halcyon days an important part of its formula was the cartoon strips. Before television they were the *Coronation Street* and *EastEnders* of their day.

In Field Marshal Lord Alanbrooke's diaries there is a fascinating passage. During the war years he was Chief of the Imperial General Staff. While he was visiting King George VI and the Queen at Sandringham an equerry ask him if there was anything he required. The field marshal asked for a copy of that day's *Daily Mirror*, as he hadn't read the 'Buck Ryan' detective strip that day. The equerry laughed and said but he'd see what he could do.

I once mentioned this to David Niven, who was also a *Daily Mirror* fan, and he said, 'I bet he really wanted to see Jane.' Jane, a scantily clad young lady, was the pinup of the armed forces in the war years.

In the proprietor–editor relationship the lighter burden is

always on the proprietor: he has to find only one person. For the editor, a winning staff has to be constantly invigorated with fresh talent. Sometimes it meant buying in from outside, and at other times star quality could be right there on the staff – just. Such was the case with John Pilger.

John had moved from being a subeditor to being a feature writer, but he was fed up with the sorts of jobs he was given. Then Cudlipp asked to see this youngest feature writer. The rest of the department were put out that the selection had been made on age rather than experience and all waited, fearing that Pilger would be given a job that might bestow glory. Eventually, John returned and was closely questioned.

'Some politician's lobbied him to get the *Mirror* to say something nice about the youth voluntary services,' John said.

'I know the sort of thing,' said Roy Blackman: '"Motorbike thugs decorate granny's kitchen".'

'I guess so,' said Pilger. 'I've got to give him a memo with my ideas.'

'Thank God we missed that one' was the group consensus; and, relieved, they made for the Stab.

I had a more than usual amount of work on so I remained in the features room and John disappeared to the library. He returned later with an atlas and a pile of cuttings. After a few hours John said, 'what do you think of this?' He handed me his memo for Cudlipp.

It was brilliant. He'd taken Cudlipp's idea for a modest series and wrought it into something quite different. Unknown to Cudlipp and anyone else in Fleet Street, youth volunteers were working all over the Third World: conserving animals in danger of extinction; bringing drinkable water to remote villages; fighting disease; teaching; nursing; and rebuilding communities in the most remote corners of the globe.

John proposed he visit them and report on their activities. He had taken an idea for a few worthy pieces reporting from the more depressing parts of the United Kingdom and turned it into a magic carpet to circumnavigate the globe.

'Good luck with that,' I said doubtfully.

'Yeah, I don't suppose he'll go for it,' said John. 'I'll deliver it to his office and see you in the Stab.'

The following morning John was again called up to Cudlipp's office. When he returned I asked him how it went.

'He had my memo in his hand,' John answered, a trifle stunned. 'He took that bloody great cigar out of his mouth and handed it back to me. It was signed. All he said was "Go."'

John got to see just about every corner of the world; and he won a hatful of awards with the series. It was the beginning of a distinguished career.

John once invited Sandy and me to a dinner party at a house in Hammersmith he rented from a film director. It was close to Hammersmith Bridge and rather grand. We sat in a dining room that was hung with some impressive-looking paintings. The one opposite my seat looked very much like a Turner. My gaze kept returning to it during the meal until I asked John if he knew anything about it.

'We've got an inventory for the house contents somewhere,' he said, and he fished the document from a drawer. After a moment's study he said, 'That's it : a study of the Thames by William Turner.'

All eyes swivelled to the picture and after a few seconds, with no one going anywhere near it, the heavily framed Turner fell from the wall to crash on the floor.

We examined the back of the painting. The supporting wire and the sturdy nail in the wall were both intact. It was the only 'supernatural' event that has ever happened in my life.

Women's editor Felicity Green decided that the youths of the sixties were paying greater attention to their clothes. So she hired a freelance to write a fashion column. She called me into her office, where a visitor with strikingly dissolute looks sat drinking tea. He gazed at me with deep suspicion.

'This is Mike Molloy, who will design your page,' she said. 'I'm sure you two will become friends.'

It was about the only thing she ever got right about Jeffrey Bernard. We went out for a drink and didn't return to the office that day. Jeff took me on a conducted tour of his natural habitat: Soho. We began in the French pub and spent two hours drinking astonishing amounts of whisky. Jeff had a long and unresolved argument about the works of Beckett, then, after closing time, we went on to the Colony Room, where Jeff introduced me to the notorious proprietor, Muriel Belcher.

She addressed me with her customary greeting to newcomers: 'Are you going to buy some champagne, cunty?'

'No he's fucking not,' Jeff replied on my behalf. 'We're drinking Francis's.'

Standing a few feet away were the artists Lucian Freud and Francis Bacon. Jeff leaned towards them. 'Francis, Lucian, this is a friend of mine, Mike Molloy.'

'Have some champagne,' said Bacon, and poured two glasses with the careful correctness of the deeply drunk. I was impressed to be in such company; and for a moment I thought I might learn something profound about painting, but the entire conversation was about racing, and the coming Derby.

'Charlottown is going to piss it' was Jeff's verdict. 'I'll bet my bollocks on it.'

'You've bet your bollocks so many times there nothing under your prick but fresh air, darling,' said Bacon. Before the pair swayed from the room, Bacon reached out and tucked a £50 note into the top pocket of Jeff's blazer. 'In case you have to buy anyone a drink,' he said with an affectionate pat on the pocket.

In future years I was to meet Bacon and Freud several times, but always in the company of Jeff, and each time they were astonishingly drunk, so I had to be introduced again and again. Eventually, I was to meet Lucian Freud in a club late one night and he was quite sober, but this time it was I who was the worse for wear and, tragically, the long conversation we had about his work was wiped from my memory banks.

From Muriel's we took a brief stroll to Gerry's Club, which was mostly frequented by actors, writers and general riffraff with 'Sohoitis'. People with Sohoitis are so seduced by the atmosphere of a handful of pubs, clubs and restaurants that they must spend all of their waking hours there. This makes working for a living such a boring demand that some of them give it up altogether, as Jeff had done when he was discharged from his national service.

After Gerry's my memory grew hazy, but I do recall being

in the Kismet Club, where a depressed young actor said to Jeff, 'What have I done in life? By my age Keats had written "Ode to a Nightingale".'

Morosely, Jeff replied, 'By my age Keats was dead, so I suppose I'm at least one up on him.'

Charlottown did win the Derby, in 1966. I was there with Jeff, but neither of us had a bet on it.

Chapter 15

HOSTING THE GREAT AND THE GOOD

Although Hugh Cudlipp was never editor of the *Daily Mirror* he made all the key appointments. Lee Howard conducted the day-to-day business, but the fun part of editing was all Hugh's. Occasionally, though, Cecil King would put his oar in, and remind Cudlipp who was the ultimate captain of the ship.

So we were instructed to run features on tenpin bowling when King became convinced that the pastime was about to become immensely popular in Britain and he had invested in the business. The Northern editions were left to the Northern staff, as Cudlipp hated going to Manchester.

In the early sixties the circulation began to increase steadily in the North. It happened through a combination of the popularity of the Beatles and that of booming football clubs. Bernard Shrimsley, the then Northern editor, attacked the job with a great deal of drive and eventually came to the attention of Cecil King; and King instructed Cudlipp that he must bring Shrimsley to London so he could be groomed for greater things.

The first Lee Howard knew of it was when Cudlipp brought Bernard Shrimsley into the editor's office and said, 'Lee, I'd like you to meet your new assistant editor in charge of features.'

We in the features department monitored his arrival with interest. He was unlike the usual *Mirror* executive in that he didn't drink. Geoff Pinnington didn't drink, either, but he had an excuse: he was diabetic. Shrimsley just didn't like the stuff. He also gave out a disturbing energy field, as if he buzzed with ungrounded electricity.

I have known several people with this condition in newspapers: Colin Valdar, Cudlipp and David English, whom I met briefly on the *Daily Sketch* when Colin Valdar was the editor. Interestingly, Valdar and English loathed each other; and Cudlipp wasn't too keen on Shrimsley. Perhaps their energy fields clashed.

Shrimsley was an interesting man. He told me that when he was evacuated as a schoolboy of thirteen he complained to the local education authority that he wasn't getting a good enough education. So they moved him to a grammar school. During his national service he was a sergeant setting intelligence tests for prospective officers.

'They weren't very bright,' he said dismissively. 'I set a couple of questions that none of them could solve.'

It didn't occur to him that it was possible to set a problem that was unsolvable. It was part of his character that, if he convinced himself he was right about anything, he was incapable of changing his mind

On another occasion, he tried to justify altering the words in Peter Tory's copy when he was quoting the title of Oscar Wilde's 'The Ballad of Reading Gaol' to 'The Ballad of Reading Jail', on the grounds that readers always read 'gaol' as 'goal'.

His short stay in the features department was something of a rest cure for the staff, as he insisted on doing all of the work himself, including rewriting everyone's copy. He never was happy in the London office, but Murdoch eventually hired him and he ended up editing the *Sun* and the *News of the World*.

He was chosen by Vere Harmsworth to be the first editor of the *Mail on Sunday*, to the disapproval of David English, then editor of the *Daily Mail*, whom Vere had not consulted. It was the easiest thing in the world to see what the prospective readers wanted: just a Sunday version of the *Daily Mail*. But Bernard tried to give them something bearing his own stamp. The launch was a disaster. Then English stepped in and produced the paper that became a great success.

Cudlipp loved propaganda campaigns and promotional stunts. Rupert Murdoch considered him just a political pamphleteer who used the *Mirror* to shock the public, but if the news had been dull or depressing for any length of time he would launch something that would cheer up the readers.

When the miniskirt craze was in full swing Cudlipp became aware of all the beautiful girls strolling on the streets of Britain. He ordered they should appear on the pages of the *Mirror*. The feature, called 'Gorgeous Girls', was a success, so Hugh decided to take it further. All the girls whose pictures appeared in the paper would be invited to a grand ball at the

Albert Hall, where the Beatles would play, champagne would be drunk and the gorgeous girls could dance the night away. What could go wrong?

Each *Mirror* executive was allocated a box above the dance floor, where we would act as hosts to various celebrities. I suppose it was still a sign of the times that, at a dance for teenagers, we, the *Mirror* hosts, would all wear dinner jackets, but I suspect we would have looked even more ridiculous dressed as *Top of the Pops* presenters.

Marty Feldman was in my box, a delightful man and very funny. But he really wanted to talk about politics; Frankie Howerd was the same. But then a lot of politicians like telling jokes. My other guest was Dave Lee Travis, who wore a splendid dinner jacket and lace-trimmed shirt. My own evening wear was drab in comparison. The following week I went to Austin Reed's and bought myself a fetching velvet job.

Larry Lamb, then a junior executive on the *Mirror*, but later to find fame as the editor of the *Sun*, was less fortunate in his guests: he got Simon Dee, a self-important little twerp, who actually thought he was more popular than the Beatles.

As the festivities got under way we, who were sitting above the arena in our private boxes, noticed that the gorgeous girls' dancing seemed pretty wild, and occasionally one of them would crash to the ground and regain her feet with whoops of laughter.

Keith Waterhouse, a late arrival, explained what was going on below. There were scenes of chaos in the corridors. Tommy Aitkins, the publicity director, was a broad-brushstroke man. The person he relied on to sort out the details was his organising genius, the publicity manager, John Jenkinson. Jenks was always immaculate and unflappable. It was he who'd pulled off the masterstroke for the evening by booking the Beatles to play. The trouble was, each of the three hundred or so gorgeous girls had got the idea they were going to meet their idols – and even dance with them.

Tommy Aitkins was arriving just as Jenks was explaining to a mob of sulking girls that they would see the Beatles only on the stage. So obvious was their disappointment that Tommy Aitkins commanded Jenks to give them champagne.

'Tommy, most of them are only about seventeen,' Jenks protested.

'They need champagne,' insisted Aitkins as he departed for Cudlipp's box. And then he added as an afterthought, 'And bring the Beatles up to meet Hugh Cudlipp.'

Within half an hour quite a lot of the gorgeous girls were drunk; and, as is the way with young drunks, some were happy and some sad, but all were still disappointed about not meeting the Beatles.

From our box we could see into Cudlipp's, where he stood gazing down on the whirling crowd below. It was *Citizen Kane* stuff. After a time he grew bored with the dancing below and turned away to begin an animated conversation with the political editor.

Eventually, when the Beatles left the bandstand, from the corridor outside our box we could hear a crescendo of shouting and screaming, but such was the crowd outside it was impossible to push open our door to investigate.

When the noise finally died down, a battered John Jenkinson

entered. One sleeve of his dinner jacket had been ripped off and his dinner shirt was smeared with lipstick. He accepted a large whisky from our bar and explained. 'Three of us managed to get the Beatles into Cudlipp's box. When we finally got the door shut I thought the mob outside would pound it off its hinges. Cudlipp was deep in conversation with the political staff; he looked up at the Beatles and all he said to me was, 'Get these monkeys out of here.'

Cecil King was never seen at promotional events, always claiming he sought anonymity. So many people believed he'd refused a life peerage. The real reason was something quite different. Harold Wilson told me he had offered King a life peerage, but he'd insisted on a life earldom so that he would be further up the aristocratic pecking order than his cousin, Viscount Rothermere, a man he detested.

Cecil King really was an enigma. He actually claimed he could make himself invisible and that he was clumsy with his hands because he'd always had a desire to strangle his mother. His second marriage to Dame Ruth Railton, the founder of the National Youth Orchestra, was a happy one, probably because she worshipped him. She claimed to be psychic and had visions of him achieving greatness, so perhaps it was this revelation that caused his attempt, which we'll discuss later, to overthrow the government of Harold Wilson – but it was Cecil King who had to go.

Percy Roberts, the managing director, also told me a story of King's autocratic behaviour. King called for him and said, 'Roberts, I want you to get the building resurveyed.'

'Yes, sir,' answered Percy without further comment. He was halfway to the door when King asked, 'Don't you want to know why?'

'Yes, if you wish to tell me, sir.'

'You know Dame Ruth is psychic.'

'So I understand.'

King continued: 'Last night Dame Ruth had a dream that a great crack opened in the white stone front of the building. I just want to make sure all is well with the superstructure.'

Percy had the survey done, and the building proved sound.

Some years later I told the story to a friend, Tom Pitt-Aitkin, who was a distinguished psychiatrist. He showed some interest. 'Was Cecil King under any kind of threat at the time?' he asked.

'Yes,' I answered. 'It wasn't long before King was deposed by the other members of the board.'

'Was the building identified with King?' Tom asked.

'Oh, yes, he was very proud of it.'

'I would guess she was picking up unconscious signals from the other board members,' said Tom. 'Some women pick up nuances of speech and behaviour men miss. King *was* the building; her subconscious translated a danger to Cecil King into a danger to the building.'

It wasn't the last time Tom Pitt-Aitkin told me something fascinating about one of my masters.

Chapter 16

'MIRRORSCOPE'

In 1967 Tony Miles and I were summoned by Cudlipp and told that he wanted to start a new section in the paper. It was to be called 'Mirrorscope' and it would be a pullout on Tuesdays and Thursdays. Cudlipp said he would leave the job of designing the section to me, which was flattering.

One day, just before we decamped to our new 'Mirrorscope' office on the floor above the newsroom, a chance occurred to strike a childish but satisfactory blow against Pinnington's cohorts. The men who staffed the back bench prided themselves on their accuracy and the checks they brought to scrutinise each story. One day, Derek Pryce handed me a news page proof, saying, 'Look what those prats are putting on page seven. Shall I go and tell them?'

At the bottom of the page was a picture from a Cairo newspaper depicting a 'Merman' washed ashore on an Egyptian beach. The picture showed a creature with the lower half of a human being and the upper half of a fish.

'Let's leave it for a bit,' I answered.

When it was getting closer to edition time I had Derek stroll over to the back bench with the page proof.

'Yes?' said a minion, with the usual disdain shown to anyone from the features department.

'It's about this picture of the merman,' said Derek helpfully. 'I thought you might like to know it's not the real thing. It's actually a painting by the Belgian surrealist René Magritte.'

The back bench sat stunned for a moment, and then three men ran towards the composing room in satisfactory panic.

Cudlipp was delighted with the reaction to 'Mirrorscope'. It was greeted by the media pundits as a breakthrough in popular journalism. It won prizes and was hugely popular with everyone – except most of the readers of tabloid newspapers, who found it too demanding. But it did serve a useful function for Rupert Murdoch. He became even more convinced that the *Mirror* was leaving an enticing slice of the readership to be snapped up by the *Sun*.

At that time George Gale joined the *Mirror*. He got the job because Cudlipp, liked the idea of putting the heading GALE FORCE 8 on the top of the page. But the readers were puzzled by Gale's column, which might be a discourse on playing tennis with Peregrine Worsthorne, or even a poetic description of distant youths returning from shooting ducks on the autumn marshes. Some people thought we were going upmarket too fast.

But George was great fun. He once accompanied a team of us from 'Mirrorscope' who had gone to Paris to cover the student riots. We had a grandstand view of the events from the third-floor balcony of our hotel.

It was an enthralling spectacle, until clouds of teargas floated up from the street. George prowled restlessly about the room until the gas, riot police and the students had finally cleared from the streets.

'Right,' he growled when all was clear. 'Who's coming out with me to destroy some expenses money?'

Having been gassed, albeit from a very safe distance, we decided to treat ourselves to a night on the town. I can only say that to enjoy Paris on unlimited expenses is an experience to be remembered.

In 1972 George Gale became editor of the *Spectator* and hired Michael Wynn Jones as his deputy. When the job of literary editor became vacant, George and Michael decided to advertise the job, saying only those with an Oxford or Cambridge double first need apply. To their astonishment they got a reply from a brilliant young man called Peter Ackroyd, who had been to both Oxford and Yale.

But Ackroyd was incredibly nervous at the prospect of working for the *Spectator* and, getting cold feet, decided to deliberately fail the interview. He was shown into George's office where George and Michael sat together.

'So,' George growled, 'you took a first at Oxford and then did a postgraduate degree at Harvard.'

'Ssright,' slurred Peter Ackroyd nervously, having taken a bit to drink before the interview. 'Look, there's something I ought to tell you,' he added.

'Yes,' said George.

'Well, I've never had any kind of a job before, I'm not sure I'm up to it,' said Ackroyd.

'We can give you a hand, can't we, Michael?' assured George.

'Oh, yes,' replied Wynn Jones.

'Well,' said Ackroyd, feeling around for another excuse, 'I've got to tell you, I'm homosexual.'

George cleared his throat, 'Oh, in this day and age . . . All liberal about these things now, you know.'

Michael said he could see Ackroyd was trying really hard to lose the job. 'There's something else I feel I must tell you,' he continued.

'Yes.'

'I'm an alcoholic,' said Ackroyd, in desperation.

George and Michael exchanged significant glances.

'Well, you should fit in here pretty well,' said George.

Four months after the launch of 'Mirrorscope' the paper ran a front-page leader signed by Cecil King with the headline ENOUGH IS ENOUGH. Disenchanted with the Wilson government, King resolved to form one of his own. The Mirror Group board decided enough was enough all right, but the man to go was Cecil King, not Wilson. Hugh Cudlipp took over as chairman, and an early decision he took was to sell the *Sun* to Rupert Murdoch.

Meanwhile, working on 'Mirrorscope' was enjoyable, but there could be the odd problem. We ran a weekly profile that we illustrated with a portrait by a different cartoonist. One week the subject was Chairman Mao and the writer his fervent admirer: Edgar Snow. The piece he submitted was so sugary with praise I decided to get Gerald Scarfe to draw Mao in order to add a bit of counterbalance.

Scarfe always worked on a large scale, drawing on huge sheets of cartridge paper. Having received the work by cab I unrolled the drawing. It was startling: a portrait of a naked Mao presented like a woman giving birth to the Chinese nation pouring from between his legs. It certainly caught the eye.

I carried it to where Tony Miles was working and he looked up. He was silent for some time. 'I think we'll show this one to Cudlipp,' he said, reaching for his hotline. Cudlipp answered.

'Hugh,' he began, 'Mike and I would like to show you a remarkable drawing.' Then he turned to me and said, 'He says we're to go up.'

As he was senior man I held out the drawing. 'Do you want to carry it?' I asked.

'No, *you* carry it,' he insisted, as if I'd offered him a blanket infested with smallpox.

We were shown into Cudlipp's office with me bearing what looked like a roll of white lino. Cudlipp was entertaining Tommy Aitkins. We were also given glasses of champagne and cigars. Then Cudlipp said, 'Let's see this drawing.'

Cudlipp and Aitkins stared at it silence for nearly a minute. I could see that Cudlipp hated it, but he said nothing. Finally he took the cigar from between his teeth and said, 'This drawing is crude, ugly, offensive – and brilliant. Print it!'

I rolled it up and tucked it under my arm. When we were

halfway to the door, we heard Tommy Aitkins ask, 'Hugh, why are all those people marching up Chairman Mao's arse?'

A few weeks later I was talking to John Jenkinson about Tommy Aitkins's question.

'Don't underestimate Tommy,' he said. 'Let me give you an example of how well he understands Cudlipp. When Hugh fired Cecil King he was to take over the chairman's office, but Cudlipp loved King like a father. He couldn't go into the room until Tommy had the room gutted, the fireplace removed, the antique furniture sold and the ceiling lowered.

'Cudlipp told me to show him some pictures from the *Sunday Mirror* Children's Art Exhibition to decorate the walls. One of the biggest ones was a class project of a crowd for a football match. It showed hundreds of figures looking out of the painting and raising up their arms in joy or anguish. I got it framed and it cost a bloody fortune. It was delivered to Cudlipp's office and he called in Tommy. "What do you think of that?" he asked.

'Tommy looked at the picture and said, "Are you sure you want all those people looking down at you Hugh?"

'Cudlipp turned to me and said, "Get the bloody thing out of here. I never want to see it again."'

Cuttings are a valuable source of facts, but can also be a deadly source of inaccuracies. I experienced the 'curse of the cuttings' when I wrote a profile for 'Mirrorscope' of the sculptor Henry Moore. I was troubled by the fear that he would be a disappointment, but I need not have worried. He was a sturdy, friendly man who apologised for keeping me waiting. When he realised that I'd actually come to ask him about his work, rather than how galleries could charge millions for his holes, he extended my time to include the entire afternoon.

Finally, when I had to catch my train, he added, 'Could I ask one favour?' At that point I would have given him the shoes from my feet. 'People often write about me and they nearly always say, "Henry Moore carves stone just as his father, who was a miner, carved coal."'

'Yes,' I said, having already read similar passages several times in the cuttings.

'Well, it is true that my father started life as a coal miner,' he continued, 'but he worked very hard to qualify as a mining engineer, and he was proud of that too. If you mention him will you say that he was a mining engineer?'

'Of course,' I assured him.

When I handed in my copy the chief sub glanced through it and said, 'A bit laudatory, isn't it, old man? Never mind, we can take care of that.'

The following day I didn't see a proof of my piece until the page was nearly due to be off the stone. As expected, it bore only a distant resemblance to my copy, and near the end had been inserted the deadly sentence, 'Henry Moore's father had been a coal miner, how many times he must of thought of that heritage as he hacked holes into a piece of marble.' With a high-pitched scream I ran to the composing department and begged the printer to allow me to cut the line; mercifully, he did.

Then I made for the pub, swearing I'd never write about someone I admired again.

Chapter 17

BIRTH (AND DEATH) OF A MAGAZINE

O ne day in 1966 Lee Howard mentioned quite casually that he thought eventually I would be editor of the *Mirror*. I was astonished. Until that moment I had never even considered such an eventuality.

'When you are editor, don't expect any justice,' he warned me. Then he told me of the first Saturday night he edited the *Sunday Pictorial*.

'Tommy Aitkins sent John Jenkinson to tell me that I had to go to Wembley Stadium that evening to present the trophy for Greyhound of the Year, as it was a *Sunday Pictorial* promotion.

'"Can't *you* present it?" I begged Jenks, but he was adamant. "It's the big event of the dog-racing calendar," he explained. "It's got to be you, but I'll see you get away by nine o'clock."

'So off I went and I kept wondering what was going on back at the office while I was watching these bloody creatures chasing a mechanical rabbit. Then I was told there was a call for me.'

'I got to the telephone and it was Hugh Cudlipp. He was in a fearful rage and wouldn't let me get a word in. All he shouted was, "Listen, Howard, I didn't make you the editor of a great newspaper so you could go to the fucking dogs on the night the edition was coming out. Get back to the office before I fire you."'

I made a note of the story, and was delighted when Terry Lancaster, the political editor, told me one about Lord Beaverbrook that was oddly similar.

When the prison escapologist Alfie Hinds (who managed to break out of three high-security prisons) was on the run, Charles Wintour was appointed editor of the *Evening Standard*, which delighted him. Being cerebral and rather abstemious in his habits, he agreed with some reluctance to join his senior staff in a celebratory glass of champagne at El Vino's wine bar. Wishing he was back at the office, Wintour was surprised to be called to the telephone. The caller was Lord Beaverbrook.

'Mr Wintour,' he barked. 'I understand you're now in El Vino's wine bar. Well, you won't find Alfie Hinds in there. It's a wicked place, full of men of folly.' Then he banged the phone down. Subsequently, Beaverbrook always claimed that whenever Charles Wintour was under any kind of pressure he could be found skulking in El Vino's.

After I'd been doing 'Mirrorscope' for a year the *Mirror* board decided that a colour supplement would be produced to be distributed with the *Daily Mirror* on Wednesdays

Cudlipp selected me as a possible editor if Dennis Hackett,

the editor of *Nova*, which was the most prestigious publication in our magazine division, thought I was made of the right stuff. He dispatched me to Hackett's office, which was in a familiar building: my wife Sandy had worked there as an artist on *Woman's Own* before she left to raise our three daughters, Jane, Kate and Alex.

Nova was located in Southampton Street on the edge of Covent Garden, which was still London's fruit, vegetable and flower market. *Nova*'s floor was a comfortable warren of rooms inhabited by some of the nicest people I ever encountered in journalism. Most of them were young women, but two men were in charge: Dennis Hackett and Michael Wynn Jones.

Dennis, a Yorkshireman, had an extraordinary talent. He was the best magazine journalist of his generation, and had made his reputation on *Queen* under the ownership of Jocelyn Stevens. Michael Wynn Jones, Dennis's deputy, and I became friends from the moment we met. He and Dennis were quite different, but they worked easily together.

Michael, an easygoing individual, was the son of a Church of England vicar. He'd been educated at Lancing College and Oxford, but he was completely without pretension in dress and manner. Women fell for him like ninepins. A dedicated smoker, he told me the first time we went out for a drink that he was writing his autobiography.

'How much have you done?' I asked, impressed.

'So far, just the title,' he answered.

'What is it?' I pressed him.

'*The World is My Ashtray*,' he replied airily.

With its pleasant, undemanding atmosphere, life at *Nova* was conducted with all the hurly-burly of a palm court orchestra. It reminded me of my early days in *Mirror* features.

I spent most of my day with Dennis in his comfortable, cork-lined quarters, but we occasionally ventured out into the other offices. The art editor, Sue Wade, had also gone to Ealing Art School, but a few years after me. It was hard to judge what she looked like because she dressed in baggy, army-surplus fatigues with her hair tucked into a woollen helmet liner.

An aspect of Dennis's genius was his ability to find new talent. Irma Kurtz, Jeffrey Bernard, Molly Parkin, Peter Martin, John Sandilands – they all blossomed under his patronage. He was as generous and encouraging to those he discovered as he was difficult, contrary and downright rude to those who were set above him

The days at *Nova* drifted past, except for about five days a month, when Dennis would erupt into a frenzy of activity, laying out the pages and writing all the headlines for the current issue. Then we would revert to the usual gentle pattern of life. But he was always sceptical about the chances of *Mirror Magazine*'s getting off the ground. Then, one day, Cudlipp said he wanted a dummy of the magazine prepared.

'It looks as if they might be going to do it after all,' said Dennis.

With a little gentle help from Wynn Jones and me, Dennis produced the dummy. I was confirmed in my future editorship when Dennis was stuck for a headline of a lioness and her albino cub that the mother was rejecting because of its white fur.

'Pride and prejudice?' I suggested.

'You'll do,' answered Dennis. 'I'll tell Cudlipp you've got the job.' And that was as close as he ever got to praise.

Birth (and Death) of a Magazine

Hugh Cudlipp decided that Dennis would leave *Nova* to be the director in charge of the *Mirror Magazine* project as well as becoming the publicity and promotions director of Mirror Group Newspapers. I would be the editor. Michael Wynn Jones was a natural for the deputy editor's job. From *Nova* we also took for my secretary Vera, a striking girl who looked and dressed like a gypsy princess; Sue Wade in her battle gear; her deputy, Carol, who also turned heads in a pub; and Lynn White, another beauty, who was a talented subeditor.

Bill Hagerty, already on the *Mirror*, was made assistant editor. Eve Pollard came to see us from *Honey* magazine and got the job after a moment of confusion when Dennis and I nodded to each other.

'So you want that one?' Dennis said when Eve had left.

'I thought you wanted her,' I answered.

'Well you've bloody got her now,' said Dennis philosophically.

Cudlipp decided Keith Waterhouse would produce a column. For regular writers we took on Russell Miller, Colin Bell, Jeffrey Bernard and John Cruiseman. Patric Walker joined as our astrologer. All we needed was someone to do the cookery column.

Wynn Jones and I tried all the regular cooking writers with no luck, so we rang Debbie Owen, the literary agent, and asked her if she had anyone. 'Not really,' she answered, 'but I met a girl recently called Delia Smith. She's never written anything, but there's something about her.'

'Send her along,' I said.

The following day a nervous, pretty girl was shown into my office. I liked her immediately. She was a girl of the suburbs, the kind of girl I'd grown up with – the kind of girl I'd married. The first thing she said was, 'I must tell you, I've never written anything before.'

'That's all right,' I said. 'I've never edited anything before. We're not looking for long pieces. A couple of hundred words and a recipe. That's all.'

'When do you want it by?'

'As soon as you like.'

When she'd gone I reflected on the meeting, and realised what a lousy brief I'd given her. It was the casual way I would have commissioned a newspaper feature writer with decades of experience.

The following day she returned and handed me a couple of sheets of copy. It was terrible. She'd started in a way beginners often do: 'Gosh! I gulped when the editor asked me . . .'

I gave her another brief. 'It's all there,' I said, 'but you've tried to be too clever with it. Relax for a couple of hours, and then just write it as if it were a postcard to your mum.'

She nodded and folded the rejected piece into her handbag. She returned later that afternoon. This time the piece was perfect. It was a friendly chat to the readers.

'This is just right,' I said, and I escorted her to Michael Wynn Jones's desk.

'This is Michael,' I explained. 'He knows far more about cooking than I do. He'll be in charge of your copy.'

'Does this mean I've got the job?' she asked.

'Oh, yes,' I answered.

She got more than the job: that evening she cooked Michael a meal and they were together ever after.

We did have one minor disaster with the column, however, later, after the launch, when we published Delia's Christmas cake recipe, I arrived the morning after publication and found Vera full of woe.

'The telephones haven't stopped ringing, Mike,' she wailed.

'What's up?'

'It's Delia's Christmas cake. She didn't say when to put the nuts and fruit in, so they all left them out.'

I had a lot of letters to write that week. Later in the same day I saw Hugh Cudlipp for a drink and confessed our transgression. 'That's nothing,' he said. 'When I was editing the *Sunday Pic* we told readers to save coal by wrapping coal dust in wet newspapers and burning the results on a hot fire. A scientist rang me up and said if they did that it will explode like a bomb – but I got away with it.'

Years later Michael told me that Delia had learned a valuable lesson from the incident. 'She realised you have to tell people *exactly* how much, and *exactly* when you add the ingredients. Just saying add a pinch of this and a dash of that and then put it in a hot oven until it looks done just won't do.'

Apart from Delia and Michael I acted as matchmaker to another couple. Sue Wade, of the baggy combat uniform, had joined me for a drink in the Stab one evening when John Hill, a graphic artist on the *Mirror*, joined us.

The following morning I was astonished to be greeted warmly by a fantastic-looking girl with long gleaming hair who wore white tights and a Biba dress. It took me a moment to recognise her. Gone were the baggy combat uniform and the woolly hat, and a long-legged butterfly had emerged.

'It's me, Sue,' she said. 'I've decided I'm going to marry John Hill.' She did, too.

During the planning stage of *Mirror Magazine* Cudlipp relinquished the chairmanship of the International Publishing Corporation and allowed Reed International to make a takeover. The men who controlled Reed were businessmen and to them the newspaper industry, with its festering union problems, diverted them from their real interest, which was simply to make profits. In the new Reed structure, Mirror Group Newspapers ceased to dominate. Paper manufacturers and packaging companies now called the shots.

Before the first issue of *Mirror Magazine* was printed, once again Dennis Hackett told me there was no way it could succeed financially.

'I was right: the unions have taken too much. It can't make a profit,' he said. Well, it lasted for a year before Dennis's prediction came true. But we had a hell of a good year. The readers and the advertisers loved us. The only people who hated *Mirror Magazine* were the majority of the *Daily Mirror* staff. Most of us on the magazine were under thirty, and so happy we could feel the jealousy in the air.

The last issue we produced but never printed was a *Mirror Magazine* guide to sexual knowledge. It was pioneering stuff then, but tame by today's standards. The one illustration I did decide to show to Hugh Cudlipp was of an erect male penis as part of a guide showing how to put on a condom. Cudlipp looked at it for a few moments, but there was none of the bravado he'd shown towards Scarfe's drawing of Chairman Mao.

Birth (and Death) of a Magazine

'Maybe we could print it upside down,' he pondered. Then he decided to bring the closure of the magazine forward by a week.

Of the tiny staff we had on the magazine, in later years Bill Hagerty became editor of the *People*; Michael Wynn Jones founded the *Sainsbury Magazine*; Delia Smith became a national star on television and sold more than 20 million cookery books; Eve Pollard edited the *Sunday Mirror* and the *Sunday Express*; Herbert Pearson became editor of the *European*; Jeffrey Bernard wrote a famous column for the *Spectator* and had a hit play, *Jeffrey Bernard is Unwell*, written about him (more on that later); Colin Bell became editor of the *Scots Independent*; and Russell Miller became a successful author. Not a bad result in the long run.

The closure of most publications usually follows a similar pattern. There is a fairly drunken party where all swear to keep in touch and then everyone goes off to start a new life.

Bill Hagerty and I returned to the *Daily Mirror*, I as an assistant editor and Bill as features editor; Eve Pollard went to the *Sunday Mirror*; Michael and Delia bought a cottage in Suffolk with Delia's payoff (they live there still, although the property has been extended somewhat); Keith Waterhouse took his column with us to the *Mirror*; Colin Bell found a new life in Scotland; and Jeffrey Bernard went back to Soho.

Chapter 18

OUR GREEN AND POISONED LAND

L ee Howard had welcomed me back to the newspaper, but my relationships with other executives, and a lot of the older staff, were a little frosty. I was in a sort of limbo for a time, and I suppose still grieving over the closure of *Mirror Magazine*. I began to get used to the sarcastic remarks from other people on the paper and I'd developed an even thicker skin, but it was a depressing time. I couldn't see another job like the one I'd just lost anywhere on the horizon.

At that time, something changed with many of the working-class readers who'd remained loyal for so long. The *Sun* was beginning to edge up and the print unions were in a state of permanent hostility.

Cudlipp, bending with the times, held a series of meetings with groups of the editorial staff, where they were invited to put forward suggestions. Hugh hated these sessions. For the past thirty years he'd simply dictated what he wanted done. He was pleased enough if people had bright ideas; but he hated subordinates suggesting what should be the policy of the paper. Meanwhile, I languished in the doldrums with little to do, unsure of my future.

Then one day at the editor's conference it was announced by Lee Howard that he was resigning and Tony Miles would take over as editor. All departments were astounded and Lee's farewell was fabulous. I don't think I ever saw a more heartfelt goodbye. The ceremony took place in the newsroom and, in tribute, gift after gift was piled on the back bench. To cap it all, shortly after his farewell, he left his third wife on amicable terms, and, piling his twenty-two stone into a Mini, drove to Rome. There, he was to live with Madeleine Dimont, daughter of Penelope Mortimer and stepdaughter of the playwright John Mortimer. It was a happy ending in anyone's book.

Tony took over, but his time as editor was not a happy one. However, no matter how grim his regime, there were passages of sudden humour. It was Bill Hagerty's task, as features editor, to present, after morning conference, the dummy of that day's paper. One morning, before he'd opened the pages, Bill said, 'By the way, have you put Eric Wainright on any special project?'

'No, why?' Tony asked abruptly.

Bill shrugged. 'It's just I haven't seen him in the office for about a month.'

A deep silence fell upon the room; the same thought struck us all. Eric was known to lead a rackety private life. Suppose he'd died somewhere in some rarely visited room and, on the discovery of the body, there followed a coroner's inquest. What answer could there be if the coroner asked how it was that his employers had no idea of his daily whereabouts? But Tony had a flash of inspiration.

'Check with the cashiers,' he instructed.

Bill left the room to return and say, 'Eric cashed a chit for an advance on his expenses two days ago.' Our relief at the news was palpable.

Margaret Thatcher's guru, Sir Keith Joseph, came to dinner one evening and over drinks his first question was, 'And how do you find dealing with the unions?'

Tony Miles replied without hesitation. 'Easy,' he said, 'we give in to them.'

Joseph shook his head at the news. 'I think I'd better sit down,' he said weakly.

In cases like that of Eric Wainwright, a sort of *noblesse oblige* had existed for *Daily Mirror* editorial staff. It was as if Eric had become shell-shocked after years on the paper and was allowed to live out his own version of early retirement. But gradually the National Union of Journalists' demands grew more and more lavish and the old ways gradually began to fade away.

My star had been waning after *Mirror Magazine* but an odd set of circumstances came about, and once again I felt the earth spin. Hugh Cudlipp had held another ideas meeting with editorial staff and the father of the chapel (print unions' equivalent of a shop steward), Bryn Jones, had suggested that the *Mirror* produce a shock issue on pollution. Cudlipp loathed the idea.

'The fucking father of the chapel wants me to produce an issue of the *Daily Mirror* about shit,' he shouted. 'Well, some other bastard can do it, I'm not.'

So Tony Miles sent for me.

Not having been to Cudlipp's meeting with the staff, I had no idea what he meant when Miles said, 'Cudlipp wants you to do a shock issue about shit; you'd better get on with it.'

'Can you tell me a little more about what he wants?' I pleaded.

'Don't ask me,' stormed Miles. 'Ask Bryn Jones.'

Slightly bewildered, I found Bryn, who was quite lucid about the idea.

'We're poisoning the whole bloody planet, Mike,' he said. 'People should know about it.'

I thought for a couple of days about what to do and then called a meeting of the photographers. Luckily, the *Mirror* photographers were quite a different breed from the miserable old bastards I had known on the *Sunday Pictorial*. They were a highly talented bunch and responded to my ideas enthusiastically.

Two weeks later, all the pictures I'd asked for were in and I briefed the caption writers and laid out the whole issue, the way Cudlipp had taught me. Then I went to see Tony. 'I've done the shock issue,' I said. 'Do you want to see it?'

'I don't want to see the fucking thing,' he said, as if I'd suggested showing him some particularly deviant selection of pornography. He snatched up the hotline and called Cudlipp. 'Hugh,' he growled. 'Mike Molloy's done the shit issue; do you want to see it?'

He slammed the phone down, saying, 'He's on his way, and he's got to go out in half an hour.' He indicated a coffee table. 'Stick it down there.'

Moments later Cudlipp appeared and, as was his habit, he talked about other matters for a few minutes before saying, 'OK. Let's see this crap.'

He stood in silence while I went through the issue page by page. Then he walked to Tony's hotline and called his secretary. 'Beryl,' he instructed, 'cancel my next appointment. I'll be in the editor's office.' Then he turned to me and said, 'Take me through it again.'

The photographers had followed my brief perfectly. On the front page was a little girl wearing a World War One gas mask walking across a meadow, the headline read, OUR GREEN AND POISONED LAND.

Other pictures followed: rivers filled with poisoned fish; children drawing species of wild life that would soon be extinct; a family standing in front of a mountain of dustbins indicating the rubbish they disposed of in a year. And the centre pages showed a jumbo jet appearing to rise from a suburban back garden.

Cudlipp was delighted. He had all the senior executives called in and he told them what a brilliant job I'd done. With Cudlipp's sudden benediction, they were all loud in their praise. He then took me off to see the Minister of the Environment, so I could show it to him too.

In the next few days people who had not spoken to me for some time invited me to lunch, or to join them in a drink, and Hugh proclaimed he was going to make me an editor as soon as a post fell vacant.

For a short while I was referred to as the Comeback Kid – but in a friendly fashion.

As an assistant editor I also got to know better one of my heroes in journalism: Sydney Jacobson, Cudlipp's close friend and by now editorial director of the *Mirror*. Sydney had loved the army and won the Military Cross fighting in France. Late at night, when we were in the appropriate surroundings, he would get me to sing with him the soldier's songs I had learned from my father. He could also tell a good story.

It was a curious tradition that nearly all art editors in Fleet Street were bad-tempered. When Sydney was on *Picture Post*, the art editor, of whom he was very fond, was a man known as Grumpy. One day Sydney asked if he was coming to the pub. Grumpy replied, 'Nah, Sid, I've got to go home. The wife moved us into a new house today and I promised her I give a hand with getting the furniture sorted out.' Then he paused and said, 'Well, maybe I'll come for just the one.'

At ten o'clock Sydney said his goodnights, noticing that Grumpy was still in the bar and still going strong.

The following morning Sydney got a call from Grumpy.

'Sydney, do you fancy a drink?'

'I'm up to my eyes in work.'

'Last night I pissed on my mother-in-law.'

'I'll meet you in the King and Keys.'

Five minutes later Sydney was at the bar with Grumpy. 'Tell me what happened,' said Sydney.

Grumpy began, 'I was late and it was the first night we were going to sleep in the place. Anyway, I managed to open the door with my new key and I go upstairs, very quietly, and I even remember where the wife had chosen for our new bedroom, so I didn't disturb her as I got into bed.'

'Go on.'

'Well, I wake up in the middle of the night dying to have a leak. And I don't know where the lavatory is. I blunder about in the moonlight opening doors until I suddenly see something white. I point myself at the white and let go, then, gradually, my eyes get used to the moonlight and I see my mother-in-law sitting up in bed looking right at me.'

'And?'

'Well, she doesn't say anything, and I don't say anything. I just find me way back to bed.'

'What about this morning?'

'I go downstairs and they're all having breakfast. Nobody speaks to me, but I'm used to that. I think maybe it was all a dream. then I look out of the window and I can see the mother-in-law's sheets flapping on the line.'

Chapter 19

THE ENTERTAINING MR CUDLIPP

C udlipp enjoyed entertaining. Occasionally, when the mood took him, we, the executives, would be summoned to his favourite restaurant in Soho, where, in a private room, we would feast and listen to Hugh tell anecdotes. His story of how, when he was a young reporter in Blackpool, he persuaded the unfrocked Rector of Stiffkey to improve his side-show act by introducing a lion was very funny – even though the lion eventually attacked the vicar and killed him.

Hugh also invited an impressive list of people to be entertained in his private dining room. One of the most enjoyable guests was Roy Jenkins, the then Home Secretary. Over the dinner table he seemed more like the master of an Oxford college than someone busy climbing the greasy pole at Westminster (as it turned out, he was later to be Chancellor of Oxford University). He was polished and suave – in spite of a minor speech impediment that saw him pronouncing his *r*'s as *w*'s – and the atmosphere of the senior common room clung to him like aftershave.

Having been often entertained by Harold Wilson, we were all familiar with the generous measures poured for his guests. Roy Jenkins made his generosity sound sinister. 'I knew Hawold wanted to betway me the moment he poured me one of his barbwous whiskies,' he purred.

On another occasion he was asked by Cudlipp how he would respond if he and his group were put into resigning positions because of their support for Britain's entry into the Common Market. Jenkins shrugged and said, 'We all hope that when cornered we would fight like tigers, but I fear most of my colleagues would behave more like cornered wats!'

Ted Heath was also quite different from the man who appeared on television. The *Guardian* writer Alan Brien once said he reminded him of a cocktail sausage, but in real life Heath was a burly, tough-looking individual. The first time I met him he was completely devoid of charm, or any ability to make small talk. Instead, he just made what sounded like speak-your-weight statements.

But later, when he wanted me to print his article attacking one of Margaret Thatcher's policies, he did show an eerie sort of charm, and even made a few body-shuddering jokes. It was like being entertained by a zombie programmed by Frankie Howerd.

Heath turned out to be a fan of the comedian Dave Allen. They met in a hotel lift and Heath asked him to his suite for a drink. They were actually in Ireland and Heath asked him what should be done to solve the troubles in his homeland. Dave's solution was precise: 'Burn all the churches,' he advised.

The actress Shirley MacLaine was in town and my colleague Donald Zec urged Hugh Cudlipp to invite her to dinner. The invitation was extended to me, too. As I had been smitten with her since my early teens I looked forward to the meeting. Sadly, she was nothing like the girl I had mooned over in *The Apartment*. I don't remember a smile throughout the meal. Instead, a rather serious-minded woman spent the entire meal lecturing Hugh on the theme that cannabis should be legalised throughout the world. She claimed that 'the best medical evidence' supported her position. Hugh, who had no particular strong feelings about the subject, finally asked her, 'Who provided this medical evidence?'

'Many of California's leading psychiatrists,' she answered triumphantly.

'Psychiatrists!' Cudlipp replied scornfully. 'We use psychiatrists like stair rods in this building.'

I have never heard anyone else use the phrase, but it finally stunned her into silence.

It was in Hugh's dining room I met J K Galbraith, who had known every Democrat president of the United States from Franklin Delano Roosevelt to Lyndon Baines Johnston. We could tell that he'd liked John Kennedy a lot.

'Jack was a civilised man,' he said, 'but he was a hell of a good politician as well. He knew how you got things done. Let me tell you one thing about his style. I was born a Canadian but I became an American citizen. Canada and America had a mild dispute about air routes between the two countries. It was all technical stuff, but the experts were getting hot under the collar about the matter. Jack called me in and said, "Ken, I want you to represent the United States in these talks."

"'Mr President," I answered, "I've already agreed to represent Canada."

"'I know," he said. "It'll be a big help your knowing their guy so well."

"'Do you think it will be fair, Mr President?"

"'Ken, remember Scott Fitzgerald," he replied. "The test of a first-rate intelligence is the ability to hold two opposed ideas in the mind at the same time. Is there any doubt you have a first-rate intelligence?"

"'I hope not, Mr President.'"

Galbraith continued: 'I told the Canadians and they were quite tickled by the idea, so I went ahead with the work. Actually, it was quite easy and in a couple of weeks I'd finished my paper and I showed it to Jack. He read through it fast and then handed it back to me. "This is good stuff, Ken. How long did it take you to do?"

"'Nearly two weeks."

"'Well, let me tell you, if I present this to the committee and they see it's been done in two weeks they're going to crawl over every sentence and argue for about a year before the talks begin. Take it away and think about it all for another six months and then bring the same paper back to me and I'll get it through by Christmas.'"

'What was President Johnson like?' somebody asked.

'A tragedy, really,' answered Galbraith. 'Probably the last man in America to believe the generals: they kept telling him we could win in Vietnam and he gave them more and more. It broke him in the end. But in his time he was a good man.'

'You liked him too?'

'I did. He was brilliant at making the system work. He acted the part of the foul-mouthed Texan hick, but he was a pretty shrewd operator. None of the Ivy League boys could figure him out, so they always underestimated him. One night I was sitting in my room at Harvard when the phone rang and he said, "Ken, it's me."

'"Yes, Mr President," I answered.

'"Ken, I've got this fucking economic statement I've got to make and none of these useless assholes working for me can write something that a normal fucking citizen could understand. Can you help me out?"

'"I'll do my best."

'"I'll get someone at the White House to deliver it. I need it tomorrow." Then he hung up. An hour later the secret service delivered the document. It was dense stuff, but I managed to iron it out. The following morning I rang the White House and they said, "The President is at his ranch in Texas. Would you like us to patch you through?" And a few moments later LBJ was on the line.

'"Ken," he said. "What the fuck do you want?"

'"I've got your economic statement."

"Oh, yeah, I knew you could do it. None of these useless sons of bitches can hold a candle to you."

'"Would you like to send someone for the document?"

'"No. I want you to be there when I read it. I'll get *Air Force One* to pick you up."'

Galbraith shrugged. 'I was wearing a tweed suit when I got on the plane. In Texas the weather was boiling hot. The car was air-conditioned, but when I got out at the ranch it felt like a hundred degrees. LBJ was holding a party and there were all these characters in cowboy hats. There was a Mexican band playing and they were roasting a couple of steers. I was practically melting by the time I got to LBJ.

'"Ken," he said astonished to see me. "What the fuck are you doing here?"

'"I've got your economic statement, Mr President."

'"Oh, yeah,'" he said. "Come over here."

'We walked away from the crowd and we actually leaned against a corral while he read the paper. When he was finished he looked up and said, "This is brilliant, Ken. None of those other fuckers could have done what you've done. What do you think of the sentiments?"

'"I think it's an important statement; it will have effects on the future of the country."

'LBJ nodded. "Yeah, it's important. But it'll do me no fucking good at all with the American people. That's the problem with economics, Ken. It's like pissing down your leg. It feels pretty warm to you, but it's pretty cool to anybody else."

'I got back in the car and returned home, musing that I'd been an economist all my life.'

In 1972, Hugh Cudlipp decided to shuffle the Sunday editors. Mike Christiansen was demoted from the editorship of the *Sunday Mirror* and made deputy editor of the *Daily Mirror*; Bob Edwards moved from being editor of the *People* to the editorship of the *Sunday Mirror*; and Geoffrey Pinnington was made editor of the *People*. Tony Miles was relieved to see the departure of Geoffrey Pinnington, his old adversary, but he was still no happier as editor.

The department he hammered most was the back bench. But the night editor, Mike Taylor, bore the brunt of his attacks and managed to stay sane under the nightly barrage. The problem was that Tony had ceased to like the *Daily Mirror*. Once, when he had attacked the features department with his accustomed ferocity, I asked him if there was any single thing that appeared in the *Mirror* that he liked. After a moment's hesitation he admitted there was not.

'Is there a paper you would like it to be like?' I asked.

'The *Guardian*,' he answered.

I found Mike Taylor brooding in the Stab one night and asked him what the matter was.

'Bloody Tony Miles,' he answered bitterly. 'He's just left the office. He said to me, "I'm just going out, I don't know where I'm going, but if you need me I'll ring you."'

When Hugh Cudlipp resigned in 1973 it was a cataclysmic event. He also told us that he'd approached a famous Fleet Street figure to take over his role, but could not yet reveal the name.

Then preparations began for his farewell. John Jenkinson planned the evening. We would feast and drink in honour of Hugh at the Trafalgar Tavern. The cost, £40,000, was so prodigious it appeared on the MGN annual budget.

As well as speeches, members of the senior staff would provide entertainment. Mike Taylor and I were chosen for the job. We decided we would add a little satire to the event. We would reveal what Cudlipp was *really* like in an interview with his much-loved parrot, Bertie. Mike volunteered to be the bird, and we had a magnificent parrot suit made for him. The trouble was, we'd never rehearsed the act with Mike wearing the parrot head.

When the time came Mike had had a few. When he stood in a vast hall, filled with hundreds of drunken journalists, all that could be heard from Taylor was a loud muffled sound, like a man trapped aboard a submarine.

I ploughed on asking the questions, but no one could hear our brilliant gags. By the third question the first bread roll sailed towards us, followed by a blizzard of missiles that bounced off our bodies like a biblical stoning. In total humiliation, we trudged through the hall to the gents' lavatory at the back of the hall, where Mike was to change. Once inside, he locked himself in a cubicle and wouldn't come out. Through a crack I could see him sitting on the lavatory smoking, still dressed as a parrot.

'You've got to come out and face them,' I pleaded.

'No,' he answered, 'I'm going to stay here for ever.'

By this time several fights had broken out at the back of the hall, but the top table seemed to be enjoying themselves. Hugh had been presented with a barrel organ. He stood turning the handle with a blissful expression, unaware that the hall before him had descended into chaos.

Also on the top table sat Alex Jarratt, chairman of Reed International. He'd once been a civil servant at the Ministry of Agriculture and Fisheries, and was therefore unused to the behaviour of journalists in a party mood. He watched the events unfold with a fixed smile. I often wondered if it was that night that decided him to sell off Mirror Group Newspapers.

Sydney Jacobson, now a senior journalist in the group, would often talk about Hugh and describe his unpredictable habits when they had been younger men.

'Did I ever tell of Hugh's reaction the time Cecil King banned drinking?' he asked me one day, as I poured him a large whisky.

'No, never.'

'King was having a medical checkup one day and the doctor asked him how much he drank. King told him and the doctor was appalled. He cut him back severely, and, after a week or so, King noticed that everyone in the building was drunk every day, so he ordered Hugh to stop everyone drinking. Hugh's reaction was to just drink white wine, which he considered hardly alcoholic. I cut back a bit, but Reg Payne continued as normal. This infuriated Hugh. We were due to go to Manchester for a couple of days, so we all got on the train and Hugh was in a foul temper. He wouldn't speak to Reg and when we got to Manchester he made Reg stay in another hotel

'That evening the Northern office gave us dinner at the Midland Hotel and Hugh wouldn't let them give Reg any wine. The following morning we got on the train. Reg was still sober and Hugh and I were very hung over, as we'd been drinking most of the night. Hugh insisted on the hair of the dog, but he still refused to let Reg have a drink.

'We got to King's Cross and Hugh said to me, "You've got to tell Payne to stop drinking." And he drove off. I felt awful and I could barely stand up. I said to Reg, "There's something important I've got to tell you, but I think I should lie down for a while."

'"I'd better book a room in a hotel," said Reg.

'He did so, at one of those little hotels around the stations. I lay down on the bed with a Scotch Reg had poured me from the minibar and he said, "I'm feeling a bit tired, too. Do you mind if I put my feet up as well, Sidney?"

'So there we were, like Laurel and Hardy lying in the same bed, and I said, "The thing is, Reg, Cudlipp says you've got to stop drinking."

'Reg looked up at the ceiling and said, "Yeah, I know what you mean. I wish I could take it or leave it like you and Hugh can."'

Another time I asked Sydney if Hugh had ever been angry with him. 'Once,' he answered. 'We were in Cardiff. Hugh insisted on a walk before breakfast. He was chattering like a magpie. He suddenly stopped and said, "Look at that."

'"What?" I asked.

'"That sign." He was pointing at huge lettering on the side of a pub saying WELSH SANDWICHES SOLD HERE.

'"Welsh sandwiches," Hugh mused. "I was born and bred in Wales and I've never heard of Welsh sandwiches. What do you imagine they consist of?"

'Without thinking, I said, "Two slices of bread with fuck all in between them."

'Hugh turned on me in a rage. "I thought you as a Jew wouldn't attack a minority like the Welsh. I never thought I'd hear such a fucking thing from you of all people."'

Sydney was a sophisticated man, and he taught me a good deal about tolerance.

'You know, I was quite fond of Harold Macmillan,' he said.

I was astonished, 'Surely Harold Macmillan stood for everything you want to do away with,' I said.

'Oh, no,' he replied. 'He's part of the family of Britain. He had a great love for the men he commanded in the trenches; he admired the miners, too. George Orwell got it right when he said, "England is like a family, with the wrong members in charge."'

'So you admire Macmillan?'

'I think I understand him. He's a pragmatist who was born in the reign of Queen Victoria. I was with the press corps flying about with him in Africa when he made the 'wind-of-change' speech. He was busy dismantling the British Empire in Africa and the older generation were calling him a dangerous radical. He still thought being British was to be superior to any other nation on earth. But he couldn't say that of course.' (In February 1960, Macmillan had told the South African Parliament that a 'wind of change is blowing through this continent,' in reference to the rise of African nationalism. It was ill received in a country still in the throes of apartheid rule.)

'How did you know if he never said it?'

'He hated flying. Just before we took off on any of our trips in Africa – and we were flying on a lot of colonial airlines – a civil servant would come and whisper something in his ear and you could then see Macmillan visibly relax. Finally, I asked the civil servant what he was whispering. "White pilot, sir," he answered.'

Chapter 20

REACHING FOR THE STARS

In the 1970s there was a growing interest in astrology, so Tony Miles suggested we rehire Patric Walker, who had been the astrologer on *Mirror Magazine*. Patric had become a great friend, so I was pleased by Tony's decision.

In his younger years Patric had been a theatrical manager and owned a successful gay club. In those days he had no interest in astrology. But all that was to change when he went to a party and met an impressive old lady. 'Tell me your birthday, and the time of your birth,' she said.

Patric gave her the information and she nodded. They chatted generally for a time and then she told him she was an astrologer. Then she said, 'You don't believe in astrology, do you?'

'Not really,' he answered.

'You will,' she said. 'How is your life going at the present time?'

'Pretty well,' he answered.

'That's all going to change,' she said briskly. 'I'm afraid there are bad times ahead for you; when it happens give me a ring.'

She handed him her card and he saw she was Celeste, the doyen of British astrologers.

Six months later Patric was swindled out of a lot of money, but he was determined to pay off his debts, so got a modest flat and a boring office job. Then he found Celeste's card and gave her a ring.

'Do you remember me?' he asked.

'Of course I do, Patric. I've been expecting you. Come and see me.'

When they met she said, 'You're intended to be my successor. You've got a lot of work ahead of you.'

For more than a year Patric worked at the office and in the evenings was given lessons by Celeste. Then Dennis Hackett, who had just taken over *Nova*, gave her a call to ask her if she would do an astrology column.

'No,' she said. 'I'm too old, but I've trained my successor. He's called Patric Walker.'

'Send him along,' said Dennis.

By the time I met Patric he had a comfortable flat on the top floor of the actors Jack Hulbert and Cicely Courtneidge's Mayfair town house, and a group of private clients whose names he would never divulge. He also had an income from another mysterious source.

One night Sandy and I accompanied Patric back to his flat for a nightcap and in the foyer there were wine crates with an impressive name stamp.

'Oh, dear, my wine merchant should have picked those up to store for me,' he said.

'Where are they from?' I asked.

'They're part of my inheritance, dear,' he said.

In the flat he told us the story of his mysterious private income. In his salad days he'd had a liaison with an older man from one of Europe's most wealthy families. Patric said the relationship had been like a finishing school. He'd taught him about music and painting, and they'd stayed at the great hotels and eaten in the finest restaurants.

Eventually they'd parted. Years later Patric got a letter from a firm of lawyers asking if he could call at their chambers in Gray's Inn. Puzzled, he went along and a partner told him that his old lover had left him everything. Patric sat dumbfounded while the list was read out: it consisted of a huge sum of money, jewellery, several factories, some vineyards and a vast estate.

When the lawyer finished he said, 'Of course, you realise you won't be able to keep all this, don't you?'

Patric was worldly-wise and had already guessed that the family would contest the will. 'Yes, of course,' he replied.

The lawyer smiled. 'Oh, Mr Walker,' he said. 'I'm so glad you're going to be sensible. Now, would you like to hear what the family are offering you?'

It turned out to be an income for life and a supply of vintage wine.

But the stars among Patric's friends were always Jack Hulbert and Cicely Courtneidge. Sandy and I got to know them quite well. One day I asked Jack if they'd care to join us for lunch at the White Elephant, a restaurant club close by their house in Charles Street.

He made a face. 'I'd love to, but I just can't go there, old boy,' he answered. 'Too sad for me.'

'Why?' Sandy asked, concerned.

'We used to own the very house it's in, darling,' he explained. 'It got a bit blast-damaged during the war so I sold it for five thousand pounds. Cicely wasn't too sure of the price. She urged me to keep the row of mews cottages out the back, but I threw them in too. I'm afraid they got a bit of a bargain.'

I once asked what he regretted most about the changes in London.

'Before the Great War, every evening in the West End of London was like a theatrical event. The boys and girls used to come in from the suburbs in their best clothes. The lads in hats, gloves, carrying walking sticks, and the girls in with parasols; everyone just paraded up and down, and the atmosphere was magical.'

For a few minutes Jack Hulbert had given me a glimpse of the lost city.

Chapter 21

GO WEST, YOUNG MAN

The day Edward Heath called an election in early 1974 (there would be two general elections that year), Sydney Jacobson and I were having lunch with Hugh Cudlipp, so it rather dominated the conversation. Hugh was enjoying his retirement but we could see he was going to miss leading the *Mirror*'s campaign. Heath had made mistake in taking on the miners before he had sufficient coal in stock to feed the power stations, so the country had to endure the three-day week.

We traded headline ideas for the front page for the following day and Hugh suggested, AND NOW HE HAS THE NERVE TO ASK FOR A VOTE OF CONFIDENCE. It was the clear winner, and became the last headline Hugh was to ever write for the *Daily Mirror*. To Harold Wilson's own astonishment, Heath scraped home.

After the election Sydney decided I should go to America for a month on an educational trip. Starting with a couple of days in New York, I was going on to Washington, then Los Angeles,

San Francisco, Las Vegas, Dallas, New Orleans, and back to New York, where Sandy would join me for a final week.

Mirror staff visitors to New York always trod carefully because the head of bureau was Ralph Champion, a man who had created an enduring legend for being difficult. Ralph looked like an ambassador. Tall, silver-haired and elegantly dressed, he had lived in New York for more than twenty years and was proud of the fact that he hardly ever spoke to Americans.

His entire focus in life was to keep Hugh Cudlipp happy and poison anyone else's chances of getting his job. Champion and Cudlipp had worked together in their boyhood; hence Ralph's posting to one of the glittering prizes the *Mirror* had to offer.

To be a member of the New York staff was a fabled appointment, even with Ralph as the boss. And there was a cost-of-living adjustment to the salary that meant staff reporters could live in some splendour. Because of the time difference, copy had to sent early in the day, meaning evenings were usually free.

The junior member of Ralph's staff was to go early each day and secure a special seat in Costello's, the bar used by the press corps. Costello's was a low-ceilinged, crowded saloon where the walls were covered with drawings by James Thurber. At the far end of the bar was a restaurant presided over by an ancient Austrian called Herbie, known as the world's worst waiter.

The seat reserved until Ralph arrived was at the bend in the bar where the telephone on the wall was located, so the office secretary, Barbara, could patch any call from Hugh Cudlipp to Ralph's seat. Since Hugh called only about once a year it said a lot for Ralph's caution.

It was one of Cudlipp's quirks that he never visited New York. He pretty much limited his frequent world travels to locations that were once part of the British Empire. Australian, South African and Canadian newspapers all look to Fleet Street for their style, so Hugh was a mighty figure among Commonwealth journalists. In America he was unknown; the only British newspaper Americans had ever heard of was *The Times*.

Since I was from London, I was automatically regarded by Ralph as a potential enemy, but when I finally convinced him I was not there to seize his empire he became less hostile. He even became cooperative when I told him I wanted to stay at the Algonquin Hotel.

'Why do you want to say there?' he asked puzzled. 'It's full of writers.'

John Smith, an old hand in the New York office, explained how weird Ralph was. 'He's a hypochondriac,' said John. 'He called everyone into his office one morning and said he was suffering from a dreadful disease he'd read about in *Time* magazine. A major symptom was that one foot swelled painfully.

'"I've got it," he said in a pitiful voice. We all looked down and saw the shoe on his left foot was one belonging to his son and was two sizes smaller.'

Smith continued: 'He does have one genuine condition, though. He has a compulsion to jump from high places. He has a fear that he'll come back from lunch and throw himself from the window. So he arranges the furniture so that he won't have a direct run to the window. Tony Delano [then another *Mirror*

Above left: Photographed on the roof of the *Mirror* building, aged sixteen.

Right: I occasionally did some modelling to supplement my meagre wages as a messenger boy on the *Sunday Pictorial*.

Below left: Me (*centre*) with Paddy O'Gara (*left*) and Derek Pryce in art-school days. Later, we all ended up on the *Mirror*.

Above: Christmas Eve 1982: 'the news desk staff of the *Daily Mirror*, led by a reporter playing the bagpipes, paraded around the newsroom and in and out of my office.' The piper was Alastair Campbell. (© *Mirrorpix*)

Below: From left to right: Kent Gavin, Stella Bingham, me, Keith Waterhouse, Tony Delano, Sandy, John Pilger and Judy Bachrach. The team from the *Mirror* celebrating America's bicentennial anniversary in New York, 1975. (© *Mirrorpix*)

Above: The Queen visits the *Daily Mirror* offices in 1976. Later Her Majesty spotted a proof with the headline reading: PROSTITUTE WHO POSED AS A NUN, which elicited a small sigh from her.   (© *Mirrorpix*)

Below left: Me (*left*) with Tony Miles on the Great Wall of China, *c*. 1983.

Below right: . . . and, on the same trip, in Hong Kong, then still a British Dependent Territory.

Above: With Mother Teresa in Robert Maxwell's London apartment, April 1988.
Her message to Maxwell was that God wanted him to give her a million pounds
to start a hospice in England.
(© *Mirrorpix*)

Below: With Paul and Linda McCartney at the *Mirror* Pop Awards. On being
introduced, Paul clipped me on the head, saying 'Nice to know you, head hitter.'

(© *Mirrorpix*)

Above: My wife, Sandy (*left*), with Roger Moore, then the James Bond of the day, and the *Mirror*'s women's editor, Felicity Green, at the Cannes Film Festival.

Below: With the then Labour Prime Minister, Jim Callaghan and his wife, Audrey: 'As Jim Callaghan became warmer in his relationship to the *Mirror* I was invited to more and more receptions, lunches, cocktail parties, and dinners at 10 Downing Street.' (*© Mirrorpix*)

Me beside my portrait by Michael Frith. The painting was shown at the National Gallery to celebrate the art of portraiture, and is now in the National Portrait Gallery collection. (© *Mirrorpix*)

Above: A duet on
the harmonica with
Keith Waterhouse:
'Whenever I think of
Keith Waterhouse, I
smile, and quite often I
burst into laughter.'

(© *Mirrorpix*)

Left: On board Robert
Maxwell's private jet
heading for Moscow
in 1986. By then I was
beginning to feel the
strain of working for
the monster.

(© *Mirrorpix*)

Left: With Jeffrey Bernard, who may or may not have been unwell: on our first meeting, Jeff and I 'went out for a drink and didn't return to the office that day.'

Below: With my former employer, Robert Maxwell, at the launch of my novel, *The Century*, in 1991. 'Maxwell ... made a brief speech commanding the audience to buy the book. I had every confidence he would never read a word of it.' Which was probably as well, as the villain of the piece was modelled closely on him.

(© *Mirrorpix*)

staff writer] used to wait until he'd gone and then rearrange it to give him a clear passage.'

It was in Costello's that I first made friends with Brian Vine of the *Daily Express*, who invited me to have lunch. 'Mind your manners,' Brian demanded of Herbie. 'My companion is from London and used to proper service in restaurants.'

'Velcome to New York, young man,' said Herbie in a thick accent. 'Vot can I get you?'

I ordered a hamburger and Brian Vine said, 'Poached salmon – I love poached salmon. I'll have that.'

'Ve don't have no poached salmon,' said Herbie.

'Then why the fuck do you put it on the menu?' bellowed Vine.

Herbie looked down on him with a gleam in his eye. 'Because I know you like it,' he said.

Later, I stopped at a jewellery store in Grand Central station and asked the proprietor if he had any cheap watches. It was as if I'd struck him a blow in the face.

'Sir,' he answered, 'we only have inexpensive watches.'

When I got to Los Angeles I first had to pay a call on the sheriff's department as I'd been given an introduction by Tom Tullet, the *Mirror*'s crime correspondent. They took me on a tour of the Los Angeles County Jail and I joined the inmates for lunch. It was interesting to eat fried chicken and sweet corn amid a mighty sea of black convicts.

After booking in to the Beverly Hills Hotel I called Richard Gully, who joined me in the Polo Lounge for a drink. He was a delightful Englishman who exuded the grace and charm of a natural public-relations officer. His Hollywood credentials were impeccable. For twenty years he'd been personal assistant to Sam Goldwyn; and in his youth his closest friends had been Errol Flynn and David Niven. He was now press officer to the aristocracy of Hollywood, who paid him mostly to keep their names *out* of the papers.

Shall we have lunch?' he asked. 'I've booked a table at L'Bistro.'

In the foyer of the hotel, Richard stopped to introduce me to Natalie Wood and Robert Wagner; they treated Richard like a favourite uncle. At lunch, Richard's stories of old Hollywood enthralled me. I had grown up in the cinema; my mother had taken me for the first time when I was a babe in arms.

In the days when studios had morality clauses written into their stars' contracts the famous used to go to Mexico to misbehave; and no one misbehaved more than Errol Flynn. Richard finally asked me whom I considered the greatest Hollywood stars. I thought for a few moments and then said I thought Fred Astaire epitomised the golden days.

'Fred?' he repeated. 'Fred Astaire?'

'Yes, Richard,' said a strangely familiar voice at my elbow.

I turned to my left and found I was actually sitting on a banquette beside my hero. He seemed incredibly small.

'Fred,' said Richard. 'Allow me to introduce you to one of England's most brilliant young men'

'Mr Astaire,' I said, awestruck grasping a tiny hand. 'I'm your fatest gran.'

He introduced me to the ladies with whom he dined. They were Gloria Romanoff and Barbara Marx, two of Hollywood's aristocrats.

'Come to dinner tonight,' said Gloria Romanoff.

'He can't, darling,' said Richard. 'He's having dinner with Hank Fonda.'

It was the first I'd heard about it. Here I was in Hollywood, with people who called Henry Fonda Hank. He turned out to be as pleasant as I hoped, and a convinced Democrat. I asked him about his friendship with James Stewart, who was a noted Republican supporter.

He grinned. 'Well, you know, Jimmy's an Air Force general on the reserve. He actually flew missions over Germany. I guess that entitles him to be a bit conservative, but he's one of the finest men I've ever known.'

Somehow, what he'd said reminded me of Sydney Jacobson talking about Harold Macmillan. He was also an accomplished artist, having studied architecture at college. I asked him what got him started again.

'I was in a play on Broadway,' he explained. 'Peter was a little boy then and he'd left some crayons and paper in my dressing room. I just picked them up, and I guess I haven't put them down since.'

When I thanked him for such a pleasurable evening he said he was delighted to meet a newspaperman who didn't want to ask him about Jane.

The following day I rang someone to whom Donald Zec had also given me an introduction before I left the home office: the unforgettably named Beldon Kattleman.

'Come to my home for dinner at seven o'clock,' he instructed, and gave me the address. I was late because the 'inexpensive' watch I'd bought in New York turned out to be a cheap one after all and had ceased to work. Beldon's house was extraordinary: a billionaire's bungalow that seemed to be mostly a conservatory that was half concealed in a densely planted tropical garden. Beldon answered the door himself. 'Mike,' he said. 'Where the hell have you been?'

'My watch broke, Beldon.'

It was as if we were instantly old friends. 'A guy's got to have a watch,' he said. 'Come with me.' He led me into a study, where there was a display case full of wristwatches. He handed me a black-faced example that appeared to have chips of glass instead of numerals. It looked like the sort of thing you won as a prize in a fairground. I strapped it on and followed him to the living room. On the way we passed a beautiful blonde woman with whom he exchanged icy greetings.

'My wife,' he explained. 'I really wanted to marry someone else' – a remark that he didn't explain.

The dinner, unattended by his wife, was impressive and discreetly served by a silent butler. The man sitting next to me was dressed in casual clothes and sporting a stubble beard. When we were introduced he turned out to be Father Lloyd, who was the Vatican's adviser to Hollywood.

'Molloy, that's an Irish name. Are you a Catholic?'

'No, Church of England,' I answered.

'Good,' he said. 'Some Catholics can act kind of strange when they meet a Hollywood priest.'

He told me that, when he'd been the adviser on Franco Zeffirelli's movie *Brother Sun, Sister Moon*, Zeffirelli had given him a Ferrari as a present. 'I had to give it to the church, of course,' he said. 'But I didn't hand it over for a couple of weeks.'

Before I left that night Beldon made me promise to come back the following evening for another dinner.

When I got to my room I found a copy of *Time* magazine. Flipping through it, I saw a photograph of a similar wristwatch to the one I was wearing. It seemed the casing was platinum and the chips of glass were diamonds. The watches were the big fashion item of the season and sold at Cartier's for $30,000.

At the following night's dinner party the guests were writers, agents, studio executives – the infrastructure of Hollywood that runs the business. The successful in Hollywood have a special look. Their tans seem deeper; their hair is perfectly arranged; their teeth dazzling white. Their casual clothes have that brand-new look, as if they'd been bought that afternoon. One man seemed familiar, but he didn't look like the others. He wore a plain grey suit and tie, and listened without saying much. When we sat down to dinner he was placed directly opposite me and I finally recognised him. It was Dane Clark, a movie actor I'd seen in films going back to my childhood.

We started a conversation and I was surprised that he knew all about the Jeremy Thorpe case that had dominated the British newspapers; but was an unknown story in America. (Thorpe was leader of the Liberal Party in the late sixties and early seventies, and was cleared at the Old Bailey of conspiracy and incitement to murder.)

'How do you know so much about Britain?' I asked.

'I like England,' he answered. 'I made a movie there once, with Margaret Lockwood, she's a great girl.'

As a film buff I wanted to know about how he got to Hollywood, so he told me how he'd taken a law degree, but he'd liked the idea of acting and begun to get small parts on Broadway. Then he signed with Warner Bros and made movies with Cary Grant, John Garfield, Humphrey Bogart and Bette Davis.

'You knew Clark Gable?' I asked. Gable had been my mother's favourite actor and I would've been in trouble once home if I didn't find out as much as I could about him.

'Sure,' he said. 'Clark was a good friend of mine.' Then he added, 'But once I thought he wasn't.'

'I don't follow.'

'Clark joined the Army Air Force after his wife was killed in a plane crash,' Dane continued. 'A lot of people thought he wanted to die, and there was a good chance he would, serving as a gunner in a Flying Fortress. I was in Paris towards the end of the war and I was walking through a restaurant when I saw Clark in uniform sitting at a table with a very pretty girl.

'We'd been close friends at home, so I was about to stop and talk to him but he looked right through me. It just wasn't like him, and I wondered what I'd done. The following day I got a call at my hotel.

'"It's me," said Gable. "You saw me in that restaurant yesterday."

'"I did."

'"I guess you're wondering why I didn't speak."

'"I did think we were friends."

'"Let me explain, Dane. After Carol died I wasn't interested in dames for a while. Then things gradually changed."

'"I'm glad."

'"But the trouble was, girls thought they were going to get

Clark Gable, the movie star. I just couldn't live up to that, if you know what I mean."

"'Sure.'"

"'So I hit on this idea. I told the girls I took out I was just some ordinary guy in the Air Force. I just happened to look a lot like Clark Gable. They'd believe it, and then I was all right. So that's the reason I didn't talk to you."

"'Let me get this straight,' I said, 'the girl you were with didn't think you were Clark Gable."

"'That's right.'

'I remembered the way the she'd looked at him in the restaurant and I said, "Clark, believe me, that girl knew you were Clark Gable."

'He didn't speak for a while, and then he just spoke one word: "Damn!" And he said it with a lot more feeling than when he used it in *Gone with the Wind.*'

'Tell them about meeting Nixon,' urged Beldon.

'It's a long story,' said Dane.

A chorus urging him to tell the tale rose from the table.

'OK,' said Dane. 'I was making a television special in Washington and they allowed us to film at the White House. Then Nixon was passing. He glanced toward us as he got into the elevator and then we continued filming. When we were wrapping up for the day a secret service agent came and said to me, "If you're free, can you spare a few minutes for the President?"

'I was no supporter of Nixon, but, still, it's not every day you get to meet the President. I was shown to a small office where Nixon sat at a plain desk. The only thing on it was a lined yellow legal pad and a jar of pencils. The walls were painted tan and the window looked onto thick foliage a few feet from the glass.

"'I'm sorry about how dull the room is," he explained. "I can't work if there's any kind of distraction."

"'Its fine, Mr President," I said, and I was thinking, Here I am in the White House, talking to the President of the United States. We chatted for about fifteen minutes. He knew I'd boxed and played professional baseball. Then he talked about some decision taken by the Supreme Court and I realised he knew I'd studied law. He must have been given a brief.

'After a time I thought, Good Lord, I've spent thirty-five minutes talking to the President. Then, eventually I thought, I've spent an hour and a half talking to the President. Then, after more than an hour, he eventually said, "I hope you shouldn't have been anywhere."

'Without thinking, I said, "Yes, I have a dinner date."

'He apologised for having kept me and shook hands. And I kept thinking, I'm making excuses to leave the President, so I can have dinner with the guys I work with every goddamn day.

'The following morning I was on a TV show and the interviewer says, "So, Dane, did you meet anyone interesting while you were here?"

"'Yes, I met the President."

"'The President? What did you think of him?"

'At that time he was pretty unpopular, and I'm a lifelong Democrat, but I told him what I thought. I said, "He seemed like a nice man. It's a pity everyone in the country can't meet him."

'That day I flew back to the coast, but a few weeks later I got a call from the secret service. "Mr Clark," said a guy, "did you appear on television on a recent trip to Washington?"

"'I did."

"'And can you confirm you made the following remarks about the President?"

'He then read a transcript of the interview.

"'Yes, I said that."

"'In that case, the President would like to know if he can put you on a list of friends of the President."

"'I guess so," I said. After that, every three or four months I'd get an invitation to go to the White House to have dinner with the President of Venezuela or the chairman of the United Nations, people like that.'

On Beldon's insistence I was the last to leave. I was due to get a flight to San Francisco the following afternoon, so, as Beldon bade me good night on the doorstep, relieved to be free of the burden, I handed him the Cartier wristwatch.

'Thanks so much Beldon,' I said. 'It was good to know the time, at least for a few days.'

'Hey, Mike, that was a gift.'

'I can't take it, Beldon, as much as I'd like too. The *Mirror* rules are that we're strictly forbidden to accept gifts.'

'Even from friends?'

'Particularly from friends.'

He looked at the watch for a moment as if he was suddenly quite moved. 'Don't go to San Francisco tomorrow. I want you to come to dinner again.'

He'd been so kind, and I didn't know anyone in San Francisco, so I agreed to delay my journey for another day.

'Come at six o'clock, I want to take a look at your itinerary for the rest of the trip. Incidentally, what are you doing for lunch tomorrow?'

'I'm having lunch with Cubby Broccoli at the hotel. I was going from there to the airport.'

'Then I'll see you at six. Are you sure you don't want the watch?'

'No, thanks. Here's my cab.'

'What the hell are you taking cabs for?'

'I can't hire a car: I left my driver's licence at home.'

'I'll see you at six. Give my love to Cubby. He's a great guy.'

Chapter 22

THE NAME'S BROCCOLI, CUBBY BROCCOLI

'Give my love to Beldon, he's a great guy,' said Cubby Broccoli when we met in the Polo Lounge. I was delighted to see Cubby, as ever. He was a warm, amusing man. As the producer of the Bond movies he sat near the top of the Hollywood heap and he was fascinating about the business of making films: the craftsmen hired, running a budget, choosing the director and stars, the music. He told me that for each Bond film Sean Connery's suits were made in Savile Row, and he got to keep them after the film was finished.

'What about when Bond gets thrown into a shark tank?' I asked. 'Doesn't Sean Connery resent having his free suit destroyed?'

Cubby smiled. 'When the suits are made in Savile Row we send them to Hong Kong to have copies made for the rough scenes.'

On another occasion we were waiting in a private viewing

theatre in the West End so he could show us *Live and Let Die.*
By this time Roger Moore was playing Bond. The team who
had been renting the theatre before us were Michael Medwin,
Lindsey Anderson and Malcolm McDowell. They'd been
watching the finished cut of their film, *O Lucky Man!* and they
were obviously pleased with their work. Cubby introduced us
and chatted for a few minutes. Donald asked who else was in
the movie.

'Ralph Richardson, Rachel Roberts, Helen Mirren, Arthur
Lowe . . .' Michael Medwin continued to reel off an impressive
cast.

'And how long is it?' asked Cubby.

'Just over three hours,' replied Medwin.

'Well, good luck with it,' said Cubby, and they vacated the
room. 'All that work and I doubt if they'll make money with it,'
he added.

'Why not?' I asked.

'You can only get one showing a night with a three-hour
movie. Two hours is good, like this,' he said gesturing towards
the screen as the title *Live and Let Die* came up.

When we were seated in the hotel restaurant and Cubby had
finished waving to familiar faces around the room, I said to him,
'What does Beldon actually do?'

'He was a lawyer – and he owned a hotel in Las Vegas. He
does a lot of things.' Then, changing the subject, he said, 'Did I
ever tell you about the phone booth outside this hotel?'

'No, Cubby.'

'That's where I really got my big start.'

'In a phone booth?'

'Sure. I had an option on a book for a couple of hundred dollars; it was the last day of the option so I decided to give it a shot. I got a couple of rolls of nickels from the desk clerk and went to the booth and called Alan Ladd. He was a big star in those days and a good friend of mine. So I said to him, "Alan, I've got a great part for you. Can I tell a director I know that you're interested?"

'"You can, but you know Richard Mailbaum has got to write my stuff."

So then I called Terence Young, a director I knew, and told him Alan Ladd is going to play the lead in my new movie, and he says he'd like to do the job. So I've got a star, a director and a writer, so all I need now is seed money and I'm flat broke. But I know Howard Hughes is good for it and he owes me a favour. I go to his mansion and the butler says he's on the can. So I go to the door and shout, "Howard, it's Cubby here. I need seed money for a movie." And he says, "Jesus, Cubby, I've got to see a script."

'So I say, "There's no script yet and I need the money today."

'He says, "I can't let you have any money unless I see a script."

'So I lean on the door of the can and I shout, "Howard, you're not coming out until I get the money."

'He laughs and says, "You've got the money. It better be a good movie."

'So that's how I made *The Red Beret*, and that's how I started working in England. We shot it there.'

When I turned up at Beldon's house early that evening a

manservant showed me to his study, where he was dictating to a secretary.

'Show me your itinerary,' he said and when I gave it to him he handed me a document. 'Here's your driving licence,' he added.

'I thought I had to take a test.'

'Ordinary people do,' he said easily. 'Friends of mine don't.'

He glanced at the itinerary and said to his secretary, 'Call Paul in San Francisco, tell him a friend of ours is coming on Friday.'

He turned to me and puzzled, said, 'They got you down for a motel in Las Vegas. That can't be so.'

'The New York office couldn't get me a booking anywhere else.'

'Call the Riviera Hotel and tell them a friend of ours will be in. Call Jack in New Orleans, a friend of ours will be at the French Quarter. We don't know anyone in Dallas. New York, Earl Wilson will contact you when you get to the Algonquin. Type the details up and give them to Mike before he leaves.'

When I got to Las Vegas I realised what life must be for royalty; and it was the same at all other cities I visited. Very rich friends of Beldon would buy me lunch or dinner, invite me to parties and make sure I saw the best of their home towns.

When I got to New York, and Sandy joined me. Earl Wilson, the columnist, got us tickets for the musical *Irene* and afterwards Debbie Reynolds, the star of the show, joined us for dinner. We were also presented with tickets for *A Little Night Music*. Earl had insisted that we go backstage to say hello. Glynis Johns (who won a Tony for her portrayal of Desiree Armfeldt) was polite and offered us a drink; we congratulated her on her performance and departed. The following day she rang the Algonquin Hotel in something of a panic. She apologised profusely for not being more hospitable and asked if we could come to dinner that night. I explained we had to catch a flight home that evening, but I had to assure her she'd been very kind to see us at all.

Some time later in England I was having a drink with the actress Valerie Perrine, who had been a showgirl in Las Vegas, and I mentioned I'd been regally treated in Las Vegas and all over the States, except for Texas, where Beldon had no friends.

'Which hotel did you stay at?' she asked.

'The Riviera,' I answered. 'Why?'

'It's a mob hotel,' she answered. 'Were you introduced as a friend of ours?'

'Yes, I was.'

'It figures.' She smiled. 'You were connected with some pretty powerful people.'

Chapter 23

UNDER SIEGE

The seventies was a time of sieges, and a time when John Penrose, a young *Mirror* reporter, came into his own. He was there at the Spaghetti House Siege in Knightsbridge, when gunmen attempted to rob a restaurant; and at the Balcombe Street Siege, when the provisional IRA held hostages in a council flat near Marylebone Station. But his finest moment came at the bank siege in Stockholm where the hostages formed a friendly relationship with their captors and gave birth to the phrase 'Stockholm syndrome'.

The siege was under way when John flew in. The bank was surrounded by police, and the press had a grandstand view from the wide window of a café. Two other veteran reporters had also hired a flat above the café, and, as Penrose was known as a congenial companion, they agreed he could share the accommodation.

As the siege continued, a deep lethargy settled on the press.

Pub games were played with coins and beer mats, and great exploits of the past recalled. Veteran 1 and Veteran 2 boasted of the women they had conquered around the world: beauties seduced in the Transvaal during the apartheid troubles; in the cotton fields of Mississippi during the civil-rights struggle; in the bawdy houses of Saigon during the Sino-Indian war; and in the Latin Quarter of Paris during the 1968 student riots. Wherever disaster had struck in the past two decades, the veterans had been there and left women who had cause to remember them.

'That's the trouble,' snarled Veteran 1, eventually: 'there's no bloody women in Stockholm.'

'Too right,' answered Veteran 2. 'What a lousy town for crumpet.'

Penrose, who'd kept his own counsel until then, said, 'I might know some girls in Stockholm.'

'Bollocks,' Veteran 1 replied firmly. 'How could a little fucker like you know women anywhere. You've never been further than Croydon on a job.'

Penrose said in a more assertive voice, 'If I can get some girls, will you two pay for my share of the flat?'

'If you can get some girls, I'll *buy* you the fucking flat,' said Veteran 2.

John went to the telephone and made a call to London. 'Phil,' he said to a friend, 'do you remember the names of those two Swedish air hostesses we met at the Hilton? . . . Do you have their Stockholm number? . . . Great.'

He made another call. 'Hello is that Helga? Do you remember me? John Penrose from London? . . . You do! Great! Lovely to hear your voice as well. Listen, I'm in town with two friends. I wonder if you and Karen can find another friend and come to a party.'

He returned to the veterans, who regarded him with contempt. 'No luck, eh, you cocky little sod?'

'Three air hostesses are coming at six o'clock for a sex party.'

'You fucking liar,' said Veteran 1, astounded.

When he had finally convinced them that he was telling the truth the veterans began to prepare for the promised event. Veteran 1 had a haircut and a massage; Veteran 2 had his suit cleaned. They bought drink and peanuts for the flat, and at six o'clock they sat downstairs in the bar waiting until three stunning-looking girls entered. The girls kissed Penrose enthusiastically and were then introduced.

'Shall we go up?' suggested Veteran 1 in a strangled voice.

Once in the flat, Helga said, 'Let us have a drink, then we shall have the sex party.'

With trembling hands the veterans prepared the drinks and, just as they raised the glasses to their lips, there came the crash of an explosion from across the street. The police were storming the bank!

Penrose and the veterans ran to the scene of the story, where they spent the following hours describing the events, interviewing the police and politicians at the scene, as well as onlookers and participants. Eventually, with their copy filed, they made their way back to the flat.

But the peanuts were eaten, the bottles empty, and there was no sign of the air hostesses.

When Idi Amin was dictator of Uganda, Penrose came to his attention. He wrote unflattering things about Amin. The dictator decided he must be expelled and decided to do the job in person. He drove Penrose to the airport in his Range Rover, a vehicle he was so delighted with he decided to demonstrate its versatility by taking a detour over a golf course, where he scattered players as he dipped in and out of bunkers.

Penrose didn't enjoy the experience as much as he might, because Amin was in the habit of putting people who had displeased him onto aircraft that exploded soon after takeoff. But it must have been a day when he was feeling generous.

Richard Stott was a contemporary of Penrose and they became close friends when Penrose first joined the *Mirror*. Stotty showed him how to do his expenses, and there can be no stronger bond between journalists.

One of the things that often attract people into journalism is the nature of the job. General reporting requires quick wits and cunning, but Stotty also had the gift for investigative reporting, which is not the glamorous work portrayed in movies and on television.

Investigative journalists are a special breed. Most reporters have a short attention span, and a long job is measured in days. An investigative journalist needs the ability to endure obstruction and blind alleys for months on end. Another quality that Stotty had in abundance was a lack of awe for those in authority. This lack of respect was also extended to include a few *Mirror* executives.

It is fascinating how those who are corrupt in public life always demand deference. No matter how big the target was,

Stotty would drive them crazy with what they considered his ruthless impudence.

He was funny, too, and occasionally used to write gags for his brother-in-law, the comedian Dave Allen. The best crack I ever heard him deliver was to a less than charming Chinese waiter.

'Wha' you wan'?' demanded the waiter impatiently.

Stotty looked up from the menu and said, 'Fish lips and duck feet.'

As the waiter walked away he called after him, 'And don't get them the wrong way round.'

From the moment I met him I knew he had a great future on the *Mirror*, and so it proved to be. I suppose I changed his life, as he was going to work for the BBC at one point, but I persuaded him to stay.

We all bump around like snooker balls in life, colliding into each other and careering off in new directions.

Chapter 24

RISING THROUGH THE JAM FACTORY

In 1974 the unnamed man to whom Hugh Cudlipp had offered his crown had finally refused the job. It turned out to be Harry Evans. So Tony Miles got the job, and, to his relief, relinquished the editorship. Mike Christiansen was appointed in his place and I was made deputy editor.

I was deeply fond of Mike Christiansen. He was another character who made working for newspapers fun, and his occasional crazy decisions at least gave a dangerous kind of spice to life.

As editor of the *Sunday Mirror* he'd come close to disaster on one particular occasion. Cyril Kersh, his features executive, had challenged Mike by lying on the floor of the editor's office and balancing a golf ball on his forehead, insisting he use him as a human golf tee. Using a number-seven iron, Mike had attempted to drive the ball out of a window over Holborn

Circus, but instead hit Cyril on the temple. Cyril survived, but with his reputation a little dented.

Mike was a man of big ideas, as soon as he was appointed he cast around for suggestions, while at the same time accepting the role in his village's amateur dramatic society's production of J B Priestley's *An Inspector Calls*. Mike was cast as the father and several of us from the office went to the first night in his village hall.

Then Mike announced he'd had the Big Idea: a massive series of reports from all over Europe telling how the Common Market had affected the lives of ordinary people. Mike instructed me to get on with it. 'Think big,' he said. 'Be bold. This will dominate the paper for weeks.'

When the series was about to launch, Mike had the brainwave of going to Paris to supervise the last stage. Impressive numbers of *Mirror* staff were now spread over the face of Europe. Mike Taylor, by now an assistant editor, had accompanied Mike Christiansen to Paris.

I then got a call from Tony Miles. The *Mirror*'s chief cashier had written to him to enquire if he knew what a vast sum the *Mirror* staff had already spent in Europe. 'What's going on down there?' asked Tony. 'The chief cashier says you've spent the whole of the year's budget already and it's only the end of April.'

'It's the European issues,' I answered.

'Issues,' he repeated. 'I thought it was only going to be a couple of pieces. How many issue are there going to be?'

'Mike intends to run it for a whole month.'

'Let me speak to Mike.'

'He's in Paris.'

There was a long pause. 'Get all the material together. I'm coming down with Sydney Jacobson.'

By the time they'd arrived I'd spread piles of copy and pictures over the floor of the editor's office. Tony and Sydney paced among the piles with grim faces.

'When's Mike back?' asked Tony.

'He wants to be here for your wedding celebrations tomorrow,' I said.

Tony was marrying Annie, the girl who had been Rex North's secretary on the first day I had arrived on the *Sunday Pictorial*. Their wedding breakfast was to be at the Café Royal. Annie had eventually become Lee Howard's secretary when Tony had taken over and she'd stayed on. At first she'd found him rather grumpy, but after a time they'd started a secret romance. It had remained so until they had been televised holding hands beneath the scoreboard at Wimbledon; and then the whole office was in on the secret.

Edward Pickering was not at the celebration because he was in China as a guest of the Chinese government. It was an enjoyable party until I got a call from Mike Taylor in Dover. 'Something's wrong with Mike Christiansen,' he said in a worried voice. 'He insisted on driving us back from Paris, but he can only use one arm.'

I told Tony as he was leaving for his honeymoon. Then, full of foreboding, I returned to the office. Eventually, the two Mikes arrived. It was clear Mike Christiansen had had a stroke. We persuaded him to go to Bart's Hospital, where he was kept for observation. I remained in the office brooding about the future, knowing big changes were inevitable.

Over the next few weeks Pick returned from China and Tony from honeymoon. It was a melancholy time. Pick was particularly affected because he'd been on the *Daily Express* when Mike's father had been stricken by a heart attack, so it was history repeating itself.

It was clear that Mike would never be able to edit the paper again. It's not a job for someone who has suffered a stroke. I knew that there was a good chance I would be made editor, and I felt wretched. Much as I hoped I'd get the editorship Mike had been a major influence on my life and I admired him greatly.

The following day Felicity Green came into my office. 'How do you feel?' she asked.

'Lousy,' I answered. 'I feel ashamed at wanting the job so much.'

'Get over it,' she said. 'It wasn't your fault. My father always used to say, "Every new pair of shoes has a stone in them."'

So there it was. I was in the hot seat. Senior members of the staff kept asking me if I was all right, and how I was coping with the strain; but the truth was, there was no strain at all. I was thirty-four and had been nineteen years in the jam factory; by now I knew how it was made.

Morale on a popular newspaper is a palpable thing, but the morale of the *Mirror* had taken some heavy blows. After years of brushing off the *Sketch* like a bothersome wasp , Murdoch's *Sun* had begun to make some serious inroads. A new generation of readers had emerged who didn't much like the Labour Party. They wanted entertainment and bare boobs – even the women readers among them.

I had to get the staff cocky again. Luckily, it was a fairly easy job. The thing about journalists is that most of them are smart and tend to be quick on the uptake. However, they do need direction, otherwise they continue doing the same thing as they were last instructed to do.

So I decided that we'd just produce the best paper we could and enjoy ourselves in the process. I did have a terrific staff: we had Marje Proops, greatest of the agony aunts; Donald Zec, the best show business writer; John Pilger as our chief foreign correspondent; Joyce Hopkirk, launch editor of British *Cosmopolitan* magazine, as woman's editor; Richard Stott the finest investigative journalist in popular journalism; Kent Gavin, chief among a dazzling group of photographers; Reg Smyth drew 'Andy Capp', the most successful cartoon in the world; Keith Waterhouse was considered by the whole of Fleet Street to be the best columnist alive. For political advice I had Terence Lancaster, the political editor, and Geoffrey Goodman, the industrial editor, both highly regarded men.

But to counterbalance the talent we also had a motoring columnist who was banned from driving, and a five foot tall slimming editor who had steadfastly remained a stone and a half overweight; our gardening editor had only a window box in her Balcombe Street flat; and our travel editor was banned from flying with British Airways, after a falling out with cabin staff.

I remembered Felicity Green's words: there were plenty of stones in the new shoes.

Chapter 25

LEGENDS FROM THE NORTH

Harold Wilson called another election in the autumn of 1974 and didn't expect to win it. I made the whole front page the headline,

FOR ALL OUR
TOMORROWS
VOTE LABOUR
TODAY

We'd seen Harold Wilson a few days before the election and he looked worn out. His hair was limp, his complexion grey, and even his suit looked badly creased. Two days after his win he invited us around to Number 10 for drinks and he was a man transformed. He now appeared to be in robust health with a good colour, hair gleaming; and even the same old suit looked brand new. Victory was obviously a powerful pick-me-up.

General elections are a major interruption to the usual flow of daily newspapers. The truth is, elections are bad for business. So general elections are the only time when editors conspire to put their circulations down. Once the election was over I tried to inject something more cheerful and entertaining into the paper, and some of my staff were entertaining in themselves.

Derek Jameson was one. He was Northern editor of the *Mirror*. Born a cockney, he nonetheless managed to thrive amid the northerners who staffed our Manchester office. Derek was a master self-publicist and would issue press releases about the imaginary contribution he was making to the success of the paper.

The greater part of the *Mirror* content was produced in London and sent north to be printed. But there were pages that were specifically for the Northern editions. So a large editorial staff had been recruited. They were well paid and lived in some splendour because property was much cheaper in the delightful countryside around Manchester.

The Northern office had pretty much always been left to its own devices because Hugh Cudlipp had disliked Manchester and its inhabitants. Few people came down to big jobs in London, although many were exiled to the North. I thought I'd go and take a look.

Derek was a good host and over a splendid meal told me some of the legends of the Northern staff. After the port, at my urging, he began.

'When Chris Buckland joined the Manchester reporters, Maurice Wiggleswade took him under his wing. The first night he took him to the Press Club and filled him with pints of bitter until three in the morning, all the time giving advice about his future career, which included urging him to wed a good Northern lass.

'Finally, he insisted that Christopher Buckland come home with him to have a cup of tea and one of his wife's legendary mince pies. Arriving at his house, Maurice shouted up the stairs, "Darling, I've brought young Christopher home for a nice cup of tea and one of your special mince pies. We'll be in the front room. "You see," said Maurice when they were seated, "that's what you get when you marry a good Northern lass: sweetness itself."

'A few minutes later a sleepy-looking woman in a dressing gown entered bearing a tray. Maurice looked at the contents and his face darkened. He seized a huge mince pie from the tray and hurled it against the wall. "You've put too much fookin' sugar on them again," he snarled.'

Derek continued: 'Then there was the case of Martin Keats's secretary. He had a temporary girl doing the job at the time of the Christmas party. Martin was going home early and found one of the reporters making violent love to the temp on his desk. "I'm so sorry," said Martin, backing out hastily.

'The following morning the red-faced secretary brought him a cup of tea, and Martin looked down at his desk top and said, "Well, Susan, you might have changed the blotter."'

Chapter 26

SEX, SATIRE AND RUPERT MURDOCH

In the middle of the sixties, Britain had suddenly, and incredibly, shrugged off the last vestiges of the Victorian age and embraced the shock of the new. Sex was now on the agenda. But, even so, the subject of the contraceptive pill was treated like a hand grenade with the pin pulled.

Fleet Street tiptoed into the water concerning homosexuality and eventually all papers pretty much came to the conclusion that it was all right what 'they' did – as long as they did it in private.

Satire was another matter: the Establishment was suddenly fair game for ridicule, and people who'd thought of themselves as being too powerful to be criticised were jeered at by the masses.

The cast of *Beyond the Fringe* and the television show *That Was the Week That Was* were in the vanguard. Fleet Street was slower to change because the majority of the readers were still pretty reactionary. But change they did; and the engines that did more than any other to instigate the changes were *Private Eye* and Rupert Murdoch.

Private Eye was a publication that baffled the proprietors of the established press. It was stuck together in an attic, mostly by ex-public-school boys. No one was safe from their mockery. They even lacked respect for that defender of the well-connected, Lord (Arnold) Goodman, Harold Wilson's lawyer and political adviser, whose name was enough to cause most of Fleet Street to cringe in fear.

The *Eye* could be cruel and unmerciful, and occasionally wrong, but it was fearless, and, apart from the hilarious gossip and cartoons, it did carry a good deal of real investigative journalism. We all looked forward to each new issue with pleasure, anticipating the discomfort of others, and a fair amount of relief if we didn't get a kicking ourselves.

Murdoch was another matter. He was loathed by the Establishment for other reasons. He thought Britain was a dismal sort of place ruled by Neanderthal trade unions, a fading aristocracy and a gutless political class, window-dressed with a toy-town Royal Family. For him, nothing was sacred.

It seems extraordinary now to remember the power of the unions in the seventies. The leaders, who had secured for themselves inflation-proof pay deals comparable to the conditions enjoyed by senior civil servants, simply followed the wishes of the rank and file and led their mass members on a yellow brick road that ended directly at Margaret Thatcher's door. But on the way they instigated terrifying inflation and a destabilisation that nearly destroyed the Labour Party, before finally putting the wind up the voters.

Chapter 27

A MYNAH OFFENCE AND A TRIP TO TINSELTOWN

The first day I came to work I walked up Fleet Street and passed the legendary journalist and critic Hannen Swaffer. Swaffer had defied convention by remaining famous for several generations, and by the look of him was still wearing the same overcoat he'd owned when he worked for the *Daily Mirror* before World War One. In later years I got to know one of his friends, Stanley Bonnet, who'd been a young reporter on the *Daily Herald* when Swaffer wrote a column for the paper.

Stan told me that Swaffer had once told him that he thought there were too many Scotsmen working in Fleet Street. 'I tried to thin them out,' Swaffer said, 'by putting down bowls of poison porridge at King's Cross, but the bastards were so mean they were getting off at St Pancras because the fare was a farthing cheaper.'

In her day, whenever comedians needed the name of an agony aunt, they always used Marje Proops. The daughter of a Hoxton publican, Marje had gone to art school and started her career as a fashion artist. I asked her how she'd started in Fleet Street and she told me a rather wistful story.

'I worked in a freelance agency,' she began, 'and one morning the boss said, "Go up to the *Daily Mirror*, there's a man called Cudlipp who wants a girl artist." I rushed up to Fetter Lane and was shown into a room where he was dictating a letter to a beautiful secretary. As he paced up and down it was as if sparks were coming off him. I could see the secretary had stars in her eyes.

'After frowning at my portfolio, he said, "How old are you?"

'"Eighteen," I whispered.

'"Do you think you could represent the *Daily Mirror* at Royal Ascot today? You'll have to dress up and wear a big hat. I want fashion sketches of the smartest ladies."

'"Yes," I said. "But I haven't got a big hat."

'He waved the cigar dismissively. "I'll get you an office car. Pick up a new dress and a big hat on the way. The *Mirror* will pay."'

Marje loved Hugh Cudlipp from that day on. Her long marriage was never very happy and she had affairs over the years, but for the rest of her life she always saw Hugh as that young man with sparks coming off him. Apart from the countless readers she advised, Marje helped dozens of people on the staff. Over the years, she was unofficial counsellor to secretaries, executives and reporters, and she never broke a confidence.

But she was not perfect. One year I wanted to give her a

special Christmas present, so I asked her if there was anything she wanted.

'I've always wanted a mynah bird,' she answered.

So I asked my assistant to buy one and planned to give it to her at the editor's Christmas lunch. When the lunch was finished, the toasts made, and I'd said a few words of appreciation, my assistant appeared bearing the bird cage shrouded in a cloth. 'And now a special Christmas gift for the girl who has everything,' I said.

The mynah bird was unveiled and stood on its perch blinking suspiciously at Marje. Marje blinked suspiciously back. It was hate at first sight.

Time passed and I suddenly remembered the bird, so I invited Marje into my office for a drink. 'By the way, how's the bird getting on?' I asked.

Marje looked shifty. 'Well, dear,' she began. 'I'm afraid I've had to find him a new home.'

'Really, why's that?'

'Did you know mynah birds will imitate the sound of anything, a gate squeaking or a passing car?'

'Actually, yes, I did, Marje.'

'Well, the bird developed a particularly unpleasant habit.'

'Go on.'

'Whenever we held a really smart dinner party it would wait until there was a lull in the conversation and then say in a loud cockney accent, "Oh, well, I can't 'ang about 'ere, I've got to go to the fucking airport."'

The bird was found a new home with a boy in Marje's street. Presumably, his family didn't have smart dinner parties.

Donald Zec was still at the top of his form in my day, although he had been a young reporter on the *Mirror* before World War Two. In those days the paper was ruled by Harry Guy Bartholomew and, although only semi-educated, he was considered something of a genius.

Beginning his career in the engraving department, it was Bart who developed the *Mirror*'s famous strip cartoons and instigated the transformation that saw the paper go from a genteel, Tory-supporting picture paper into the razzle-dazzle tabloid that changed the game in Fleet Street.

As a very young reporter Donald had been sent North to find human-interest stories. In his absence Bart announced to his executives that there were too many old people in the paper, and from then on he only wanted to see stories about the young.

Donald was having a thin time in Leeds until he called into the local police station to ask if anything was happening. As he was talking to the desk sergeant a young constable brought in a little old lady. He'd found her curled up in a doorway saying she wanted to die. When asked why by the young copper, she said her sister had bought her a new hat for her birthday and the wind had blown it from her head.

While Donald was still making notes a dustman came into the police station with a hat in his hand. He said he'd been told that an old lady was looking for a flowered hat and was this it? The old lady was so pleased to see her missing headgear she regained the will to live.

Later in London, Bart was on the prowl in the newsroom.

'Got anything good?' he asked the newsdesk.

'Not much, sir,' replied the news editor.

'What about that young lad, Zec?'

'He filed a story, but it's about old people, so we spiked it.'

'Show it to me,' ordered Bart.

The spiked copy was produced and Bart stood reading it. Gradually, a tear trickled down his cheek and, finally, he looked up and said, 'This story is brilliant. Why did you spike it?'

'But, sir,' wailed the news editor, 'you told me we mustn't have any more stories about old people.'

Now a look of dark anger came to Bart's face and he thundered in a voice loud enough to rattle windows, 'Don't you *ever* do what I tell you to do again.'

As a volunteer in the Territorials, Donald had been called up when war was declared. His unusual name came to the attention of the drill sergeant, a grisly Regular soldier.

'Zec, is that really your name?'

'Yes, Sergeant.'

'How do you spell it?'

'Z-E-C, Sergeant.'

The NCO pondered this information and then said, 'Z-E-C. Blimey! Well, I feel sorry for you, son. Do you want to know why?'

'Yes, Sergeant.'

'We're all going to be killed in this war, and when they put your name on the war memorial Z is going to be right down at the bottom, where all the dogs will piss on it.'

After six years as a weapons instructor, Donald returned to the *Daily Mirror* and eventually graduated to write about show business. British film stars seemed remote; the demigods of Hollywood might as well have existed on another planet.

One day in 1947 Donald was called to see the editor, Sylvester Bolam. He greeted Donald with the words, 'Ah, Zec, you have heard of Shirley Temple, I take it?'

'Yes, sir.'

'I've received letter from a reader saying that she isn't the young child we are given to believe. In fact, he claims she's a midget.'

'Shall I write and make enquires?' asked Donald.

'No, this is such a good story I want you to go in person. Take a boat and spend a couple of days in New York on the way.'

Donald reeled from the office unable to believe his luck. Today, we can fly in a gigantic jet to California in twelve hours, but then travel was closer to the nineteenth century. It took a couple of weeks' journeying by ocean liner and transcontinental railway before Donald arrived at the Beverly Hills Hotel.

His room was filled with baskets of flowers, crates of spirits, bowls of fruit and a table overflowing with telegrams. All of the messages were similar: Welcome to Hollywood, give me a ring – Cary Grant; Let's get together and have a drink – Humphrey Bogart; Thrilled you're in town – Bette Davis. All the great stars had sent greetings.

One of them he already knew. It was from David Niven, whom he'd met in London several times. He called him first.

'Donald,' said Niven. 'Come over for a drink tonight.'

'I've got messages from every star in Hollywood; I'd better ring them first.'

Niven laughed. 'That's not a problem. I'll tell you how it works here. Did you write to the studios before you came?'

'I did.'

'All those messages are from the studio publicity departments. They're the people who run the stars. Tell them who you want to see and they'll arrange it. If I were you I'd relax and have a swim for now. See you at six.'

'What's your address?'

'The taxi driver will know.'

The taxi driver did know. He could also reel off the addresses of all the other stars. The house was comfortable, but not as grand as Donald had somehow expected. Niven sensed Donald's surprise and said, 'Bit like a bungalow in Finchley with palm trees, isn't it?'

Over a drink, David Niven told him some surprising truths about the lives of Hollywood film stars.

'None of us have any real money,' he said. 'It sounds like a lot but when the agent has taken his cut, the cost of keeping up a front with the right clothes and address, there's not much left. If your studio lends you out to another studio the fees are enormous, but we don't get any of that.'

'But, surely some of you are rich?' said Donald.

'Oh, yes, Bing Crosby, but he makes vast sums from his records, and he has his own radio show. Bob Hope is the same. But we studio hacks work like dogs doing picture after picture. Still, it's a pretty good life.'

While they were still at Niven's house Donald got a call. It was Humphrey Bogart. 'I knew you fucking Brits would be getting together,' he said. 'Listen, I hear you're a good guy.

Would you like to come out on the boat tomorrow? After that I've got to go out of town on location.'

'I'd love too,' said Donald.

'I'll pick you up at your hotel at seven o'clock – that's in the morning.'

At 6.30 the following day there was a rap on Donald's door. Bogart looked around the Aladdin's cave of publicity-department gifts and said, 'Jesus, look at all this booze.'

Donald nodded. 'I'll never drink it all.' Then he said tentatively, 'Would you like some?'

Bogart took a pull on a cigarette and said, 'I think I can help you out with that case of Scotch.'

They had breakfast together and Humphrey Bogart confirmed all that David Niven had told him. 'Christ, I can just about afford my boat,' said Bogart. 'Thank God Lauren works, too.'

Finally, they set off for Malibu, where Bogart kept his yacht. It was a longish drive. They were halfway there when Bogart suddenly slapped his forehead. 'Jesus, we forgot the Scotch.'

To Donald's amazement he turned the car around and returned to the Beverly Hills Hotel for the forgotten free whisky.

With the kind of access to the stars the studios provided, Donald amassed a pile of material by the time he headed for home. He was about to leave when he remembered one fact he'd forgotten to check. He telephoned David Niven.

'David, is there any truth in the story Shirley Temple is a midget?' he asked.

'Has that one finally got to England?' said Niven.

'You mean there's something in it?'

'It came out of Sweden.'

'You're kidding.'

'A journalist was sent from Stockholm to interview Greta Garbo. Of course, she wouldn't see him, but the *Hollywood Reporter* had just run a story with the headline, SHIRLEY TEMPLE IMPERSONATOR IS A MIDGET. The Swede filed the story after Errol Flynn had got him pissed, and left out the word "impersonator".'

'Is that true?'

'As true as anything that comes out of Hollywood, old boy.'

When Donald got home he tried to interest the features editor in the fact that most Hollywood stars were broke, but couldn't raise any enthusiasm.

'People want magic from Hollywood,' said the features editor. 'Life's depressing enough without you tarnishing the tinsel.'

Oh, well, thought Donald, and began his story: 'David Niven angrily denies that Shirley Temple is a midget . . .'

Chapter 28

THE ECCENTRIC
MR WATERHOUSE

Whenever I think of Keith Waterhouse, I smile, and quite often I burst into laughter. His life was devoted to cheering people up, and he was very good at it. From real poverty in Leeds, he became a top journalist, a bestselling novelist, an award-winning playwright and a noted Hollywood screenwriter.

Keith was contrary, curmudgeonly, mischievous, generous, parsimonious, argumentative – and immensely gifted. One of the pleasures I had as editor was reading his copy before anyone else. It was always immaculately typed, without any alterations; there was no chance of any interference from the 'inky fingers of mediocrity' in Keith's work.

Keith lived his life in self-contained units, rarely mingling his friends in journalism and show business. He worked until six o'clock. By that time his wife, Stella, would have chilled two substantial dry martinis so he could 'catch up' with the rest of the drinking world.

Some days he would relish a lunch with chosen companions that might easily last until the small hours of the following morning. It was another quirky aspect of his character that he enjoyed lunch so much that he virtually ate nothing at all.

His choice of homes was also eccentric. Keith was a wealthy man, but he liked to live in very small flats or houses in the less smart neighbourhoods. However, they were comfortably stuffed with leather furniture, and lined with books and pictures. He had no interest in sport at all.

When he shared an office with his writing partner Willis Hall, they would frequently carouse around town. One December Keith had bought a Christmas tree and they took it to the Kismet drinking club, where they had the tree enrolled as a member. Keith had also bought a painting by Lowry, which he presented to a particularly fetching actress who had joined them.

When Willis went back to live in the North, they continued their writing partnership. I was once at Keith's house when they held a telephone conversation about a script. The journalist and eventual chat-show host Michael Parkinson also shared the same experience. Although we had both clearly heard their voices, because they were on loudspeaker telephones, neither actually said anything coherent at all. The conversations were pretty much as follows:

'Hello, Willis.'

'Hello, Keith.'

'About page, um, I think it sort of needs . . .'

'Yes . . . And in the middle there should be more sort of . . .'

'There's a bit there that works, but after that it needs . . . you know . . .'

'Is the later part, shall we give it more . . .?'

'I think so.'

'Goodbye, Keith.'

'Goodbye, Willis.'

Waterhouse and I were once in Birmingham, where we'd been invited to take part in a daytime television chat show hosted by Anne Diamond. On the train with Keith and my personal assistant, Neil Bentley, I told Keith it was essential we should keep a low profile on the trip because *Private Eye* had been reporting some of the wilder exploits of the *Mirror* staff.

'Let's just have a quiet dinner and then a few drinks in the hotel,' I pleaded.

'Suits me,' said Keith.

'Anything you say, boss,' said Bentley, who looked like a six-and-a-half-foot bank manager.

The TV spot with Anne went well, and we went for a drink in the BBC bar. Then a call came for Keith. He returned in a hurry, saying, 'Drink up, I forgot I'd said we'd have dinner with Anne Diamond. I've already called for a cab.'

We arrived at a Greek restaurant with a huge poster in the window announcing,

THE MIDLANDS AMATEUR BELLY DANCING
CONTEST!
FINALS TONIGHT.

I entered with some foreboding, already imagining *Private*

Eye headlines. The room was filled with many curvaceous ladies wearing very little by way of clothes, who were in a party mood. Within a few minutes, Waterhouse had a belly dancer on each knee and was pouring champagne into their toeless slippers.

As the night progressed, many people the worse for retsina were carried out shoulder high. I finally lost my nerve, and, like Mike Taylor at Cudlipp's farewell, I hid in the lavatory.

In the taxi on the way back to the hotel Keith suggested we have a nightcap. I agreed, relieved to have left the excesses of the Greek restaurant behind us. The residents' lounge was quite lively. There were tables packed with members of the Birmingham CID, who were a good crowd, and a group of young men who had been taking part in a snooker championship.

After a time, Waterhouse announced he would perform the 'egg trick'. Keith requested a box of matches, a biscuit-tin lid, a box of fresh eggs and a pint glass of water. He immediately had the full attention of the room. When the props were assembled, Keith placed the tin lid on top of the pint of water, took the sleeve of the matchbox and put it end up on the biscuit-tin lid, then placed a fresh egg in the recess of the matchbox sleeve.

'Gentlemen, I need your complete silence and your total concentration as I perform this astonishing phenomenon,' announced Waterhouse.

Removing his shoe, he struck the edge of the biscuit tin lid which flew across the room leaving the matchbox sleeve to topple sideways and drop the egg into the pint glass of water. The applause was tumultuous. Keith's bow was interrupted by one of the young men, who tugged his coat and said, 'I'm the Junior Welsh Snooker Champion. Let me have a go.'

Keith set the trick up again and the youth took a deep breath and with a swift motion struck the edge of the biscuit tin – and a table full of Birmingham CID men sat splattered with raw egg.

'How do you do it, what's the trick?' demanded the Welsh champion, distraught that he had been defeated.

Keith put his arm around the youth's shoulder. 'You have to be over fifty,' he said sympathetically.

The political party conferences provided the backdrops to many Waterhouse escapades. One evening in Brighton we got into a poker school and the foreign editor cleaned us out. It was only when we counted the pack of cards we realised we'd been playing with nine aces, and seven kings.

Even so, Keith remained quick-witted. He reeled from the table and asked a white-coated man for a cheese sandwich and a cup of tea.

'I'm the waiter, sir. That's the night porter's job,' he said.

'Give me his telephone number,' said Waterhouse.

He called the number and said, 'I'm a guest. I know it's four o'clock in the morning but you do advertise as a twenty-four-hour service. I would like a cheese sandwich and a cup of tea in the residents' lounge.'

There was a pause, and then Waterhouse continued: 'In that case, I would like seven hundred cheese sandwiches and seven hundred cups of tea.'

He sat down again and said, 'That wasn't the night porter: I woke up the banqueting manager.'

We didn't bother to go to bed that night and after a cup of coffee at 6.30 we decided we needed a Turkish bath. In the

September sunshine on the seafront we found a burly man in a white T-shirt and matching trousers who was sweeping the pavement before the Turkish bath.

'All right if we come in?' Keith asked.

'Suit yourselves,' he answered with a shrug.

He supplied us with towels and keys to the locker room and we changed and took our places on a tier in a white-tiled room. We sat in silence for quite a time, as we had exhausted our small talk throughout the night. Then we finally realised that the room was, if anything, getting colder.

Keith pushed open the door and shouted to the white-clad man, 'It's bloody freezing in here.'

'What do you expect?' he answered. 'We don't turn the heating on until nine o'clock.'

Our stargazer Patric Walker had met Keith only a few times and was in Langan's Brasserie having dinner with a friend, Martin Thomas, who did not know Keith at all. They saw him enter.

'There's Keith Waterhouse with Stella,' Patric said. 'He's very shy, but I'll see if I can persuade them to join us.'

They did so and the evening was going rather slowly until the eccentric proprietor, Peter Langan also decided to join their table. A jeroboam of champagne was rapidly dispatched and Waterhouse made some disparaging remark about Irish dancing. Langan challenged him to demonstrate a clog dance, which Waterhouse claimed was superior. Waterhouse did so on the tabletop.

Martin Thomas, a fastidious man, sat at his feet watching the clumping figure for a few moments, and then said to Patric, 'I can see what you mean about him being shy, dear.'

The ability to goad people into bizarre wagers was another of Keith's gifts. He and I were having dinner in a smart restaurant in Brighton with Peter Tory, who was in those days writing the *Mirror* diary page. Tory had once been a member of the Royal Shakespeare Company, so his knowledge of the Bard's works was extensive. But he fell for one of Waterhouse's traps. Keith bet his own trousers against Tory's that there was a crab in one of the plays. A telephone call established that there is: a dog called Crab in *The Two Gentlemen of Verona*.

Gleefully, Waterhouse took Tory's trousers to the bar at the Grand Hotel, where he introduced them to several leading lights in the Conservative Party. Cabinet members were seen politely shaking a leg. It didn't end there. Over the following weeks Tory received postcards from his trousers sent from Bruges, where the trousers claimed they'd had a brief romance with a lace table cloth, and then from Paris, where the trousers had fallen in love with a pair of French knickers.

One night Keith had arranged to meet me in Soho and failed to turn up. He was usually reliable, so I waited into the small hours in the company of actor, Tom Baker, then famous as the current Doctor Who, Sandy Fawkes, the columnist, and Terry Saunders, an executive in MGN publicity department.. Finally, Waterhouse arrived with profuse apologies. 'I'll buy champagne in the Candy Box,' he offered.

The Candy Box was counted as one of the last refuges of late-night drinkers. It was located down a dank alley; its formidable door was equipped a sliding peephole.

Our polite knocks had no effect, so Sandy Fawkes banged on the door with her shoe. The peephole slid open, a pair of sinister, Oriental eyes peered out and a voice shouted, 'What you want?'

'Open the door,' Sandy commanded. 'I am here with two major newspaper executives, Fleet Street's top columnist, and the finest actor in England.'

The Oriental eyes swivelled to examine us, and, before the peephole was slammed shut, the voice shouted, 'No Doctor Who?'

Tom Baker is a genial soul and when he wasn't working could often be found at the Coach and Horses in the company of Jeffrey Bernard's coterie of revellers. One morning, while they chatted, a silent man arrived and, producing a tape measure, began to make notes on Tom's dimensions.

'This is my tailor,' Tom explained. Then he looked disapprovingly at Jeff's ancient jeans. 'When you've done me,' he continued, 'measure up Mr Bernard on my account. I'd like to see him in a decent suit for a change.'

For each generation of regulars, Soho eventually becomes a haunted house. Throughout most of my Soho years Jeffrey Bernard was a regular fixture, like one of the ravens at the Tower of London. He was the epitome of a real Bohemian. For Jeff, every night was a new venture that could sometimes bring joy and just as often tragedy.

Friends would let him sleep on their sofas and spare beds, and he would set them alight with his cigarettes. A string of women imagined they could heal the hurt they thought they saw in his eyes. Jeff soon set them right. In drink he could be viciously sharp-tongued, or astonishingly amusing. He was endowed with a dazzling array of talents and he could write at short length with great style. He should have been a superstar. The problem was that he was born with the worst case of writer's block I ever encountered. Publishers were always giving him advances for books that never materialised. He could just about squeeze out a thousand words when the wolf was really at the door, and the stuff he did produce made you want to weep at the waste.

I got him to write for all the publications I ever edited, knowing that giving a commission to Jeff was like buying a ticket to a lottery. We remained friends because I never put any pressure on him to deliver and I ignored all his transgressions.

Finally Alex Chancellor, best of the *Spectator*'s editors, realised the same truth about him and made it a virtue. Whenever Jeff failed to deliver he would print the euphemistic line, 'Jeffrey Bernard is unwell' in place of his undelivered column.

Keith Waterhouse and Ned Sherrin realised there was a gold mine in the weekly catalogue of failure, and with Jeff's permission Keith fashioned it into a work of art, a play set in a pub where the eponymous hero reviewed his unconquerable condition.

I was responsible for a few lines in the play. Jeff had printed a letter in the *Spectator* saying he'd been again commissioned to write his memoirs, so if anyone could remember what he was doing between 1965 and 1979 would they please contact him. I replied, saying that on a certain night in 1969 he'd rung my mother and threatened to murder her only son (he was pissed at the time but my mother didn't know it).

Keith told me he'd sent the play to Peter O'Toole, whom he'd known since they'd both worked on the same local paper in Leeds. A few days later he got home late and found a message from O'Toole on his answering machine.

'Keith,' he said, 'you bastard. I was intending to take a year off, but I've just read your fucking play. Now I've got to do the bloody thing. It's brilliant.'

At the party after the first night, O'Toole was introduced to me and for a moment a flicker of fearful surprise showed in his eyes. 'You actually exist,' he said.

'Yes,' I answered.

'Christ, he croaked. 'For a moment I thought you were just a figment of Waterhouse's imagination. Now you've come to life like a fucking Irish ghost story.'

At Jeff's funeral I told a story about being with him at the Ascot races. We'd arranged to meet the trainer Bill Marshall in the champagne bar and we chatted for a while until he said, 'I'm going to the owner's ring to see the runners in the next race.'

'I'll come with you,' said Jeff.

'Where's your hat?' asked Marshall.

'What do I need a fucking hat for?' asked Jeff.

'Suppose you meet the Queen, what will you raise?'

Jeff didn't hesitate, 'Well, there's always the case of my knighthood,' he answered.

Chapter 29

THE PEN IS MIGHTY

How writers produce their work has always interested me. Peter Tory chipped his elegant prose from granite – apt, really, as he was descended from stonemasons. For others, words flow like water, or in some cases champagne. I once spent an evening with Stephen Fry in Groucho's Club and, although he was initially a shy man, I was entranced by his gift of speaking prose. A lot of people are capable of managing decent sentences, but Fry delivers complete paragraphs of coherent thoughts. You may disagree with what he's saying, but by God it's a pleasure to listen to him.

Peter Ustinov was another who could write at the same pace as he thought. I once asked him what he wrote with and he held out his ballpoint pen.

'With this. Dictation takes place in my head,' he explained. 'I can just about keep up with the speed I receive it.'

Kingsley Amis used to enjoy teasing earnest women of

the atheist persuasion when they asked him where his ideas came from.

'Oh, God, I suppose,' he would reply artlessly.

The most enviable writer to watch was Alan Coren. When he was editing *Punch*, I waited in his office a few times while he finished his weekly piece. Alan would sit before his typewriter, lace his hands behind his neck and stare into the middle distance. Then, after about ten seconds, he would unclasp his hands and deliver a violent flurry on the keyboard before pausing again. Once finished, he would rip the finished article from the typewriter and never give it a second glance.

When Margaret Thatcher quite unexpectedly became leader of the Tory Party in 1975, Edward Pickering asked her to dinner. She arrived with fellow politicians Willie Whitelaw and Michael Havers. For our side Pick fielded Tony Miles, Terry Lancaster and me.

It was a pleasant enough encounter. But it was made slightly awkward by Thatcher, who obviously felt she was in enemy territory and seemed rather formal and strained. Ostensibly, the visit was for her to inspect our new technology, which was about as interesting as viewing a bank of filing cabinets.

After the meal she became bored with the conversation and demanded that Pickering show her the new equipment. 'Are you coming, Willie?' she asked.

Whitelaw blustered, 'I thought Michael and I would have some talk with the chaps, Margaret,' he said.

Thatcher managed to snap her handbag shut with quite a loud bang and actually said, 'Humph!'

Then she stalked off with Pick. As she left the room Whitelaw let out an audible sigh of relief.

'She's still got that strange voice,' said Lancaster.

Michael Havers explained: 'The problem is, she started out with a Lincolnshire accent, then she was given rather bad elocution lessons, then she attempted to add an Oxford accent on top of the pile. Now it's hopelessly entangled. All we've been able to do is make it a little less shrill.'

Their attitude towards her was fascinating, like managers bewailing the faults of a new pop singer. That night it didn't seem possible that the time would come when she was treated with adoration – or dread – by the Tory Party grandees

Harold Wilson's resignation in 1976 came out of the blue. The first I heard was when Terry Lancaster told me.

'Why?' I asked.

'He said he's had enough,' said Lancaster bitterly.

As far as 10 Downing Street goes, whoever the occupant, a thick fog of deceit always lies over the truth. Those journalists who are admitted to the magic circle around the incumbent prime minster are trusted only if they tell no one what they know – even their editors.

But towards the end of Wilson's reign it was widely known in Fleet Street that the atmosphere in the inner sanctums reeked of poison gas. The top of the Labour Party was divided into those who were friends of Marcia Williams, Wilson's secretary (later Baroness Falkender) and those who were opposed to her.

Now rumours abounded: Wilson was getting out before a devastating scandal broke; Wilson had been a spy of the

Russians. Joe Haines, his press secretary, steadfastly maintained that it was a planned departure, but no one believed him.

Wilson came to power on a wave of goodwill, but he did nothing about the corrosive power of the unions and so the frightening troubles continued. It really did look for a time that there might just be a revolution in Britain brought about by economic collapse.

One evening Bruce Page of the *Daily Express* and I, along with other representatives of the press and the BBC, were invited to a dinner hosted by Sir Val Duncan of Rio Tinto-Zinc, where we were asked if we would guarantee to continue the printing of the newspapers and radio and television broadcasting if Duncan formed a revolutionary government. Shades of Cecil King, I thought. Afterwards Bruce Page and I walked through Trafalgar Square still unsure we hadn't been part of an expensive practical joke.

Wilson prevailed and the elected government staggered on; but who now? Well, it turned out to be Sunny Jim Callaghan, a man who, like many politicians, wasn't anything like his public persona. Jim was on the strait-laced edge of the party. Popular papers, including the *Mirror*, seemed totally trivial to him, and he didn't approve of topless girls at all. His press secretary, Tom McCaffrey, persuaded him to invite me for a drink, but it wasn't a very warm occasion.

Meanwhile, Joe Haines had written a book. Joe had educated himself at the local library and got a job as a messenger boy on a newspaper. He eventually became a reporter in the House of Commons and came to the attention of Harold Wilson. Later, he was appointed Wilson's press secretary. A lean, plainly dressed man, with gleaming spectacles and a constantly wary expression, he was once compared to one of Oliver Cromwell's puritan generals. He was not well disposed towards Marcia Williams and her coterie of wealthy friends for what he saw as her destructive influence over Wilson.

When Wilson resigned he thought he no longer owed him his pledge of *omertà* and, when the notorious resignation honours list was produced Joe had had enough. He wrote his book, *The Politics of Power* and offered it to the *Mirror* for serialisation.

There, in the middle of a well-written and rather scholarly account of the government of Britain, was a lengthy section that was wonderfully scurrilous. Joe pulled no punches, and Marcia was his target. My first thought was how we would ever fight off Arnold Goodman.

'Won't they take out an injunction, Joe?' I asked.

'I don't think so,' he answered easily. 'They know the stuff I can prove that I haven't put in the book.'

It was a fraught time leading up to the publication. To prepare the series for publication I sent Lancaster and Haines to the Swiss Cottage Holiday Inn for a week and sat back in cheerful anticipation of their copy. They returned with the various episodes, and I sat down to relish the tale

I couldn't have been more wrong.

Because of their old loyalty to Wilson they had produced the dullest copy imaginable. All the bite had been removed; the gossip and the best details obliterated. I was stunned with disappointment. We had paid £60,000 for an exclusive story that now contained all the explosive power of a Christmas cracker.

I sat slumped at my desk, when the solution to my problem

walked into my office: Joyce Hopkirk, the women's editor. Joyce is one of those people who lift your spirits when she enters a room. But, despite a gift for creating hilarious catastrophes, she was a shrewd judge of copy.

'Joyce, I've got a task for you,' I said, handing her the manuscript of the book with the marked chapters and the episodes Haines and Lancaster had extracted. I asked her to make a list of all the most interesting material that had been left out. Then I waited overnight for the list, anticipating the rage I could expect from Haines and Lancaster. I knew they considered Joyce far too trivial-minded to interfere in political copy.

When I presented them with Joyce's appraisal the following day, Lancaster and Haines were incandescent with rage. It wasn't that they disliked Joyce – on the contrary, they both loved the company of women and counted many of them among their friends – but it was the fact that I had given their *political* copy to the *women's* editor!

But when they'd read her long list of the omissions they'd made they reluctantly admitted that she was right. I handed the whole package to John Patrick, our best subeditor, and he knocked together the series I'd originally hoped for.

Tony Miles came down to my office to read the finished copy with Joyce, Haines, and Lancaster in attendance. 'Good stuff' was his verdict. In the conversation Joe added that he had seen a copy of the honours list written on Marcia's notepaper. 'It's a pale-purple colour,' he added.

'Do you mean lavender?' said Joyce, and so the term 'the Lavender List' was born. We inserted it into the copy; from there it passed into common usage.

The Happy Hack

Mary Wilson was unperturbed by the debate over Marcia. I met her several times at cocktail parties and lunches, invariably accompanied by the Labour MP, and my old colleague, Gerald Kaufman.

She did on one occasion act in a manner for which I complimented her. The disgraced Labour minister John Stonehouse, having faked his death and disappeared, was discovered in Australia and he returned to England to face trial. But, before appearing in the dock, he turned up at the Labour Party conference in Blackpool. Stonehouse took a seat in the body of the hall and immediately his old colleagues moved away, leaving him in a sea of empty seats. It made a good picture and the photographers were clicking away when Mary Wilson passed. Seeing he was deserted, she stopped and spoke to him. A look of pitiful gratitude passed over his face at this kindness.

Later there was a pre-lunch drink for Harold and Mary. I approached her as she stood a few feet from Harold, as always talking to Gerald Kaufman, and said, 'I thought that was very decent of you to acknowledge Stonehouse.'

She answered quite passionately, 'Wasn't it disgraceful the way they were all treating him? And he hasn't been found guilty yet, you know.'

'I think he will be, Mary,' said Gerald.

'Well, it wasn't the worst of crimes,' she said, 'and when I think of what some of the others have got away with . . .'

I was about to question her closely on what the others had got away with, but Harold, who obviously had the ability to listen to two conversations at the same time, intervened: 'Mary,' he said quite sternly, 'come along, it's time for lunch.'

The Pen is Mighty

When we published the first instalment of Joe's series it was as if we'd dropped a bomb on the opposition. That day Terry Lancaster, Tony Miles and I had lunch at the Reform Club. We passed within inches of Harold Wilson on the great staircase, but he ignored us and looked grimly ahead.

'Do you think he saw me?' asked Terry.

We assured him he had.

Actually, it was all a bit sad, because when Harold had resigned he'd insisted on inviting me to dinner at Kettner's restaurant with Joe, as a thank-you for all the *Mirror* support over the years; as well as for my personal work for the Labour Party. It was an entertaining evening.Wilson was a brilliant mimic and, particularly good at imitating Churchill, whom he greatly admired.

'I knew him well when I was in Attlee's government,' he said. 'On one occasion we were both on a trade mission to Liverpool. There was a formal dinner and Winston was enjoying himself greatly, talking to a group of Northern magnates. Eventually, a civil servant came to me and said, "Mr Wilson, we're worried about the time. We're all due on the midnight train to London."

'"Well, I'm ready, you'd better go and tell Winston," I said.

'The civil servant then confessed they were afraid of him.

'"Then I'll tell him," I said, a bit irritated.

'I went to his table and he invited me to take a glass of brandy. "The civil servants are anxious about the time, Winston," I said.

'"Why?" he asked.

'"The train's due to go at midnight."

'Winston didn't bat an eyelid. Casually, he just said, "Tell them to hold it."

'I was dumbfounded. It never occurred to me that you could just order a train to be kept waiting. In my book, if you were late they went without you.'

'Tell Mike about the message to Mary,' said Joe.

Wilson nodded. 'When I resigned from the Attlee government over health charges I saw Churchill in the corridor of the House of Commons and he stopped to talk to me. "Young man," he said [and now Wilson managed an extraordinarily good imitation of Churchill], "you have made a brave sacrifice for your principles, and I admire you for it. But, in these grave times, I always remember the women who wait for us, and serve our cause so nobly. When you get home please convey to your dear wife my deepest felicitations for the sacrifices she too will also be called upon to make in the coming weeks."'

Harold continued: 'When I got home to Hampstead Mary was reading in bed. I told her I had resigned and I said Winston had sent a message to her. When I repeated his words I saw tears on her cheeks. She wiped her eyes and said, "Please tell that wonderful man I shall always revere him for what he did for our country in our darkest hours."

'A couple of days passed and then I saw Churchill in the corridor again. I said, "Winston, I told Mary what you said, and she wept." And I repeated her remarks. As I spoke I saw tears begin to stream down Churchill's face. Then he said, "Please tell that fine, brave woman that my heart is . . ."'

'I decided there and then I wasn't taking any more messages.'

Later, when talking to Joe about Harold I said how different he was in private.

'He's superstitious, too,' said Joe. 'We were on our way to

an important meeting and from the car he saw a single magpie. "That's bad luck, Joe," he said worried, and he began to hold his lapel. Then he relaxed and said, "It's all right, I've just seen a white horse.'"

At the end of our serialisation I decided to offer Joe Haines a job on the paper.

Chapter 30

THE SWAN AND THE TEASMADE

Finally, Eric Wainwright's retirement was upon us. Eric had not produced any work for well over ten years, but Tony Miles had a deep affection for him, so we decided to see him off in style. Eric selected some of his older colleagues from the features department to attend his farewell dinner at the Ritz.

On the ground floor of the Ritz there are pleasant private dining rooms off the main concourse. We had taken one and gathered on a warm summer evening to say goodbye. Champagne was served before the occasion and Eric and I, accompanied by Arthur Thirkell, decided we would enjoy our drinks where it was cooler and stood just outside the dining room.

Arthur had been the *Mirror* theatre critic for many years and was popular with managements, who frequently invited him to attend royal visits. As Arthur, Eric and I stood side by side, we suddenly saw the Queen Mother, followed by a retinue, proceeding down the concourse in a stately manner. As she came closer she recognised Arthur and, to our astonishment, veered towards us before an equerry could intervene.

Slightly stunned, we stood to attention while she beamed expectantly at Arthur. He rose to the moment and, giving a courtly bow, shook her proffered hand and said, 'May I present Mr Eric Wainwright, and Mr Michael Molloy, ma'am.'

Finally, a courtier intervened. 'We're going to another occasion, ma'am,' he explained.

'Oh, and what is *this* occasion?' she asked

'Mr Wainright is retiring, ma'am,' explained Arthur.

'Well, I wish you many happy years ahead,' said the Queen Mother.

Another astonishing member of the staff was Peter Senn. Peter would have been perfectly at home on the pages of an early Evelyn Waugh novel. He was our arts correspondent. He also had a modest private income left to him by his father, who'd been a successful doctor.

After public school, Peter went to Oxford, which remained his spiritual home for the rest of his life. He'd retained many of his friendships from his undergraduate days and counted the historian Asa Briggs, the politician Shirley Williams, British Railways Board chairman Sir Peter Parker and other impressive luminaries in his circle.

He was a tall, rangy man, with an ageing wardrobe of Savile Row suits; but he could still cut a dash when he remembered to wear his dentures. He was a genuine eccentric and convinced he was a perfectly normal English gentleman to whom unexpected things happened.

I once received a desperate call from him from Greece, where he'd encountered a spot of trouble. Luckily, I was able to get the newsdesk to organise a rescue. Peter had been leading his elderly mother by the hand down a grand staircase in the hotel where they were holidaying, when they both lost their footing and tumbled down, knocking themselves unconscious.

Peter had come to, lying naked on a trolley in a squalid hospital. No one spoke English, and, because his father had been Indian, the Greeks had taken him to a different hospital from his concussed mother. The newsdesk sent a local reporter to rescue him and Peter was reunited with his mother, although someone had stolen his clothes.

One of Peter's colleagues on the paper was Paul Callan. When he was working on a story there was no better man to have on the job, for he was a natural reporter;. One evening I entered the Stab to find Callan, who had clearly been there some time, giving a lusty rendition of 'The Eton Boating Song' to a group of printers he'd befriended. The printers returned to the bowels of the earth and Callan joined me to reminisce wistfully about his imaginary years at Eton.

'Music soothes the soul,' he intoned, 'and nothing soothes more than the incomparable velvet tones of the cello.'

'Do you play the cello, Callan?' asked Peter Senn, who had come up on his blind side accompanied by a tough-looking type.

Callan nodded. 'I was taught in my years at the Royal Academy of Music,' he claimed.

'Oh, I haven't introduced my old chum Alan,' said Senn.

'You play the cello?' asked Senn's chum.

The Swan and the Teasmade

'Every evening when I get home,' said Callan.

'And you say you still play,' said Senn.

'Of course.'

'Well this is a bit of a coincidence,' said Senn. 'Alan has his cello in his car outside. I was just taking him back to my flat; why don't you join us?'

'Certainly,' said Callan.

I was invited to join them but I had other duties to perform.

The following day I saw Senn in the corridor and noticed he had a large red sore patch on his cheek.

'What happened to you?' I asked.

'*Mon cher*,' said Senn, 'weren't you in the Stab last night when Callan claimed he could play the cello?'

'I was.'

'Well, we went back to my flat and to my astonishment he actually could play. I was so moved by his rendition of "The Swan", I fell over and burned by face on my Teasmade.'

Senn's flat consisted of a comfortable set of rooms off Sloane Square, where he had some good furniture and impressive paintings. One day he announced he was thinking of selling his pictures.

'Why?' I asked.

'I've just seen a wonderful display at the Royal School of Needlework,' he enthused. 'I'm thinking of commissioning a sort of Bayeux Tapestry telling the story of my life. What do you think?'

'I would like to see that, Peter,' I replied with deep conviction. Sadly, he never did go ahead with the project and the world lost a fascinating artefact; Peter had led a very gaudy life.

Chapter 31

FRIENDS WHO ROCK

Some people are made for a life in journalism; others stumble through their career on newspapers never quite sure what they're supposed to be up to. One of my best friends, Peter Tory, wrote beautifully, but always considered himself a resting actor.

Anne Robinson was a natural. She'd had an interesting start in life. She was of Irish stock, and her mother started with a stall in Liverpool market and ran it up to being the biggest supplier of game in the Northwest of England. Annie was sent to boarding school, and then on to a finishing school in Paris. But her mother insisted that she and her brother work on the family stall in the holidays.

Annie took to journalism like a bolt fitting into a rifle when she went to work on a London news agency. John Penrose was already there and they began a lifelong, on/off relationship that continues to this day. Over the years they have been lovers, husband and wife and best friends.

Friends Who Rock

I consider Annie a good friend who knew my habits, so it came as a surprise to me when she wrote in her biography that, as editor of the *Daily Mirror*, I spent a great deal of my leisure time consorting with rock stars and footballers. It also taught me how little we all really know of each other. One of my failings as an editor was that I had absolutely no interest in sport at all. I only ever knew one footballer, and that was Bobby Moore, because he wrote a column for the *Mirror*, ghosted by Pat Doncaster.

As for rock stars, I did once have a truly enjoyable lunch with Paul and Linda McCartney. He started by smacking the back of my head. 'Nice to know you, head hitter,' he said jovially. 'Geddit? Geddit? Head hitter, editor?'

After that we got along very well and eventually decided that we'd like to see more of each other, but Linda came to a wise decision. She rang me after Sandy and I had arranged to meet them in Rye and said, 'Mike, you know Paul and I smoke pot.'

'Yes,' I said.

'What's your paper's position on legalising marijuana?'

'The paper's against it, Linda,' I replied.

'So, if Paul and I are ever busted, you wouldn't be able to side with us?'

'No.'

'We'd better be friends at a distance, then.'

And so we were.

Another rock-star friend was Rod Stewart. Rod and I recognised each other from the moment we met. We came from the same sorts of streets. Not the concrete canyons of the big city: Rod and I were from the leafy landscapes of suburban London. Rod was also the only rock singer whose work I truly enjoyed.

When he was in England we usually got together, and once he probably saved me from a beating. I was to buy him dinner in Rules restaurant in Maiden Lane, a quiet road that runs parallel to the Strand. Sandy had gone on to the restaurant with Rod's manager, Billy Gaff, and Britt Ekland. Rod wanted to drive me in his Ferrari, as he seldom had a chance to get behind the wheel.

A minder produced the car outside the hotel in Park Lane. We drove down Piccadilly at what seemed to be a hundred and fifty miles an hour, then around Trafalgar Square, and came to a halt near St Martin-in-the-Fields, where another minder took over the controls so Rod and I could walk down Maiden Lane towards the restaurant. Halfway down the narrow street we encountered a group of murderous Scottish football fans who had taken drink.

At first, they were furious that anyone could have the temerity to imitate Rod Stewart, then they were transported with delight when they realised they had actually encountered the real thing; then they got the idea that I was somehow his enemy and they were ready to beat me to death in his defence.

Rod calmed them with assurances that I was really his friend and not some Englishman bothering him. They patted me with horny hands, saying, 'Go on, then, Jimmy.'

He once rang me in a rage, saying, 'Mike, could I buy the *New Musical Express*?'

'Well, you know the old saying,' I answered: 'everything

is for sale at the right price. What's up? Was it the story they printed about you wearing Britt's knickers?'

'Nah,' he said. 'I don't care about that. But the bastards said I was sent off in a football match. No one in my family has ever been sent off. My dad will have read that.'

In the end the *Mirror* was offered a gossip series about Rod written by his former press officer. It wasn't very racy stuff, but it was personal and it ended our friendship. It was one of the few things I did that I still regret.

Show business does take a toll on some people. Whenever I saw the Who's Keith Moon he always seemed to be on the edge of exploding into chaotic misbehaviour, dancing on the counters of bars and challenging strangers to join him in destroying his greatest enemy: tranquillity.

But one night, in the late hours, Sandy and I were at a table in Tramp nightclub, and, when Sandy went to the loo, Keith came over and sat in her vacated chair to chat. When she returned he patted his lap and she sat on his knee. He talked quite gently to us. He seemed funny, but rather wistful. It was the only time I'd ever seen him so calm, and the last time we saw him alive.

Jim Callaghan surprised the political observers by becoming much more successful and popular as prime minister than anyone had expected. I got to know him pretty well and he gradually warmed towards me.

There was no doubt where Jim Callaghan stood when he became prime minister: right of centre, and the left hated him for it. They hated the *Mirror* as well. We were always accused of being 'the Running Dog of Capitalism' which was perfectly true. The paper believed in a mixed economy, support of the Common Market, the abolition of Clause Four from the Labour Party manifesto.

It was unpleasant enough being loathed by the far left, but then the IRA sent me a chilling message. They took umbrage against a *Mirror* leader, so they took one of our staff reporters for a ride in Belfast and put a shotgun against his head, saying, 'Tell your editor we can reach out to him in London.'

Getting a threat from the IRA was frightening. My house was in an ordinary suburban street. I realised how vulnerable we were. As a family, we moved out for a few days, and then, rather sheepishly, moved back. But the worry was still there, until months later we changed the paper's policy and declared that Britain should give a date when we would withdraw troops from Ireland and leave it to the Irish to solve the problem. It proved to be an enormously popular policy with the readers – and the IRA. A few weeks later I was sent a rather handsome relief carving of my portrait with the best wishes of the Provos. Interestingly, the Red Hand Ulster Loyalists approved of the policy as well.

During the Troubles, our staff men in Ulster came under a lot of strain, and some pretty much suffered from battle fatigue. Two of our staff men, Chris Buckland and Joe Gorrod, were once leaving the *Mirror* offices for a lunchtime drink when an enormous bomb detonated across the street and blew them both over. Having scrambled to their feet, they ran back to the office, where several telephones were ringing. Joe, a Geordie, picked one up at random and a voice said, 'Hello, this is Felicity Green from London.'

Knowing it was the women's editor, Joe said, 'I'm a bit busy now, hinny.'

'Don't hang up,' pleaded Felicity. 'This is very important.'

'Go on, then,' said Joe.

'Our *Mirror* Slimmer of the Year comes from Belfast.'

'What happened, hinny?' interrupted Joe. 'Did she have her arms and legs blown off?'

Later, when Chris Buckland had done his time in Belfast, I sent him to work in New York, but he was still a bit bomb happy. When I went over he said, 'Come on, I'll take you out for a drink.'

As we entered the bar I heard the strains of 'Danny Boy' on the jukebox and I realised he'd taken me to a bar with a counter holding Noraid collection boxes, a jukebox of Irish songs of the Big Crosby variety and a clientele of third- or fourth-generation Irish cops.

I sat uneasily at the bar as Buckland ordered the drinks. When we were served he rapped smartly on the countertop and loudly proclaimed, 'I'm going to sing you an Irish song.'

Immediately he had the attention of the whole bar. Raising his glass, he then sang them the anthem of the Northern Irish Protestants, 'The Sash My Father Wore'. To my amazement, we weren't instantly dismembered by the crowd. When he'd finished he even got a loud round of applause. Then he announced he would sing them another. I prayed for 'When Irish Eyes Are Smiling', but the first line turned out to be, 'Get back, get back, you Fenian dogs'.

'Are you trying to get us murdered?' I hissed when he'd finished.

He just laughed. 'These fuckers know nothing about Ireland. Tell them it's an Irish song and they think it's got to be attacking the English.'

And so I lived to tell the tale.

As Jim Callaghan became warmer in his relationship to the *Mirror* I was invited to more and more receptions, lunches, cocktail parties, and dinners at 10 Downing Street. Eventually, he asked me to be a personal adviser, but my duties turned out to be light. When he decided not to hold an election in the autumn of 1978 he asked me if we could do anything to persuade the unions to keep their pay claims down in the coming winter.

In order to try to help a hopeless cause, Geoffrey Goodman and I took Moss Evans, general secretary of the Transport and General Workers' Union, to lunch at the Jardin Des Gourmets, a splendid restaurant in Soho of the kind Moss favoured. When we came to the point, and asked Moss if he would stick to Callaghan's pay restraint boundaries in the coming winter, he shook his head. 'My members just won't put up with it,' he said.

'So, you'll strike?' said Geoffrey.

'If we're forced to, we will.'

'Then we've lost the election,' said Geoffrey gloomily.

'Oh, no,' said Moss, surprised. 'When it comes to the election we shall move heaven and earth to see that a Labour government is elected.' Then he beamed at us as if his resolve had already saved Callaghan's premiership.

Widespread public-sector strikes led to the so-called Winter of Discontent and Jim Callaghan's popularity began to melt away. When he did call the election his personal popularity was still greater than Margaret Thatcher's, but the public had the wind up.

When the 1979 election date had been announced I was invited to a grand lunch to celebrate the life work of John Gielgud. Jim Callaghan was to be the speaker and Lord (Louis) Mountbatten was the guest of honour. The audience hated the prime minister; you could actually feel it in the air.

When he spoke, Jim said he had particularly wanted to be at the lunch because of his admiration for both one of the theatre's greatest figures and his old friend Mountbatten. But even his friendship with Mountbatten did nothing to soften the waves of hostility. After the lunch I was moving towards the exit with the rest of the guests when we began to flow around a trio of people standing in a group. It consisted of Jim Callaghan, Lord Mountbatten and Peter Ustinov. Jim called me to join them, and we stood, like Custer's cavalry, surrounded by hostile Indians.

It was the only occasion I ever saw Peter Ustinov in low spirits; he was usually the best-tempered of men. We talked of anything but the terrible reception Jim's speech had received and then he said to me, 'Would you like to come back to Number Ten for a cup of tea?'

It was the offer of a lonely man who wanted a friend to be with him. I accepted and when we were served in his private office, he looked from the window and said. 'There's a political sea change coming, Mike. The tide's changed.'

He knew the election was lost.

Chapter 32

MISTAKEN IDENTITIES

T alking to the letters editor one day I asked what were the most common requests he received from readers.

'The words to Kipling's poem, "If" and Leigh Hunt's poem, "Abou ben Adhem",' he answered without having to think.

'Do you get many requests for them?' I asked, intrigued.

'So many we had them printed off so we can always bung a copy in with the reply,' he answered.

I thought about what he'd said on my way to lunch with Kingsley Amis and one of my assistant editors, Christopher Ward. Christopher was always excellent company and a person to whom strange things happened. He was the only person I've ever known who actually fell down a manhole. It happened in Fetter Lane when he was walking along reading and some fools had left the opening in the pavement unguarded.

We arrived at Bertorelli's restaurant and Christopher said at the desk, 'I'm Christopher Ward, and I've booked a table.'

'Yes, sir,' said the man on the desk. 'Mr Ward has arrived.'

'No said Christopher, *I'm* Christopher Ward.'

'No, sir,' said the receptionist. 'I tell you Mr Ward is at the table.'

Giving up and spotting Kingsley, we went to the table. It was close to two others.

'They refuse to believe I'm Christopher Ward, Kingsley,' he said plaintively.

'Never mind, old chap,' said Kingsley, sipping his drink.

Overhearing the exchange, a man on the next table said, 'I'm Christopher Ward.'

We glanced at him with some interest and then a man on the other table said, 'My name is Christopher Ward too.'

'I do like a good coincidence,' said Kingsley with some satisfaction. 'It reminds me of Dickens.'

I told Kingsley about the requests for the poems and he didn't seem surprised. 'All newspapers used to print poems before the war,' he told us. 'They went out with newsprint rationing and never came back.'

After we'd started on the third bottle of wine I suddenly decided I would like a poetry column in the paper, the verse to be chosen by Kingsley, with a short couple of paragraphs about the poem. He agreed, and we ran a half-page each day until it was eventually killed off by my successor. Kingsley got an anthology out of it however; he dedicated it to me.

Editors can lose touch with the general public. There's only so much you can take in. One evening I was invited with a few other *Mirror* executives to a fashionable publishing party and found myself chatting amiably to a young woman who was not exactly beautiful, but she had a certain beguiling quality that Frenchwomen often possess. Our conversation involved a great deal of hand movements and I suddenly noticed that I was being watched intently by Joyce Hopkirk.

Afterwards, in the car back to the office, Joyce asked in an urgent voice, 'Exactly what were you talking to Koo Stark about?'

'Who?' I asked puzzled.

'Koo Stark. She won't give any interviews. What did she say? You do know every gossip column in the world is after her?' said Joyce.

'Of course,' I lied.

'So what were you talking to her about?'

'Penguins,' I answered lamely. 'I'm very fond of penguins. She used to train them.'

'You had a private conversation with Koo Stark and you talked about bloody penguins!' said Joyce, sighing.

'I've been a bit busy with all sorts of important things,' I replied weakly.

As an editor, I was also accused of concealing the truth about unidentified flying objects, murders committed by MI5 on behalf of the Royal Family and a list of government secrets kept under wraps by the imposition of D-notices. It always comes as a disappointment to people when I tell them that in the years I was an editor I was never once presented with a D-notice that concealed a national secret from the public.

Sometimes you can upset influential people. In the early seventies, Princess Margaret began a public affair with a landscape gardener some eighteen years her junior called Roddy Llewellyn. Personally, I had no interest at all in how Princess Margaret conducted her private life, but the group of *Mirror* executives who made up the leader committee voted that the paper should say she ought to stop making a laughing stock of the Royal Family.

Some time after the leader was printed, Percy Roberts asked me to accompany him to a charity lunch, as Mirror Group Newspapers had contributed to the cause being celebrated. It transpired that Princess Margaret was the royal patron and Percy was to sit beside her at the top table. I was somewhere below the salt in the company of two jolly ladies-in-waiting.

After the lunch Percy asked me how I had enjoyed the occasion and I said I had a fine time. How about him?

'Well, it was extraordinary,' he said. 'Princess Margaret ignored me throughout the meal and pointedly kept her back turned to me. She finally embarrassed the lady to her other side, who leaned right across Margaret and said, "This is a wonderful occasion, don't you think, Mr Roberts?" and I said yes.

'Then Princess Margaret finally turned to me and said, "You're Roberts?"'

'Yes, ma'am,' said Percy.

'Oh,' she said. 'I thought you were Molloy.' She then included him in the conversation.

That wasn't the only time my name was confused with somebody else's. Lord Harmsworth's irrepressible wife, known as 'Bubbles', was a frequenter of press events and nightclubs, where we would see each other. One evening there was an anniversary event at the Press Club and I was seated at one end of the top table next to the Bishop of London, who was resplendent in his purple regalia. Lord and Lady Harmsworth were at the other end. Before the first course, Bubbles, on her way to the ladies' loo, squeezed behind the bishop and me and stopped to say in quite a jolly fashion, 'I heard on good account that you were seen in Soho last Tuesday, haggling with a whore.'

She passed on, leaving the bishop and me at a loss for words. On her return journey she waggled a finger at me playfully and repeated, 'Haggling with a whore.'

'What time was this incident supposed to have happened, Lady Rothermere?' I asked.

'Three o'clock in the morning, according to Nigel Dempster.'

'Then it couldn't have been me,' I said. 'I'm always in bed by two o'clock.'

'Don't try to wriggle out of it, Jameson,' she said.

A few days later I saw Derek, who was now editor of the *Daily Express*. I told him what Bubbles had said. 'I wasn't haggling with a whore,' he protested indignantly. 'I was having a row with my wife.'

Chapter 33

JUST LIKE THAT!

S ometimes, when news schedules fall into the doldrums, papers try to think of a idea that will intrigue the readers. So, when Uri Geller visited the office one day in 1977 I thought of a stunt. Geller – the man who'd intrigued the nation by seemingly being able to bend cutlery by mind power alone – claimed he could broadcast images that people could pick up. So, I asked him to do it for the *Daily Mirror* readers and we would publish the results. He decided to broadcast from Blackpool Tower, where he would send out his picture messages, and the readers would send us the drawings they'd made of his thoughts.

To act as an umpire I'd given the job to my personal assistant Neil Bentley. After the event Geller would return by private plane and we would review events. That lunchtime I pocketed a heavy teaspoon from the Savoy Grill to see if Geller could bend it for me. Neil was the first to arrive, saying that Geller gone for a ten-minute nap on the sofa in the ladies' lavatory because he was exhausted.

Neil was clearly disturbed.

'So, what happened?' I asked.

'I don't know what to make of it,' he said. 'We got to Blackpool and he said, "Go around all the repair shops you can find and collect any clocks that aren't working. The shopkeepers will sell them to you for a couple of pounds."

'He was right,' Neil continued. 'I got together a box full of old alarm clocks and wristwatches. When I presented them to him he just picked them up and squeezed them. Some started working again, others seemed to spring apart, or the hands curled up. It was a damned clever trick.'

'You think it's a trick?' I asked.

'It's got to be.'

Then Uri Geller came into my office looking quite drained.

I took the teaspoon I'd taken at lunchtime and handed it to him. 'Can you bend this?' I asked.

He held it for a moment and said, 'Yes, I think so.' Then he began to rub the stem as I'd seen him do on television. In a few seconds the spoon drooped out of shape as if the stem were made of rubber. He handed it back to me without any expression.

The news editor entered my office with a couple of other executives. They began to clamour for him to bend things. Then the news editor said, 'I hear you can move a compass point.' He held out a compass.

'I will need to rest it on something metal,' said Geller. We placed my typewriter on my chair with the compass resting on the metal casing.

'I'll need all your help for this,' Geller said. 'Gather around and concentrate your thoughts.'

We did as instructed and the compass needle quivered. 'One more big effort,' urged Geller, and this time the needle swung a quarter of the way around the face of the dial.

He then said he was very tired and asked to go to the hotel room we had provided.

Uri Geller had left his set of drawings he'd broadcasted to the nation. But they were pretty general sketches of a house by a stream, a cow in a field and a sailing boat on the ocean, so no one was surprised when a lot of drawings, mostly from children, were a close enough match.

We all forgot about the incident, and then, one evening, some months later, I got a call from photographer Kent Gavin. 'Michael,' he said. 'Come over to the Stab, there's someone here you'll like to have a drink with.'

Gavin was right: when I entered the pub he was standing at the bar with one of my heroes, Tommy Cooper.

'Mr Cooper, you are one of my heroes,' I said. 'May I buy you a drink?'

'That's very, very nice,' he answered. 'I'll just have the one.'

Three hours later the pub was crammed with fans. Gavin, Tommy Cooper and I were crushed at one end of the saloon bar while the mighty Cooper drank prodigious amounts of lager, told endless jokes, and demonstrated inches from my face incredible feats of conjuring with tricks he took from the pockets of his tentlike sports coat.

He made objects appear to pass through his hands, disappear, reappear and turn into other objects.

The Happy Hack

Finally, I said to him, 'If you ever wanted to show people how you could move a compass point, how would you do it?'

He smiled. 'I'd get everyone to concentrate on the needle point then I'd use the magnet in my hand,' he said.

Another pleasure in being an editor is that you sometimes get the chance to ask your own questions of famous people. Sidney Bernstein, the founder of Granada Television, was something of a legend. I met him at a reception in Downing Street. Bernard Donoughue,adviser to Harold Wilson, told me Sir Sidney was unwell and couldn't stand for long. He asked me if I'd sit and talk to him. I was happy to. Knowing he had an impressive collection of art, I wanted to ask him about the first painting he'd ever bought.

'I can remember as if it was yesterday,' he answered. 'I'd been on a walking tour of Southern Germany and I was passing through this little town when I saw a painting in a gallery window. It was by Max Ernst. It was love at first sight. The trouble was, I was flat broke, but I knew I had to have it.'

'So, what did you do to get it?' I asked, expecting to hear a story about how he'd washed dishes in a local hotel or chopped great piles of wood to raise the cash.

He looked at me, puzzled. 'I wired my brother for the money of course,' he answered.

Margaret Thatcher was prime minister, Michael Foot leader of the Labour Party, and inflation was still ravaging Britain. In those trying times the management of Mirror Group Newspapers continued to blunder along.

In some parts of the world, however, the Mirror Group still clung to a reputation formed in the past that we were the most modern newspaper on the planet. Tony Miles rang me one day and said, 'You've got to come to lunch today, cock. We've got some important Japanese visitors coming.'

'I have no sympathy for the Japanese, Tony,' I replied. 'They were very cruel to my uncle Mike when they captured him on Java.'

'Forget the war, cock,' he instructed me. 'These are the new men of Japan.'

He couldn't have been more wrong. We assembled in the chairman's office, where Ted Blackmore, the production director, was to explain before lunch the sophistication of our printing operation.

Four tiny, aged figures were ushered into our presence and after much bowing we realised there was a problem. Our Japanese visitors spoke no English and the only member of their party who knew a foreign language spoke German.

Luckily we remembered that the *Mirror*'s Polish butler, Alfred, spoke excellent German. But he could only translate between serving the lunch, which was further complicated by the Japanese never having mastered the art of eating with knives and forks.

So, when one of the Japanese wanted to make an observation or ask a question, he would ask their interpreter, who would ask Alfred in German. Alfred, between performing his butler's duties, would translate the German into English. Then, with the reply, the reverse would happen. The conversation didn't exactly flow.

The Happy Hack

Finally, with utter confusion over the role of saddles on the machines, which became confused with the saddles used by cowboys, I was overcome with the desire to burst into snorting schoolboy laughter. Knowing that to be laughed at was the ultimate insult for the Japanese, I stumbled to the bathroom off the dining room and succumbed to helpless chortling.

Splashing water in my face, I pulled myself together and re-entered the dining room, where I saw one of the Japanese visitors attempting to insert a large piece of poached salmon into his mouth with the aid of two fish knives. I caught Tony's eye, and, seeing he too was on the edge of exploding with laughter, I crashed back into the bathroom.

After the visitors had departed we turned to Ted Blackmore and said, 'Why did you invite them?'

'I didn't invite them,' he answered indignantly. 'I thought you had.'

We never did find out how and why the Japanese had come. Good old Mirror Group Newspapers.

Chapter 34

HOUSE OF FUN

Ted Blackmore was one of the more enjoyable companions among our fellow directors. And he did have a good wartime story. One night in the seventies I was vainly trying to dig interesting information out of Ted Pickering about his time on Eisenhower's staff and he mentioned that he'd visited Hitler's bunker. Just then, Ted Blackmore came into my office for a drink and said, 'What are you talking about?'

'We're talking about the Führer,' Pick answered.

'The Führer,' Ted said. 'I arrested him when I was a major in the military police.'

'No, no, Ted,' said Pick, ponderously, as if he were addressing an idiot child, 'the Führer died in the bunker.'

'I don't mean *Hitler*,' said Ted triumphantly. 'I arrested Grand Admiral Doenitz, whom Hitler appointed to be his successor.'

'You actually arrested him?' said Pick.

'Well, nearly,' said Ted. 'I rang the bell to his flat and when he answered the door in his pyjamas I said, "Grand Admiral Doenitz, I arrest you in the name of the Allies." Then Doenitz looked me over and said, "You're only a major. I demand to be arrested by someone of field rank." So I said, "Do you mind if I use your telephone?" I can tell you, it was bloody difficult to find a colonel of the Military Police in the middle of the night.'

Ted finished his drink and departed. Pick looked after him for a moment with slight rancour and said, 'Another bloody triumph for the production department.'

It wasn't just the management that contributed to the Ealing Comedy world we lived in. I decided to hire John Edwards, back from the *Daily Mail*, but the news was taken as a dire insult by Paul Callan, as they both specialised in colour reporting. ('News colour' involves reporting a hard-news story as if it was a feature, as if the reader was an eye-witness to the event.)

John Edwards and Paul Callan both became fine exponents of the style. So, when Edwards turned up early to see me, he went into the Stab, where Callan barracked him with accusations of inventing copy.

Edwards departed from the pub and, when he reached me, I took him up to the ninth floor to see Tony Miles, who was also an old friend. We were drinking to John's arrival when the door of the chairman's office door burst open and Callan stood quivering with rage on the threshold.

'You fucking imposter,' shouted Callan. 'I haven't finished with you yet.'

Whereupon Edwards fell upon him and they rolled out of the chairman's suite and into the executive corridor like a sequence from a *Tom and Jerry* cartoon. Doors all along the corridor opened to see what caused the affray and Miles called out, 'Just a spot of editorial fun' to the puzzled management men.

Callan had always lived dangerously. When he first worked for John Junor, doing casual Saturday shifts with Peter Tory on the *Daily Express*, he and Tory had taken much drink in the *Express* pub Poppin's. It was a warm summer night and Callan persuaded Tory to lie down in the gutter outside the *Express* building. Junor came out on his way to supper and looked down on them.

'What are you doing lying in the gutter, lads?' he asked gently.

'Sir,' Callan answered, echoing Oscar Wilde, 'we may be in the gutter, but we are looking at the stars.'

'Carry on, then,' said Junor.

One Christmas Eve, overcome with seasonal exuberance, some of the editorial staff, led by a reporter playing the bagpipes, paraded around the newsroom and in and out of my office. It all added to the festivities, I thought, having rather enjoyed the skirl of the pipes. I made a note of the piper: one never knows when a skilled musician may be needed.

That summer I was on holiday in the South of France with Sandy and my daughters, Jane, Kate and Alex. One evening we decided to take a drive along the coast to have dinner in Cap Ferrat, a town we'd never visited before. It turned out to be a lively place, filled with buskers dressed as troubadours and minstrels, playing various stringed instruments for customers seated outside the cafés. After the meal the unmistakable sound of bagpipes came to us.

'I haven't heard the sound of the pipes since a reporter played them in my office last Christmas,' I told my family. I glanced over my shoulder towards the sound and saw a half-familiar figure who now began playing 'Scotland the Brave'.

'The reporter looked a bit like him,' I said, waving towards the piper. 'In fact *exactly* like him,' I continued.

I got up and strolled towards the source of the music. As I drew closer I saw an attractive, blonde girl I recognised as Fiona Millar passing a hat round. I dropped a coin in the hat as a look of horror came to her face. She had clearly recognised me – so had Alastair Campbell. His pipes made a dying sound as his instrument deflated.

I brought them back to where the family were sitting and that began a long friendship. Fiona and Alastair had been on the *Mirror* training scheme and Alastair had eventually got a job on the paper. I had not known him well until then, but he clearly had a remarkable personality, and it was quite obvious he was going to have an interesting life.

When he became the prime minister's press secretary under Tony Blair, the story that he'd planned the encounter with my family got around Fleet Street. According to gossip, he'd learned where I was staying and decided to cultivate me. It was absolute tosh, but journalists like nothing better than a conspiracy, particularly one supposedly concocted by a fellow hack, so the story stuck.

A Cambridge graduate, Campbell had worked as a teacher in the South of France and a croupier in a London casino, and had written freelance articles for a girlie magazine. It was clear that his interests lay in politics rather than general reporting, so I gave him a particular task: to cultivate Neil and Glenys Kinnock, as it looked possible then that Neil would become prime minister.

Alastair and Fiona practically became part of the Kinnock clan. When Alastair left the *Mirror* and joined Eddie Shah's relatively short-lived daily newspaper *Today*, where he eventually had a breakdown through drink, Neil and Glenys helped him a great deal to get through this bad patch in his life. As did Sid Young, one of my favourite district reporters. It was a fair example of how friends can make a difference in a troubled life. Alastair hit bottom. But he pulled himself up again and went on to fame and fortune.

Chapter 35

WAR STORIES, REVOLUTIONARY SOCIALISTS AND ROYALTY

I was going to have lunch with the author Len Deighton in 1982 when he called. 'Come and have a drink at my London place,' he said. 'There's someone I think you'll like to meet.'

'What's your address?' I asked.

'It's not shown on the *A–Z* guide,' he said mysteriously. 'Come to the German Embassy and ask for me at the gate.'

It was typical of Len to be living in London, but technically to be in Germany, I thought, as we drove to the embassy. The mews house where he was staying turned out to belong to his father-in-law, who'd been a Dutch diplomat. The person he wanted me to meet was a slight, tweed-clad figure, who was one of my boyhood heroes: Eric Ambler, author of wonderful thrillers and a member of the Crown Film Unit along with Peter Ustinov and David Niven. It's odd how people you admire can come in clusters.

'Tell Mike the story you just told me,' said Len when we had glasses of champagne in our hands.

'I was in the Royal Artillery at the beginning of the war,' said Ambler. 'They put me in charge of the anti-aircraft guns at Chequers. Churchill used to love them. Whenever he had an important guest he would come out after dinner with a glass of brandy in his hand and say, "Ambler, fire the guns."'

'So I would send up probably several hundred pounds' worth of high-explosive shells as a fireworks display for the old boy.'

I knew Eric Ambler's old wartime companions Peter Ustinov and David Niven but I had no knowledge of what they'd been like as young men, so I asked him. He was warm about them both, but said how totally different they were in life.

'Because Peter had such an impeccable accent people imagine he's thoroughly English, but nothing was further from the truth. He did love England, but as an eccentric foreign country. He was cosmopolitan in the real meaning of the word, just as much at home in Paris, New York or Leningrad.

'David was the absolute reverse. He really was an English gentleman who lived abroad: self-deprecating, beautifully mannered, and very tough. He had a bizarre war, serving in the commandos, and then taking long leaves of absence to make those Crown [Film] Unit films we did. But he really did fight in the war and he would never say a word about it. I admired him greatly.'

Later, I tried to question Niven on the fighting he saw, but he would only make jokes and change the subject.

Most of the revolutionary socialists I met were dreadful people.

They always seemed chillingly composed about the need for executing or imprisoning anyone who opposed their political ideology, but Paul Foot was an exception. Paul was one of the most decent people I ever knew.

Educated at Shrewsbury with his lifelong friend Richard Ingrams (who would become editor of *Private Eye*), he started out, like most of his family, as a dedicated liberal. Then, after Oxford, because of his family connections, Cudlipp gave him a job on the *Daily Record* in Glasgow, where he was converted to socialism.

Had Paul joined the Labour Party, his abilities would have taken him to the very top, but he chose the far left and hoped for revolution to bring him to power.

As a relentless investigative journalist, he already had an impressive reputation when I met him at a *Private Eye* lunch. We liked each other immediately, and eventually I invited him to write a column for the *Mirror*. I did add one rider: that he must not use the *Mirror* to promote the Socialist Workers Party. He accepted the deal.

Paul was always a bit embarrassed about his upper-class upbringing, but he would occasionally stumble when he was attempting to adopt working-class manners. One day in a restaurant his request for chips came out as fried potatoes. Richard Stott, by now features editor, and a former public-school boy himself, pounced and started to give him a working-class lesson about how to hold his knife and fork and talk to waiters

Later, Stotty found a photograph of Footy in officer's uniform with sword drawn in charge of a guard of honour. It had been taken when he was doing his national service. Stotty pasted it on his office wall.

My own moment came when I explained all the privileges he was entitled too as a columnist.

'Your salary will be forty thousand pounds per annum,' I began.

'Oh, no. Oh, God, that's far too much,' he protested.

'You will charge a minimum of three thousand pounds per annum expenses.'

'Oh, no.'

You will have a private office.'

'No. No,' he protested.

'With a carpet,' I added, piling on the agony.

'No.'

'And you will have an office car up to the value of a Ford Mondeo.'

'No, Mike,' he said firmly. 'I draw the line at a motor car.'

'You do realise your union has fought for these rights. It's your duty to take them,' I said.

'All right, everything but the office car.'

A few weeks later he came to my office and said, 'Mike, about the office car.'

'Changed your mind?' I said.

'No, no. But would I be able to have an Underground Tube pass? It would be so convenient not to have to queue at the ticket office.'

'I'll see what I can do,' I said. I rang the managing editor and said, 'Paul Foot wants an Underground pass.'

'Well he can't fucking have one,' he said. 'Tell the bastard we don't do Underground passes.'

I rang Paul and said, 'Sorry, you can't have an Underground pass. Just buy one and put it on your expenses.'

'Can I do that?' he said.

'Paul,' I said, 'you can do anything you like.'

I was intrigued to receive an invitation to lunch with Prince Charles and Princess Diana at Kensington Palace. When I rang the bell I made a note to remember as much as I could, because I'd been ordered by my wife, daughters and mother to recall every detail of the event. A butler answered the door and I knew from our cuttings library that he'd once worked for Bing Crosby.

'My name is Molloy,' I said. 'I'm invited to lunch.'

'Of course you are,' he said rather chirpily. 'Nobody turns up here unexpectedly, you know.'

I was led upstairs into a comfortable, average-sized living room, furnished with understated English taste: oriental carpets; inviting sofas and armchairs; side tables with personal ornaments; silver-framed photographs; traditional pictures; and flowers. Princess Diana entered alone and I was struck by how young she was, and what a beautiful complexion she had.

I was served a rather 'barbwous whisky' by a footman, which I downed rather quickly while the princess and I made small talk about the traffic and weather. I noticed her voice and realised how much the accents of the upper classes had changed. While not exactly sounding like a shop assistant, she certainly had none of the precise qualities required by the nanny who had briefly schooled me.

Price Charles entered. A slim figure, he looked fit and wore a good-humoured expression.

'I'm so sorry I was delayed, Mr Molloy,' he said, and took my glass to give me a refill. I was surprised that he did this himself, rather than ringing for Bing's butler. As he handed me the drink, I noticed his hands. They were workmanlike and powerful, with stubby fingers, more like a builder's than those of a prince.

As we talked it became apparent why he'd invited me to lunch. He knew the answers to the questions he asked. Mostly, they were about the areas of interest newspapers always have in the pursuit of royalty. Clearly, this was all a lesson for the princess on the motives of the press.

'Why are you so fascinated by our private lives, Mr Molloy?' she asked when we were served a very light lunch of chicken and salad with a small glass of delicious German wine.

'Because you are the most glamorous couple in the world, ma'am,' I replied.

'Do you really think so?' asked Prince Charles. 'Is there a list?'

'Oh, yes,' I answered. 'Once it was Charlie Chaplin and Paulette Goddard, then the Prince of Wales and Wallis Simpson, Laurence Olivier and Vivian Leigh, then Princess Margaret and Lord Snowdon, Richard Burton and Liz Taylor. Now it's you.'

'So I follow in the steps of Charlie Chaplin,' said Diana, looking up from a slightly lowered head to give me the full blast from her remarkable eyes. It was a glance that was to make a long list of men go weak at the knees, and gladden the hearts of the world's paparazzi.

'It will pass ma'am,' I assured her. 'It always does.'

The meal ended with Prince Charles urging me to try some cheese from the country of his Gurkha equerry. I chewed on a lump of compacted fat that had the flavour and consistency of Plasticine.

'Yak cheese, Mr Molloy,' Prince Charles said with a gleam of pleasure.

The next time I encountered anyone in the Royal Family was when the national newspaper editors were summoned to Buckingham Palace. The request also concerned Princess Diana.

Michael Shea, the press secretary, waited while we were all seated around a long table in a large, plain room. Before us were pencils and lined pads. Michael Shea's statement boiled down to a simple message: due to recent newspaper speculation Princes Diana was finding it difficult to cope. So, could we all take it easy, please?

Rumours had gone the rounds concerning a fall down a flight of stairs that might have been deliberate; and gossip had it that not all was well in the marriage.

Barry Agnew, then editor of the *News of the World*, asked if Princess Diana had thrown herself deliberately down the stairs. Michael Shea hotly denied the possibility.

David English, editor of the *Daily Mail*, asked the most questions, and Harry Evans, editor of the *Sunday Times*, took the most notes. John Junor, sitting next to me – who after more than twenty years as editor of the *Sunday Express* was the elder statesman present – carefully drew a very small house on his pad; then, after some further thought, filled in the roof. I wonder why he chose to draw a tiny house, perhaps because he had grown up in relative poverty and now found himself in Buckingham Palace, I speculated.

Anyway, he glanced at me and I nodded in approval; he then said, 'So what you're asking, Michael, is that we give Princess Diana the same consideration we would to any young lassie who was feeling the strain?'

'Yes, John.'

We all murmured our agreement and then we were shown to a reception room, where the Queen, Prince Philip and Prince Andrew joined us. The usual stiff royal-household drinks were served.

Barry Agnew had a question for the Queen. 'Princess Diana complains that every time she goes to the village shop to buy sweets for her children a horde of press photographers take pictures of her. Why doesn't she just send a footman?'

'Mr Agnew,' she replied, 'may I say that is a very pompous question.'

A battery of editors laughed heartily at Agnew's putdown. Actually, it turned out much later, Barry Agnew had been right in his earlier question to Michael Shea: Princess Diana, in a bid for attention, had thrown herself down the stairs.

On a visit to Fleet Street, the Queen toured the *Daily Mirror* and I was to show her over the newsroom. Then there was to be a reception in the boardroom to meet members of the staff, before a visit to the library. Her time with us was to end with a visit to the offices of her favourite newspaper, the *Sporting Life*.

I led her to the newsroom and she stopped before a subeditor I'd known for nearly twenty years, yet his name was suddenly wiped from my memory.

'May I present . . . er . . . Bruce Cooper, ma'am,' I said, making up a new identity.

Seeing a chance to make someone happy, I led her to the reporters' area. Peter Prendergast was a firm royalist, and he was delighted that I introduced her. But there on her desk, was a page proof of the story he was working on. It bore the headline, THE PROSTITUTE WHO POSED AS A NUN.

'A pity people are interested in such stories,' she said with a slight sigh. Then she looked over to where the Duke of Edinburgh was laughing at a selection of pinups on the picture editor's desk.

Finished on the editorial floor, we headed for the boardroom. There were further introductions to staff members, and a general conversation began when suddenly the Duke of Edinburgh looked down on Holborn Circus, where, a statue of a uniformed Prince Albert, seated on a horse, was raising his hat.

'Who's that?' he asked sharply.

'Prince Albert,' I replied.

'Why is he raising his hat? He's dressed in a field marshal's uniform,' the duke remarked, quite annoyed by the seeming breach of protocol. 'Look down here,' he now instructed the Queen.

'Why is he raising his hat? He shouldn't do that while he's mounted,' said the Queen, equally unhappy with the offence. I was beginning to feel responsible for the sculptor's work.

'I'll find out and let you know, ma'am,' I said, relieved that it was time for the caravan to move on. At their next stop, the library, the chief librarian had heaped all the *Mirror*'s stock pictures of the Queen on the visitors' counter. It was a massive pile, and it sabotaged the timetable of the visit. The Queen and the Duke couldn't resist the pictures and stayed long after their allotted time, chatting and exclaiming to each other over long-forgotten incidents from their past.

No one works harder than the night editor, who is in charge of producing the news pages each evening. When Phil Walker was doing the job he stopped me one day in 1981 and said in rather a belligerent fashion, 'I want a night off, Mike.'

'Sure,' I said. 'Will tomorrow do you?'

'Yes,' he said with even more force. 'I'm going to behave like a normal person. I'm going to take my wife to the pictures.'

'Good for you.' I said.

Phil and his then wife had a colourful life. They had a refrigerator jammed halfway through their kitchen window after Phil had attempted to throw it out because of its lack of capacity. They had also once owned a ferocious bull terrier called Bill, who had left home and was last seen making his escape by boarding a night bus at Notting Hill.

Phil returned after his day off and I asked him if he'd gone to the pictures as planned.

'I saw a wonderful picture,' he enthused. 'Anthony Hopkins in *The Elephant Man*. Have you seen it?'

'No, but I hear it's terrific.'

'It is. There's one scene where a crowd of tormentors pursue the Elephant Man and he finally turns on them saying, I am not an animal: I am a man!'

For the rest of the day, about the newsroom, I would hear Phil relating the scene to people, his eyes filling with tears each time he delivered the line about being a man.

Time passed and Hercules the Bear came to Fleet Street to open a pub called the Cartoonist. Hercules, a full-grown grizzly, was cherished by his owners, Maggie and Andy Robin from Scotland. For Phil it was a clear case of love at first sight.

He'd gone to see the bear with Paddy O'Gara and Derek

Pryce. On discovering that Hercules drank beer, Phil bought him many pints and matched each with one of his own. Finally, Derek and Paddy brought Phil back to the office. Unsure where to put him, they laid his now slumbering body beneath the art desk, next to the back bench, so he could sleep it off.

Later in the afternoon, Douglas Long, the managing director, came to see Paddy about designing a pamphlet he wanted to issue to the staff. While he was discussing it, a loud groan came from beneath the art desk.

'What the fuck was that?' asked the managing director.

'Ignore it,' said Paddy. 'It's only the night editor.'

Then a protesting voice came from beneath the art bench, saying, 'I am not a night editor: I am a man!'

In the summer of 1982 I received an invitation for my family to attend the Royal Garden Party at Buckingham Palace. I bumped into an old acquaintance, Tom McCaffrey, whom I'd last seen when he was Jim Callaghan's press officer. He was now working for Robert Maxwell.

'What's he like?' I asked.

'He's a bastard, but he's fair,' Tom answered, but I think he said it without too much conviction.

As we drove away from the Mall I thought about Robert Maxwell. His obsession to own a newspaper was well known. Maxwell was like Churchill's description of Russia: a riddle wrapped in a mystery inside an enigma.

PART II
THE SPECTRE OF MAXWELL

Chapter 36

ARRIVAL OF THE CUCKOO

In November 1980, Michael Foot became leader of the Labour Party, but the struggle between left and right continued. I went on holiday and in my absence Tony Miles and Terence Lancaster devised a leader saying Michael Foot should go.

I returned to the office and was not pleased by the decision. The problem was that, if we were going to continue to support Labour, it would prove difficult when we came to the general election to urge readers to vote for a man we had already said we thought unfit for the job.

Perhaps I was overestimating the memory span of the readership. In the event, we did urge the readers to vote Labour, and in the main they rejected our advice. But no one pointed out our own contradictory position.

Meanwhile, Sandy and I were invited to dinner at Geoffrey Goodman's home. The other guests were Neil Kinnock (the man who would succeed Foot) and his wife Glenys, Michael Foot and his wife Jill Craigie, and their dog, Dizzy.

The air was a little frosty, but after a time it plunged to subzero when Foot began to harangue me about the *Mirror*'s leader saying he should quit. Michael had been one of my boyhood heroes, so it was doubly painful to be attacked, rather like being clubbed by one's favourite childhood toy. I offered him a page to answer the attack, but he refused, pounding on the table, saying we must refute the article. Neil Kinnock had his head in his hands and a deep awkwardness descended on the dinner party.

Geoffrey walked back into the living room and I followed, whereupon we discovered that Dizzy, some kind of long-haired terrier that looked the same at both ends, had destroyed a great many of the Goodmans' grandchildren's toys that had been stored in a large box. Now the remnants lay carpeting the room. Geoffrey looked on the wreckage for a moment and said, 'I'm going to kick that creature up the arse – as soon as I've figured out what end it is.'

There was nothing to do but laugh. The following morning before eight o'clock, Michael rang me at home to apologise. 'Nothing personal, Mike,' he said. 'We all have problems with people we work with.'

The *Mirror* had agreed with the Labour MP Gerald Kaufman, when he'd said Labour's 1983 election manifesto was 'the longest suicide note in history'. But we greeted Neil Kinnock as leader of the Labour Party with more enthusiasm. The Kinnock family lived only a couple of doors away from Sandy and me in Ealing and we got to know them fairly well.

Arrival of the Cuckoo

Neil and Glenys are two of the best people I ever knew in politics. I thought it was a tragedy that Neil didn't become prime minster. I never subscribed to the conventional wisdom that the public didn't trust him. I believe Labour lost the election because John Smith announced that, if Labour were elected, he was going to put up income tax. Then, ironically, having derailed Neil's election chances, he took over the leadership.

When the Queen invited me to lunch at Buckingham Palace I had something slightly more interesting to talk about than my lack of knowledge concerning a statue of her ancestor. She'd visited most corners of the globe, with the exception of the Communist countries, so, when I told her my wife and I had toured China, she wanted to know what the highlights had been.

She kept asking questions and finally an equerry, who wished to move another guest into her presence, got quite impatient. Actually, the way the proceedings were organised was a very smooth operation. The courtiers who greeted us were charming people. They plied us with stiff drinks before the Queen and Prince Philip, accompanied by an escort of corgis, entered the reception room.

When we were seated for lunch I was placed between the composer Andrew Lloyd Webber, a quiet man, and an admiral, who was terrific company. I told him of the time I'd had dinner on board HMS *Victory* and he told me how he'd commanded ships in battle.

But all three of us were a bit daunted when the main course was served. There were some delicate little rissoles fashioned into patties and a kidney-shaped dish in which there was a thin, sweet liquid.

'What the hell do you think this is?' whispered the admiral. 'It says it's rodgrod on the menu, but I've never heard of it.'

Andrew Lloyd Webber and I confessed we were just as baffled. A few days later, at a *Punch* lunch, Stanley Reynolds, the literary editor, told me that rødgrød is a sauce made of some kind of berry. 'You may have had reindeer rissoles,' he said. 'That's what it's usually served with.'

Reed International decided to sell Mirror Group Newspapers. The technology that could replace highly paid men with computers already existed; there was just no stomach in any Fleet Street newspaper group to go head to head with the bands of militant brothers. Then, in 1986, Eddie Shah launched *Today*, which proved to be the nemesis of the luddites. *Today* was something of a disaster, despite the talented editorial staff Eddie Shah hired. The main problem was that he'd tried to save money on the technology and the public rejected a title that was so badly printed it was sometimes hard to read the text.

But putting together the paper on computers and then sending the pages electronically to satellite printing plants saved massive amounts of money. If the *Sun* and the *Daily Mirror* could shed their traditional workforce in such a way, they would tap into a river of gold. Computers, after all, didn't go on strike

Margaret Thatcher had put the necessary legislation in place by outlawing secondary picketing and Rupert Murdoch and his News International took the decision to fight it out in what became known as Fortress Wapping, a plant he'd built for such an eventuality.

Elsewhere in the printing industry, another bloody fight had been going on with the unions, but one that wasn't reported in the newspapers. Robert Maxwell had taken over the British Printing Corporation and set about hacking it into shape. He was so successful profits began to pour out of the once moribund organisation. And so the banks ignored a Department of Trade and Industry report saying he was unfit to run a public company and loaned him all he needed for future ventures.

Reed International decided that they wanted to offload us, and the best way would be for Douglas Long, the managing director, and Tony Miles, the then chairman, to find someone known and trusted in the city who could supervise a floatation. The name they chose was the chairman of the Abbey National Building Society, Clive Thornton.

He was a short Northerner with a round face and large owlish spectacles. He'd earned his solicitor's qualifications at night school and lost a leg in a tram accident. So he seemed man-of-the-people enough to reign over a Labour-supporting group of newspapers.

He decided to divide the chairman's office in two because he thought the space was too big. It took three months of union haggling to get the wall built. It should have been a warning. Someone asked why he'd been appointed the new Mirror chairman, and the answer came: 'In the land of the legless, the one legged man is king.'

Gradually, Clive Thornton's plans ground to a halt and the

massive, brooding figure of the Czech-born Ian Robert Maxwell began to loom over the *Mirror* building.

Because of his appalling reputation Reed management wanted to keep Maxwell at arm's length, so they asked if the *Daily Mirror* would approach Neil Kinnock to seek an assurance that the Labour Party would opposed Maxwell's ownership of the paper. Kinnock gave us an evasive answer. Eventually, he sent a carefully worded letter that gave no real support at all. I learned later from Michael Foot's wife, Jill Craigie, who was always wonderfully indiscreet, that Maxwell had got to Michael Foot and said that if the Labour Party didn't stand in his way of a takeover he would 'guarantee' the *Mirror*'s support at the next election.

The *Mirror* unions turned out to be paper tigers: after huffing and puffing they accepted their fate. Reed International caved in under Maxwell's pressure and in 1984 sold him the Mirror Group. We got the news at midnight and Maxwell turned up in the small hours to claim his new toy. Douglas Long invited him into his office, where Maxwell immediately demonstrated his new powers – and his lack of grace – by striding to the open drinks cabinet and pouring himself a large whisky. Then he pointedly sat down in Long's chair, squatting, like some gigantic cuckoo settling itself in a new nest. Watching him, I knew what course I must take, and so began the most bizarre chapter in my life.

Chapter 37

THE AXE THAT DIDN'T FALL

S ince the end of the World War Two, Captain Ian Robert Maxwell MC – born Ján Ludvík Hyman Binyamin Hoch in Czechoslovakia in 1923 – had made his mark on his adopted country, but not always in the way he'd intended. His attempts to emulate an English aristocrat had often ended in farcical results, except in the case of people he employed, who tended to regard him as the pigs did the Big Bad Wolf.

'Bob' – the name he eventually settled on, having rejected Ludwig, Jan, Leslie, Clive and Ian – simply couldn't understand the English. Two stories he told me demonstrated his bewilderment with Anglo-Saxon attitudes. The first happened after he was commissioned in the field. He and his men came upon a heavily defended farmhouse.

'We were getting near the end of the war,' he remembered, 'and, apart from the SS, the fight had gone out of most of the German forces. I got up close to the farm door and shouted in

German, "Come out with your hands up. You are completely surrounded." They came out and I shot them all with my sub-machine-gun. I thought my boys would be pleased, but all they said was, "That's not fair, sir, those lads had surrendered."'

He held his hands up in disbelief, saying, 'Can you understand such an attitude?'

The second incident happened when he got to Berlin. Bob had noticed that some of the upper-class British officers had gundogs with them. 'I decided to get a dog,' he said. 'But there weren't many in Berlin – most had been eaten. Then I found out that the man who'd bred Hitler's dog was still living in the suburbs. I went there and found he had one Alsatian bitch left. I took it from him, and later heard he'd committed suicide. Do you know, the other officers all felt sorry for him. Can you believe that? Sorry for the man who'd bred dogs for Hitler?' In fact, I could see that Bob felt quite sorry for himself for being so misunderstood.

I tried to lighten the rather grim moment by telling him an anecdote about his adopted fellow countrymen that I thought was amusing.

'The English are odd where dogs are concerned,' I said. 'A friend of mine served with a tank regiment in the Army of the Rhine. When they were on manoeuvres they used to drive through the German towns with their dogs sitting in the turrets wearing berets and goggles. The Germans would say, "These Englanders, they are all mad, they let their hounds drive their panzers."'

Bob's reaction was interesting. He didn't even smile. 'Typical of the bloody British,' he said rather angrily. 'Fancy letting dogs drive their tanks!'

The Axe that Didn't Fall

Finally, I realised that Maxwell had no sense of humour at all. He laughed a lot, and would tell the odd Russian-style joke along the lines, 'When the bear eats the cow, the farmer's wife takes what's left.' But, to him, humour was an alien attribute he only pretended to understand.

Perhaps it's a common with all tyrants. Hitler and Stalin only ever laughed at the discomfort of their enemies. Of course, Maxwell could be hysterically funny, but it was always unintentional; it was the grandiose pomposity of his behaviour that made people laugh, and he hated to be laughed at. That's why he reserved his greatest loathing for *Private Eye*.

Throughout the sixties he'd often popped up in the news. In 1964, he became a Labour Member of Parliament for Buckingham; and he fell foul of the Department of Trade and Industry when he attempted to merge his own Pergamon Press with an American company. He tried to buy the *News of the World* from an outraged Carr family, who were staunch Tories and appalled at the idea of some foreigner like Maxwell buying a British institution. Instead, they sold it to Rupert Murdoch, which started a feud that was to last the rest of Maxwell's life.

The first time I met him was in 1973 at the Imperial Hotel at a Labour Party conference in Blackpool. A dozen of us were with Sydney Jacobson when we were approached by an enormously fat Maxwell, who wore a suit with a pattern that looked like television interference. The strangely orange colour of his complexion, his ink-black hair and enormous eyebrows gave him the look of a music hall comedian; but his smile was like that of Richard III.

'You've put on a bit of weight, Bob,' said Sydney. 'Are you going to buy us a drink?'

'Certainly, what would you all like?' he answered in his memorably fruity voice.

The order for twelve journalists drinking after midnight will always be a complicated one: it ranged from pink gins to port, with a smattering of wines and beers. Maxwell listened intently to each selection, asked the name of the person making the request, and then left us to weave through the crowd to the distant bar.

'We won't see him again,' said Sydney. 'Bob hates buying a drink.'

But Sydney was wrong: about fifteen minutes later Maxwell returned, followed by a waiter bearing a tray of drinks. Each glass was handed to the correct person, whose name he remembered. It was an interesting demonstration of his powers of memory.

The next time I saw him was some years later, in July 1984, when he entered the *Mirror* building as the new owner. By the time Maxwell bought the papers I'd been editor for nearly ten years and I was ready for a change. I began to miss the pleasure of doing a piece of work that was all my own. Mostly, the paper was pretty different from the way I would have liked it to be.

Also, I wanted to write. So I made three hours a day for myself in the early morning and wrote a novel about starting at art school called *Pearls and Swine*. Luckily, Barry Fantoni introduced me to Giles Gordon, an agent with an impressive list of authors, and we became friends. Giles sent *Pearls and*

Swine to Richard Cohen at Hodder & Stoughton. He didn't want *Pearls and Swine*, but he did like my idea for a thriller, titled *The Black Dwarf*. I was glad of the possibility of a second career because I was pretty sure Maxwell would fire me. The first morning, he invited the editorial team to the Ritz Hotel to celebrate his takeover. Our side consisted of Tony Miles, editorial director; myself; Bob Edwards, editor of the *Sunday Mirror*; and Richard Stott, editor of *The People*.

Bob Edwards had been a friend of Maxwell's for years. Tony Miles was hostile from the outset. Richard Stott knew a bit about Maxwell's business practices, but not as an investigative reporter. Stotty's brother John owned a catering company that Maxwell had used. But John Stott had found it almost impossible to get Maxwell to pay the bills, and consequently had refused further offers to cater for him.

I was simply waiting for the axe to fall. But Maxwell assured us that we all had a wonderful future with him, including Tony Miles, who sat in brooding silence nursing a gin and tonic, having refused the Buck's Fizz Maxwell had pressed upon him.

The atmosphere changed utterly in the *Mirror* building once Maxwell had taken over the chairman's quarters: a slothful indifference gave way to a jittery sense of anticipation. Would Maxwell begin wholesale sackings, as many predicted?

The first thing he did was knock down the dividing wall that had taken three months to erect. It took forty-eight hours for the newly cooperative unions to complete his bidding. Now it dawned on us that the unions were running scared of Bob, an experience we'd never known before. He'd routed them at the British Printing Corporation, and they expected the same treatment now he owned the *Mirror*. He didn't disappoint them.

He called for me as soon as he was settled and I was fully expecting a payoff. I had no contract, but I had been assured by a lawyer friend that he would have to pay me two years' money, which was known in legal terms as 'custom of the trade'.

I was on my way to the ninth floor when I got a message to ring my dad, so I told my secretary I'd call him back. I entered the office in a nostalgic mood: I'd seen Cecil King reigning there, Hugh Cudlipp, Edward Pickering, Tony Miles and, very briefly, Clive Thornton. I'd dined with the famous, been promoted, had drunk celebratory champagne. I looked about me for what I thought would be the last time.

But Maxwell didn't want to fire me. Instead he said he wanted to tell me how brilliant he thought I was and how he was going to rely on me in the future.

'Bob, I must tell you,' I answered, 'I went to the Labour Party to try to get them to help stop your takeover.'

'I know that,' he boomed. 'You were just being loyal, and I prize loyalty above any other quality. I've got a lot of enemies, Mike, but I know *you're* not anti-Semitic. I've checked. And I know you're a Labour Party supporter like me.'

'Who did you check with?' I asked.

'I rang your father. We got on well, two old soldiers, you know.'

Back in my office, I returned my dad's call. He said, 'Robert Maxwell rang. We had a chat. He seems very fond of you.'

'Dad, I've only ever spoken a few sentences to him.'

'Is he really from Czechoslovakia?'

The Axe that Didn't Fall

'So he says.'

'He doesn't sound it, ' said Dad.

'Did you tell him you'd been a soldier?' I asked.

'No, he already knew.'

I hung up, wondering what else Robert Maxwell knew about my family.

Chapter 38

MALICE IN WONDERLAND

As a child the only presents I wanted were books. So I was delighted to be given a handsome edition of *Alice's Adventures in Wonderland*, but I found the story and John Tenniel's illustrations deeply disturbing.

The world down the rabbit hole was too close to a nightmare for my imagination. The characters Alice found there were disturbingly bizarre, and some obviously psychotic. Only her matter-of-fact attitude allowed me to finish the book. It was a good job I did, because it helped prepare me for the world Robert Maxwell created.

It took only a short while to realise that Maxwell lived in a parallel universe where his own opinions rode roughshod over the logic of the real world. He was convinced that destiny had chosen him for greatness, but he had no belief in any god in the conventional sense, more a sort of primitive elemental force that had so far protected him.

Malice in Wonderland

Within a few days he had taken Sandy and me to a casino club in South Kensington, where the food was rather good and the croupiers were well know to him. After a hurried meal he became anxious to get to the tables. He bought a vast number of chips and pressed a handful each into our hands. Then, leaving us to our own resources, he began to play three tables at the same time, piling heaps of plaques on the numbers.

We quickly lost the chips he had given us and stole away, leaving Maxwell engrossed. The following day he told me we'd brought him luck and he'd won over sixty thousand pounds.

Maxwell believed the fates were on his side, but he was tardy about paying bills. He called the Mirror Group financial director and said, 'Listen, mister, do you pay your household bills the day you get the first demand?'

'Yes,' he answered. Maxwell looked at him as if he were a creature from another world. He was so astonished by the reply that he said quite gently, 'From now on I don't want you to pay any bills until you get the final demand, understand?'

Maxwell's strangeness was not shared by his family, who were quite sane. Betty, his wife, a handsome Frenchwoman, had borne him ten children. But one daughter, Karine, had contacted leukaemia as a child and their eldest son, Michael, died after a prolonged illness after a car crash.

Betty seemed sensible enough but for one thing: she was quite sure Maxwell was without a fault in the world. She'd fallen in love with him the moment she saw him. Almost the first thing she said to me was, 'People say he is a liar, Mike, but it is not true.'

The eldest remaining son, Philip, had retired, and lived a quiet life with his South American wife.

Anne, the eldest daughter, had trained to be an actress.

The twin girls, Christine and Isabel, had married Americans and lived in the United States. Ian, a decent young man, endured crushing demands from his father, and Kevin, the youngest, who was most like a chip off the old block, had a keen and complex business mind.

Having both French and English nationality, the children were well educated and well mannered, but Bob had no manners at all, just a series of gestures and expressions he'd copied from those he considered worth imitating.

At the first lunch he held in the chairman's dining room I was first to be served by Alfred, the Polish butler. It was leg of lamb, and I helped myself to the meat cut from around the knuckle. I began talking to the person seated on my other side and when I turned back I found Bob finishing the last of the choice morsels of meat from my plate. He obviously liked the same cut as well and couldn't wait until Alfred got around to him.

In his early *Mirror* days his closest confidante was Jean Baddeley, his personal assistant, who'd been his political secretary when he was an MP. She was a small, neat woman who'd devoted her life to Maxwell and still watched over him with fanatical loyalty.

He'd confessed when he was an MP that he couldn't get on with men, who tended to be too independent for his taste. 'Women are prepared to devote themselves to serve a man in a way men aren't,' he said in a statement guaranteed to raise the hackles of every feminist in the known world.

His secretary was a feisty, freckled redhead from New Zealand called Debby Dines. She also had the ability to cope with Maxwell's roaring rages and confusing demands. 'Get me that man who I can't remember,' he would shout, and, as if by telepathic powers, the impossible request would be fulfilled.

As expected, after a few weeks, Tony Miles and Douglas Long engineered their escape, along with their Reed pensions. Tony departed from the *Mirror* after more than thirty years, leaving only a vast Cuban cigar that Maxwell had pressed on him standing like a raised finger on his otherwise empty desk.

Another surprise was Hugh Cudlipp taking on the role of a special adviser, but he soon resigned as Maxwell, true to form, simply ignored his advice and Cudlipp feared he might be blamed for some of Bob's more bizarre decisions.

It was inevitable that anyone trying to give Maxwell sane advice would be totally ignored. When he first acquired the paper he began sticking his face in it as if it were a family photograph album. Constantly, he approached me with some announcement that was dressed up as an item of news. Sometimes there would be two or three a day.

Pompous commentators faked outrage that he should be allowed to do such a thing, as if there were some kind of law that Maxwell was breaching. It seemed to have escaped their intelligence that Maxwell was the owner, and able to do what he liked with his newspaper. I, as editor, had the right to resign, which I was not prepared to do at the time; being fired was another matter.

Subsequently, I realised, Bob had only a tenuous grasp of English. When he was in one of his frequent rages, sentences would become scrambled beyond comprehension, and phrases in common usage would be recast. Thus he would shout,

'They're all running around like chickens with no necks'; 'Jerusalem wasn't built in a day'; 'They have made their apple pie, now they must lie in it'; 'They have locked the stable horse after the door was bolted'; 'There's more than one skin in catching a cat'; and my favourite: 'You can't change toads in midstream.'

One morning he called me to his office, where he jabbed with a pen at the front page of the *Mirror*. 'Which illiterate fucking idiot wrote this headline?' he demanded.

'I did,' I answered.

'Where's the apostrophe?' he thundered.

The headline ran over a picture of Prince William shaking hands with an RAF officer; it read WILLS GOES TO WORK.

'What apostrophe?' I asked, puzzled.

He jabbed the pen between 'Will' and the 's'. 'There.'

'There's no apostrophe needed, Bob,' I explained. 'He's known as Wills.'

'But there's a fucking "s" on the end,' he shouted.

'You don't always have an apostrophe when a word ends in an "s",' I shouted back.

His angry mood suddenly changed. 'Don't worry about me,' he said, suddenly tame. 'I'm just an ignorant peasant with no O-levels.'

Maxwell had an extraordinary ability to imitate. He didn't learn languages by studying their grammar and syntax: relying on his remarkable memory, he imitated them as a child does. So his ability went only as far as the spoken word. When he attempted to write a letter the result would be completely illiterate and impossible to understand. So he used the telephone for virtually all transactions and demanded a twenty-four-hour switchboard so he could call people around the clock.

At the Trade Union conference he insisted I accompany him to the 'Boilermakers' cocktail party', a good example of an oxymoron as the only thing the boilermakers seemed to drink were pints of beer followed by vast whisky chasers. A happy coincidence, really, as in America the combination of beer and whisky is known as a boilermaker.

We arrived in his Rolls-Royce at one of the modest Blackpool hotels that lined the seafront, where an icy gale was hampering the progress of a woman struggling with a wheelchair and its female occupant at the base of the flight of steps to the entrance.

'Let us give help to this woman,' Maxwell declared in a biblical manner. 'We'll do that for you, my dear,' he shouted above the howling wind, and, elbowing her aside, we hauled the wheelchair with its comatose female passenger to the top of the steps.

The woman helper was not grateful. 'Thank you very much,' she said tartly. 'It's just taken me five minutes to get her down those steps.'

Without pause, he said. 'Mike, get that wheelchair down the steps again,' before sweeping into the hotel. When I had placated the woman and struggled down the steps once more I made my way to the bar, where I found Maxwell holding a pint surrounded by boilermakers. He was addressing them in a perfect Glaswegian accent.

I have no facility with foreign languages at all, so I was fascinated by Maxwell's skills. Whenever I could I would check how fluent he was in a particular language. Victor Louise, a well-known Russian agent throughout the Cold War, told me Bob's Russian was excellent, although rusty. 'When he does speak, it is often better than many members of the Presidium,' he assured me.

Bill Davies, sometime editor of *Punch*, was German-born, and he told me Maxwell's German was perfect. 'I think it was the language he spoke as a child,' he added. His French was fluent, but, mysteriously, he chose to speak it with an English accent, so that he sounded a bit like Winston Churchill.

Joe Haines once asked him why he'd chosen to come to Britain with the remnants of the Czech army in 1940. 'Because of Churchill's magnificently defiant speeches,' he answered promptly. 'Like Winston, I wanted to fight on.'

'But you didn't speak English in those days, Bob,' said a puzzled Joe.

'No,' he answered immediately. 'But I could tell from the tone of his voice what he was saying.'

Maxwell had persuaded Joe Haines to stay, and it says a great deal about his power to charm people into serving him. I saw him do it with the formidable figure of 'Big Sam' McCluskie, the general secretary of the National Union of Seamen. Sam was a rock-hard Scot from the left wing of the Labour Party and, although he'd never met him, he loathed the idea of Maxwell, whom he considered an enemy of the trade-union movement.

Maxwell called me up one evening and said, 'Mike, do you know Sam McCluskie?'

'Yes,' I answered.

'You do?' said Maxwell, surprised. He often found it difficult to remember I'd had a life before we'd met. 'Will you do me a great favour? He's coming to see me, so I can present him with a charity cheque, but I'm running late with another meeting. Will you greet him and give him a drink in my office until I can get there?'

I got a call that Sam had arrived and I showed him to the executive lift. 'What's it like working for this bastard, Mike?' he asked in a surly fashion as we ascended. It was clear that he had no taste for the meeting at all.

'It has its moments, Sam,' I answered.

We chatted in the chairman's office for a while about the dim possibilities of another Labour government, and then Maxwell entered the huge room. As he walked towards his guest it was eerily clear that the two men had recognised some quality in each other and liked what they saw.

After a few minutes, Maxwell presented Sam with the cheque and then said they should see a lot of each other in the future. Maxwell had to return to his meeting, so I saw Sam to his car. As we went down in the lift McCluskie was silent for a few moments and then said, 'That's a man who fills a room.'

One of the most frustrating aspects of dealing with Maxwell was his attention span: he didn't have one at all. He also ignored the systems used for administration in all normal organisations. Refusing to read written information, he nonetheless still insisted that even quite minor decisions be made by him. Therefore, all communications with subordinates had to be either face-to-face or over the telephone. Queues of people would gather outside his office holding papers for him to sign, while several people at a time might actually be inside the office. Favourites would be given precedence over those in disfavour, but their supplications would be constantly interrupted by long telephone calls that Maxwell insisted on taking.

Regular trayloads of snacks would be offered to the waiting crowd and occasionally Maxwell would be reminded that he had to attend a meeting, usually with bankers, outside the building. So he would rush away leaving the wailing crowd in despair. After I'd worked for him for a few months, whenever anyone asked what the experience was like I would tell them to watch the old Marx brothers film *Duck Soup*, the scenes where Groucho is running the chaotic government of a ramshackle country called Freedonia being particularly relevant.

When business hours ended, Maxwell arranged social meetings. One evening he summoned Joe Haines and me and when we got to the outer office Debbie Dines told us Harold Wilson was inside. Joe looked disconcerted for a moment. 'I haven't seen him since I published the book,' he said hesitantly. Then he shrugged. 'Oh, well.'

We entered the room and, as Joe approached the chair Harold sat in, I could see the pair of them wanting to be friends again.

'You've changed your hairstyle, Joe,' said Wilson as an opening.

'I've just washed it, Harold,' he replied. Then it was as if no bad blood had ever passed between them; Marcia would have hated it.

Later, Harold Wilson influenced another event that was to take place in the same room. Maxwell was to sign a publishing agreement with the Chinese Ambassador. The ceremony was all arranged, when an aide called Janet Hewlett-Davies, who had worked for Wilson, saw that there were only cheap ballpoint pens with which to sign the necessary documents. There was no time to arrange anything else, so she placed her own fountain pen, an expensive Mont Blanc, on the table. The ambassador arrived and, after signing the document, he exclaimed in delight at the fountain pen.

Through the interpreter Maxwell said, 'Your Excellency, you must have it as a gift.'

Whereupon Janet whispered furiously to Joe Haines that the pen had been a personal gift to her from Harold Wilson and she wasn't going to see it given away. Joe explained the situation to Maxwell, who tried to take the pen from the ambassador, saying to the interpreter, 'Tell him I'll get him another one.'

But the ambassador hung on to the pen, saying that it would take pride of place in a museum in Peking, where such pens reposed.

For once, Maxwell was defeated; the secretary Janet went off in an angry mood and the triumphant ambassador bore his prize away.

A week later, Janet was called to Maxwell's office where she also found Harold Wilson waiting.

'I hear you lost your pen, Janet,' he said, handing her a new Mont Blanc, 'so I've brought you another.'

Chapter 39

MAXWELL PSYCHOANALYSED

Robert Maxwell decided to make his old friend Bob Edwards editor-in-chief and Bob was delighted. My deputy, Peter Thompson, was appointed editor of the *Sunday Mirror*. Bob Edwards gave me his assurance that he would always be there if I wanted to consult him on any matter, but he wouldn't interfere with the paper; and he kept his word.

Bob was a curious man, unlike anyone else I'd ever known. A friend of mine said Bob was from another planet, but he'd been badly briefed on how to behave on earth. When he was fired from editing the *Express* he was rescued by Hugh Cudlipp. As editor of the *Express* he'd earned a fearsome reputation among journalists, but he hadn't been a particularly hard master in his Mirror Group appointments.

Despite being a splendid raconteur and a generous host he had few friends, with the exceptions of Maxwell and Michael Foot. He would often lunch alone, going to the Kennel Club, which was odd because he didn't have a dog.

Revel Barker, the foreign editor of the *Sunday Mirror*, once asked him why he didn't bother to make friends and Bob was slightly nonplussed. 'I did have a friend once,' he said after some thought. 'You know, we were like brothers. We even used to go on holiday together. Which was strange because he was my deputy, but we were inseparable.' He clicked his fingers and said, 'Now, what was his name?'

One story I did like about him concerned St Dunstan's, the church at the head of Fleet Street that features two automaton figures of Gog and Magog that strike a bell to note the passing hours.

A few minutes' walk away in Chancery Lane stood the Trattoria Est, an Italian restaurant. One evening, Bob, worried about his lack of popularity with his staff, decided to take one of his writers, John Knight, to dine there and question him about the problem. John had had a difficult day and was not his usual carefree self, so Bob's searching questions about his standing with his fellow hacks did not fall on sympathetic ears.

Later, when describing the evening he said, 'I finally flung down my napkin and said, "Actually, they all hate you, Bob, and do you know what? So do I." Then I stalked from the restaurant. After a startled moment, Bob followed me into Chancery Lane as I hurried towards Fleet Street. I glanced over my shoulder and saw Bob was close at my heels so I broke into a trot.

'So did Bob. Then I saw that Luigi, the manager of the restaurant, had been so disturbed by our abrupt exit he'd followed us out, and he was now running after us as well. I trotted across Fleet Street, but finally ran out of puff opposite St Dunstan's. Bob stood panting by my side and, before either of us could speak, Luigi ran up, saying "What's the matter, gentlemen? Did something upset you?"

'Now Luigi knew everyone in Fleet Street and was a great gossip. So I said, "Mr Edwards and I have never seen Gog and Magog strike the hour; we decided to pop down and watch."

'"You know," said Luigi, "I've never seen Gog and Magog strike the bells either. I stay and watch with you."

'There we were, gazing up at the bloody clock, when, after a few minutes, Luigi says, "Hey, you know, we got to wait twenty-five minutes for the hour to strike."

'So we all trooped back to the restaurant.'

In his early days, Maxwell invited Margaret Thatcher to lunch. She'd often said he was the kind of man she wanted in the Tory party. So, over pre-lunch drinks they positively beamed on one another. It was interesting to see how she'd changed from the time her fellow Conservative grandees had patronised her on her first visit to the *Mirror*.

The lunch was a lively occasion as both had a lot to say. The trouble was, they both said it at the same time, so it was impossible to hear the points each of them was making. But it didn't seem to bother either of them, even though it made for a rather dull time for the rest of us.

The problem was that Maxwell found it almost impossible to listen to anyone; he found it equally difficult to read anything longer than fifty words. One strange thing that did happen in his office was the way the important pieces of paper would simply disappear into the morass on his desk once you'd handed them to him.

Maxwell Psychoanalysed

As the telephone rang incessantly and Bob always took the calls, you could sit numb with boredom having brought a legal letter or a piece of vital copy he had to see, while he chatted in one of the multiplicity of languages in which he conducted business. When finally hung up he would have lost the document and Debbie Dines and Jean Baddeley would be shouted for in order to excavate the piles of papers on his desk.

We editors always took priority because he relished the company of journalists, who were rarely as obsequious as the rest of the people he controlled. He would often complain to me that he was lonely. 'I have no friends, Mike, except for you,' he once claimed, as we sat in his dining room one night dipping into a vast tin of caviar. When he repeated his claim of being lonely, I asked him if he would like to meet Peter Ustinov, who was in town.

'Ring him now,' he insisted.

Peter was already fascinated by Maxwell's publicity, so he agreed to come to supper the following night.

'He's a strange man, Peter,' I said.

'I can always use another character in my work,' he replied.

The dinner was a peculiar event. Maxwell was face-to-face with one of the most amusing and interesting human beings on the planet – and he wouldn't let him finish a sentence before interrupting with his own reminiscences.

Like Maxwell, Peter also spoke several languages. He was explaining how, on United Nations business, he was translating a conversation between Presidents François Mitterrand and Ronald Reagan. In his usual style he imitated the voices of the protagonists. '"You do realise how different the world would have been, Monsieur Reagan, if Napoleon hadn't sold most of America in the Louisiana Purchase," claimed Mitterrand.

'President Reagan replied, "Yes, Mr President, but if France had owned most of America the movie business would have been—"'

Maxwell interrupted Ustinov just before the punchline, saying, 'I once told Mitterrand if the French had left Algeria earlier the history of the Middle East would have been different.'

He made the announcement as if he were imparting one of the great secrets of the Cold War. For the rest of the evening, Maxwell simply wouldn't let Ustinov complete a thought. Eventually, I dropped Peter at his hotel in Knightsbridge and we had a drink in the bar.

'That man is very lonely,' he said. 'But it must be hard work being his friend.'

The only other acquaintance I invited to meet him was Tony Armstrong-Jones – the Earl of Snowdon, former husband of Princess Margaret – but he was enchanted with Maxwell and suggested I write an opera about him, which he would like to design. The author, former MP and one-time deputy chairman of the Tory Party, Jeffrey Archer, liked him too, but he did use him in a novel based on his rivalry with Murdoch.

Maxwell was peculiar about meeting people. He always had one of three distinct reactions at any introduction. He loathed the person or liked the person, or they made so little impression on him they might well have been made of glass. Of course, the safest one if you worked for him was to be Mr Glass. He frequently turned on people he liked as if he feared he was becoming too fond of them.

One day over lunch in Langan's, Tom Pitt-Aitkins, a physiatrist friend, asked me, 'How are you getting on with your new boss?'

'He's pretty eccentric,' I answered.

'He's not eccentric, he's mad,' said Tom flatly. 'I've got people inside who are less crazy than him.'

'You actually think he's *clinically* mad?' I asked.

Tom nodded. 'Tell me,' he said, 'does he have a group of people who fulfil the following functions?' He proceeded to list them. 'Someone who is the repository for all of his secrets?'

'Yes, he does.'

'A person he only uses for sexual gratification?'

'I think so.'

'A group of executives who are bitter rivals and only answer to him directly?'

'Yes.'

'A devoted dogsbody he treats like shit?'

'Yes.'

'Does he micromanage trivial matters but leave important decisions deliberately vague and then blame others when things go wrong?'

'Yes.'

'Does he make grandiose claims for all his business motives?'

'He says he went into scientific publishing when he saw the first atomic explosion and he knew that science was the only hope for mankind to avert nuclear Armageddon.'

'That'll do. How does he treat his family?'

'Like slaves.'

'You like military history; does that behaviour pattern remind you of anyone?'

'Jesus Christ,' I realised: 'Hitler!'

'Exactly. I've been watching him for some time now: the man's off his head. He'll end up bringing his whole empire down around him.'

'He claims that he wants to leave a great heritage for his children,' I said.

Tom shook his head. 'He'll leave nothing to them, just ashes. He'll probably die unexpectedly, perhaps in some kind of explosion.'

This gave me something to think about.

'Have you met anyone else mad like this?' I asked.

'Oh, yes,' said Tom. He pointed towards Peter Langan, who was insulting a table of his customers on the other side of the restaurant. 'Peter's got the same problem.'

'As Hitler?'

'The same, only on a smaller scale. I think he'll go the same way.'

Well, Bob did leave nothing but ashes for his family. And Peter Langan lured his wife into a bedroom he'd booby-trapped with cans of petrol which he set on fire. She jumped from the window, but Peter died from his injuries.

When Maxwell took over, Sandy and I were constantly invited to Headington Hill Hall, the stately home that he leased from Oxford City Council. Just inside the security gates Maxwell had built a small industrial estate that housed Pergamon Press. But beyond were the house and parkland that had once belonged to a Victorian brewer.

Like every building I'd seen that Bob had taken over, it was decorated and furnished with an eye to economy. The fabric of the building was grand, but the reproduction furniture looked as if it had been bought at the closing-down sale of a failed country hotel. There were also some of the worst paintings I've ever seen on anybody's walls.

Ian Maxwell showed us around and in the soaring hallway pointed out where their gigantic Christmas tree stood at the foot of the staircase each December.

'We're a very big family,' he said, 'and with ten of us there were always vast heaps of presents under the tree. One Christmas Morning we all came down and found the entire hallway was knee-deep in a sea of wrapping paper. Dad had come home late on Christmas Eve and opened everyone's presents.'

'He opened the presents for all you children?' Sandy asked in disbelief.

Ian nodded. 'To understand my father you must realise he never had any presents to unwrap as a child.'

Maxwell had a hunger for publicity that he could never satisfy. His desperate need for fame caused him to leap on any passing bandwagon and try to seize the driver's reins.

I was beginning to find his presence exhausting, so I thought of an idea to get him out of the office for a while. In a general discussion about the paper I said, 'Bob, wouldn't it be great for the readers if you only had the time to travel around the country on a train, like an old-fashioned political campaigner, and met the readers and asked them what they wanted to see in the paper?'

It was like watching a gigantic salmon rising from a river to snatch at a particularly appetising fly.

'Get me John Jenks,' he instructed Debby Dines.

John arrived looking rather weary. Bob had recently added a new complication to the *Mirror* bingo game and it was causing him no end of heartache.

'Jenks,' boomed Bob, 'I want to travel around the country on a train, like an old-fashioned political campaigner, and meet the readers and ask them what they want to see in the paper.'

'Certainly, Chairman,' said Jenks, unperturbed.

In a few days, Jenks had hired the train; mapped out a route calling at all the major conurbations in the country; booked venues where meetings could be held for the vast crowds Bob expected; arranged hotels for the entourage; and arranged for local bigwigs to come aboard the train for a cocktail party at every major stop. It was a masterpiece of logistics on Jenks's part.

Then, to my horror, Bob insisted I was to come with him. Now I knew what it was to be hoist by one's own petard.

Of course, the whole venture was a disaster. A panel of us sat in a couple of virtually empty town halls while malcontents abused us for the wrongs in the world, and a few rational people objected bitterly to Bob taking over their favourite newspaper and filling it with pictures of himself.

To my further horror, after the third failure to fill a hall, he bailed out, giving the excuse that he had pressing business in London. He left me to take over as chairman and continue on the Journey of Humiliations. Wherever we went, people pleaded with me to get rid of Maxwell and return the paper to its former status. Sadly, yet another example of how people overestimate the powers of editors.

Chapter 40

DEALING WITH THE BOSS

Although he could be overbearing towards his business executives, journalists had a fairly comfortable ride with Maxwell. They saw little of him and he was yet to start thinning out their ranks. It was different for editors: we had to deal with his sudden crazed enthusiasms. But he dearly liked a celebration, particularly one where he could speak in praise of himself. So he decided to have a party in the *Mirror* building. Since he had now joined the ranks of the press overlords, it was well attended by the great and the good.

Lord Rothermere came with his wife Bubbles; they had been to some other function beforehand so Bubbles wore a Gina Fratini confection. She was also following the then current fashion of wearing trainers beneath a floor-length gown. They entered and greeted me with great affection.

Bubbles took me to one side and immediately began a diatribe about her husband, Vere, who she claimed was treating her abominably. Vere, standing a few feet away, must have overheard some of her remarks. He called out to me, 'Mike, why are you wasting your time talking to that old cow? Come and talk to me.'

'Good evening, Vere,' I replied with an unconvincing smile.

'Don't you talk to Mike,' shouted Bubbles, clutching my arm. 'He's my friend, not yours.'

'I went to his twenty-first-birthday party. Did you, you old cow?' Vere continued. 'Come and talk to me, Mike,' he urged.

Bubbles released my arm and reached out to begin battering him with her pearl-studded evening bag. Betty Maxwell had crossed the room by now and was attempting to separate the warring pair when suddenly Clive Jenkins, the union leader, prodded Bubbles quite firmly in the ribs.

She was so astonished by his presumption she stopped belabouring Vere and said, 'Yes, what do you want?' in the sort of voice she would use to an insolent footman.

Jenkins pointed down and said, 'Tell me, Lady Rothermere, why are you wearing football boots with that dress?'

This bizarre question caused everyone to pause and gave Betty a chance to bundle Bubbles into a side room.

'At least we keep our family rows private,' she said later.

The bingo problem that had so plagued Jenks was creating a winner for the *Mirror*'s million-pound prize. Then the perfect candidate qualified: a modest reader called Maudie Barrett. She worked as a charlady and had a bevy of handsome daughters and a spaniel called Trumper.

Maxwell and I, with all the *Mirror* executives, were in

Blackpool at a political conference. 'Bring her up,' boomed Maxwell. 'We'll give her the prize on Blackpool Tower.'

A team of reporters and photographers escorted Maudie and daughters, along with Trumper, to the Imperial Hotel. Baffled and stunned by events, she sat chain-smoking on her bed, when I was introduced by John Jenkinson. And then Maxwell bounded into the room and threw himself down next to her. The sudden arrival of his twenty-two stone caused the bed to rear like a boat on a heavy sea and Maudie was almost thrown to the floor.

'Maudie,' he said, edging up to her with a ghastly kind of bonhomie. 'I'm so glad you won my million pounds. Do you realise this is a tax-free sum, and if you let me invest it for you it will bring you an income of a thousand pounds a week without any reduction in the capital sum?'

He might have been talking to her in Serbo-Croatian for all the sense she could make of his words, but she smiled weakly and lit another cigarette.

'Well, I'm a busy man,' he boomed. 'I must go now. I'll see you at the presentation ceremony.' And he bounded up, causing the bed once more to rock like a storm-tossed boat. When she had settled again, Maudie glanced around the room, puzzled, to say, 'Who was that man?' She must have been the only person in Britain not to recognise Robert Maxwell.

The following day I rode to the ceremony on an open-top bus accompanied by Alan Rusbridger, a young reporter who was later editor of the *Guardian*. He was suitably enchanted by the show business of the ceremony arranged by John Jenkinson, but so far as I know he did not introduce million-pound prizes as part of a *Guardian* circulation drive.

Margaret Thatcher was an enigma but I did once see her demonstrate astonishing powers of concentration. Sandy and I were at a reception talking to Sir Larry Lamb, the editor of the *Sun*, and his wife Joan. Thatcher entered with the usual retinue of civil servants, and made a beeline for Larry; he was one of her favourite editors. I was not.

Larry introduced Sandy, but Joan Lamb and I were slightly detached so we were not greeted. I noticed Thatcher toying with her string of pearls while she was in deep conversation with Sandy – and then the necklace broke. She didn't stop talking for a heartbeat. She didn't even glance down at the floor. Instead, she cupped one hand to catch a few falling pearls and talked on, while civil servants scrambled to retrieve the rest of the missing items.

'What did you think of her?' I asked Sandy later.

'She was warmer than I thought she'd be,' she said, 'but not bothering with her pearls was strange. It was as if what she was saying was more important than anything else in the world.'

'What were you talking about?'

'She was explaining how men were hopeless at running a country because they'd never had to deal with everyday ordinary things like a household budget.'

Life with Maxwell slipped into a routine. Bob Edwards found him very hard to handle. Maxwell always treated Bob with something approaching affection, but he totally ignored his advice. The newspapers were his new toys and he wanted to play with them as he pleased, so it fell to the editors to frustrate his more outlandish enthusiasms.

Joe Haines's relationship with Maxwell was very complex

indeed. At first, he bitterly opposed his overtures, and attacked Maxwell's attempt to take over the *Mirror*. Maxwell used all his amazing abilities to charm, and gradually calmed Joe. Like the Labour Party and the Mirror Group editors, he was prepared to give Maxwell the benefit of the doubt. In those early days, people began flocking to the Maxwell banner; a successful man is never short of friends. John Pilger and Paul Foot came to see me and asked for their positions to be made clear. Like the rest of us they wanted to work for the *Mirror*, but they couldn't countenance any interference from Maxwell.

I arranged a meeting where Maxwell hosed them down with charm, saying, 'Gentlemen, you are space barons [a phrase Cudlipp had given him]: I provide the space, you provide the opinions.'

It was what they wanted to hear, but they received it in quite different ways. Both regarded Maxwell as a slippery crook who would eventually revert to type. But Paul Foot was matter-of-fact and quite happy with the reassurance. John Pilger simply glowered at him with such a look of loathing I could see he detested just being in his presence. The only other person I saw look at Maxwell with such deep repulsion was Glenys Kinnock, when she was seated next to him at lunch one day.

On first meetings, Maxwell affected people in startlingly positive ways: there were those who hated him on sight; others were paralysed with shyness; and some became embarrassingly fawnlike. Only a handful of people ever treated him with indifference.

Because Maxwell had been able to borrow millions from the banks in order to buy the *Mirror*, and he already owned an array of other successful ventures, we journalists thought he must possess some mystical powers of insight and acumen. It took some months to realise that he was simply a street trader who was mortgaged up to the hilt.

Maxwell had an astonishing memory and amazing skills in mental arithmetic, but he had no innovative abilities at all. He just had the compelling drive to imitate other successful ventures. His previous headquarters in the city had been named Maxwell House in order that fools would image he also controlled the coffee giant.

When he took over the Mirror Group he rebranded it 'MGN' with a roaring lion's head in a circle; just like Metro Goldwyn Mayer's famous Hollywood symbol. He then tried to persuade me to imitate the *Sun*. In vain I explained that the *Mirror* had proper writers because a vital part of our readership wanted something more than the stuff offered by our imitators. We were popular, but we weren't afraid to be a bit more demanding when the need arose.

To which he answered, 'But you don't sell as many as the *Sun* any more. So what they're doing must be better than what you're doing.'

Holding my temper, I said, 'Since Murdoch launched the *Sun* he's held a lower cover price than the *Mirror*, outspent us on a ratio of four to one in television advertising, printed on the best Finnish newsprint, avoided more strikes, and launched bingo. If we keep our nerve, and produce a quality popular tabloid, we'll win. If we adopt the same philosophy as Murdoch, he'll always stay on top.'

You can guess who won that argument.

Chapter 41

A NOVEL OCCASION

In his first days, Maxwell had told me he was going to retire when he was sixty-five. 'I want to smell the coffee,' he assured me. I wanted to believe him. I liked his sons Kevin and Ian. They had enough of their mother's genes to make them saner human beings. There was only five years to go, and I already had a hobby demanding enough to take my mind off the Kingdom of Maxwellia until they inherited power: as I was halfway through my first novel, *The Black Dwarf*, I thought I might just sit it out.

A few weeks after the takeover I was asked to appear on a television programme about the tabloid press and the interviewer asked me what it was like to have the paper sold from under me. 'It must be like having your country occupied by a foreign power,' he said. He was dead right. The Mirror Group had always been the business equivalent of a republic. No matter how ramshackle and inept the management had been, it was still, if not a democracy, certainly an oligarchy. Now it was a dictatorship.

Maxwell actually used to remind people who disagreed with him that he owned the very chair they were sitting on. One of the ways he established his territory was by having a pee and not always bothering to find a lavatory. One evening, his driver dropped him in the *Mirror* vanway and drove off, not realising that Maxwell had stopped to pee against the rear wheel of his Rolls. The car glided away, leaving Maxwell splashing the tarmac just as a party of Swedish students, who were visiting the paper, came through a door leading from the entrance door. Later, when he had a helicopter landing pad on the roof, he would aim down into Fetter Lane.

When the publication day of my first novel, *The Black Dwarf,* approached, Maxwell decided to hijack the occasion and throw the party in the Mirror Building, even though the publishers, Hodder & Stoughton, had nothing to do with him. Somehow, the invitation he had prepared gave the impression he controlled them. I had no objection, and there was plenty of room in the company restaurant for my friends in the rest of Fleet Street to get a glimpse of life in Maxwellia. The party was a great success, although Maxwell forgot what the actual purpose of the event was and gave a speech thanking everybody on his own behalf.

On the night, Michael Winner decided that he would like to make a movie of the book, but some months later he rang me to say, 'Sorry, Mike, but I can't raise any Hollywood money for a movie about Nazis since *The Boys in Brazil* died at the box office.'

'But it's not about Nazis, Michael,' I explained. 'It's about a modern-day hunt for a German wartime formula.'

'The book's got a swastika on the front cover. That's enough for Hollywood. Nobody ever reads the book in the movie business.'

'Jeffrey Archer liked it,' I added.

'Well there you are,' said Winner and rang off.

Then I remembered that Jeffrey Archer hadn't actually read it either. The day I'd collected the finished copies of the manuscript from a typing agency I'd met Jeffrey in Shaftsbury Avenue.

'What have you got there?' he demanded.

'Copies of my first book,' I answered.

'Give me one,' he demanded. Then he said, 'No, I know it's wonderful.'

Later, that evening, Joyce Hopkirk came into my office for a drink and said, 'So, I hear you've written a masterpiece.'

'Who told you that?' I asked.

'I saw Jeffrey Archer this afternoon. He said he's read it and it's definitely a bestseller.'

Maxwell had various ways of buying his desires. He'd banned smoking under penalty of dismissal at his other establishments, but he'd never imposed the same rule in the *Mirror* building. As a smoker, I knew he found the habit annoying, but I was damned if I was going to give up just to please him.

Then smoking came up in a conversation at one of Maxwell's editors' lunches when I was the only one at the table who hadn't kicked the habit. Bob Edwards, Stotty and Joe Haines took it in turns to tell how, with superhuman efforts of willpower, they'd conquered the addiction.

Maxwell told the story of how he'd been diagnosed with lung cancer and was expecting to die quite soon. So he'd had the representatives of the major religions to give a presentation of their version of God. None impressed him particularly. Then it turned out the lung had been peppered with shrapnel during the war and he didn't have cancer at all. But he quit cigarettes anyway.

'But I understand you find it impossible to quit, Mike,' he said paternalistically. I was smoking at the time and said dramatically, 'If I wanted to, I could make this my last cigarette.'

'I bet you five thousand pounds you can't give up for a year,' he said swiftly.

'Done,' I replied.

'But I don't mind if you smoke cigars,' he added.

I realised Maxwell had manipulated me. He still smoked cigars and after meals I'd always refuse the Havanas he passed around, contented with a cigarette. He did pay the bet, though, and, as he pointed out, it was tax-free. There was no tax to pay on money won on wagers.

At first Maxwell tried to order me to hire certain people, but I always refused, insisting it had to be in the remit of the editor to choose his staff. He went along with this. Then, one day, he said, 'Mike, is there anyone in Fleet Street you'd like to hire?'

'Yes,' I answered after a brief consideration, 'John Blake, the *Sun* show-business columnist.'

'Invite him to lunch,' he said.

John was summoned and Maxwell took to him immediately.

'Name the salary you want, John,' he boomed when the brandy was served. John was so overcome he couldn't even begin to think of a number. So Maxwell offered him a fat salary and a splendid office car, and John was delighted.

When he'd departed Maxwell poured me another brandy and said, 'Will you do me a favour now, Mike?'

'What's that, Bob?' I asked, my suspicions alerted.

'I've allowed you to hire John Blake,' he purred. 'Would you let me hire a football writer of my choice?'

'Fine,' I said, relieved. I had half expected he was going to saddle me with someone new for the political staff or a personal-shares tipster for the City office. 'Who do you want?

'Harry Harris,' he said.

'I'll get the sports editor to contact him,' I said.

'It's all right: he's waiting outside,' he said, and buzzed to have him shown in.

'Why did you want Harry?' I asked later.

'When I bought Oxford United [in 1982] a pack of sports reporters were waiting to waylay me. I brushed them off, but as I drove off my car phone rang and it was Harry Harris. Somehow he'd got the number and that impressed me. I gave him the story and told him I'd hire him one day.'

This rang true, but a lot of Maxwell's answers to stock questions had been well rehearsed, such as his fantasy that he'd gone into scientific publishing because of the atomic bomb and that he'd chosen to be British because he liked the sound of Churchill's speeches; but in the newspaper business you acquire the habit of doubting a story that doesn't quite ring true, and I was beginning to know when he wasn't lying – at least I hoped I was.

Maxwell never paid the asking price for anything, and, when it came to paying large bills, he took over the final negotiation himself. An underling would prepare a sheet of paper with the specification of the order, the company supplying and a contact number for the key person who could sanction a deal. One day I asked him how he came to decide what amount people would settle for.

'Watch and listen,' Maxwell said, picking up a sheet of paper from his desk and dialling a number. A man with a confident voice answered.

'Robert Maxwell here,' he boomed. 'You've already talked to my manager about the computer equipment you supply. You say the bill comes to one million seven hundred and eighty-five thousand pounds.'

'Yes, Mr Maxwell,' answered the man, his voice less confident now.

'I'm going to need a lot more of this equipment,' Maxwell continued. 'I will pay you one million two hundred and eighty pounds if you can deliver immediately.'

There was a pause for about five seconds, then the man said, 'That'll be fine, Mr Maxwell. We'll deliver tomorrow.'

When he hung up the phone I said, 'So how did you know what he'd accept?'

'I don't know,' he replied frankly. 'Something in his voice told me what to offer. It's all a poker game.'

Chapter 42

BINGO! AND A YEAR OF SUNDAYS

The American journalist H L Mencken once said, 'No one ever went broke underestimating the intelligence of the public' – a claim often levelled at those who produce popular newspapers. In the early sixties Cecil King said it would be impossible for a newspaper to come under the *Daily Mirror*. Within ten years Rupert Murdoch was to prove him wrong.

The fatal flaw with the pre-Maxwell *Mirror* was that we thought we had a mission to improve the country. That was fine when we had the market to ourselves, but when Murdoch came along he had a mission to produce profits. If the readers wanted topless girls, who was he to keep them out of the paper? From a journalist's point of view there was nothing more mind-numbingly boring than newspaper bingo. But a vast proportion of the readers loved it. When you're trying to keep your family's head above water, the headline FREE! YOUR CHANCE TO WIN A MILLION POUNDS is a potent slogan.

The Happy Hack

The bingo boom came about because of new technology. Someone developed an inexpensive way to print changing numbers on a bingo card without having to stop the presses. So the pop papers could distribute vast numbers of cards and print the winning numbers in the paper.

The first person to put bingo into a daily newspaper was Derek Jameson when he edited the *Daily Star*, and for some reason he was inordinately proud of the fact, but the effect on the circulation was startlingly effective.

Larry Lamb was still editor of the *Sun*, and the *Mirror* had just overtaken it once again. Murdoch took one look at the situation, fired Larry, made Kelvin MacKenzie editor, cut the cover price of the *Sun* and introduced bingo. In six months the *Sun* had put on 600,000 in circulation. The *Mirror* management responded by increasing our cover price to make us even more expensive than the *Sun*. Finally, after a long delay, we introduced bingo, but the *Sun* had stolen a march on us.

Murdoch was reputed to have said to his new editor, 'How do you feel about that, Kelvin? Six hundred thousand on the circulation and it had fuck all to do with you.'

Actually, MacKenzie turned out to be a formidable editor and the right choice for the times. The character he cultivates of being a street-smart operator from a tough comprehensive is a smoke screen. He was educated at Alleyn's, a famous independent school, and there is a shrewd mind behind the Del Boy, right-wing persona he adopts on television.

Kelvin was one of the new breed of pop-paper journalists who emerged in the seventies. He considered the *Sun* an entertainment and the *Mirror*'s political lectures hopelessly outdated. In some ways, he had a point. I had edited the *Mirror* for nearly ten years and the readers I'd originally connected with were changing. Until the late sixties there was still a vast part of the population that considered itself working class, but this pool of readers had begun to shrink like the air leaking from an old Christmas balloon.

A development that intrigued me was the sudden death of kiss-and-tell memoirs. As the permissive aged continued, revelations in newspapers that would have been considered pornographic by the men who taught me the business became commonplace. Large sums of money were paid to dubious groupies when they revealed all about the 'love rats' they'd cavorted with. Rock stars, politicians and footballers were the favourite targets.

Practically everyone (apart from the participants) is fascinated by a sex scandal. The ashes of the Christine Keeler and John Profumo story are still raked over today and few will have forgotten Margaret Thatcher's favourite, Cecil Parkinson, getting his research assistant pregnant and then being called to heel by his wife.

But, as the old song 'Does Your Chewing Gum Lose its Flavour (On the Bedpost Overnight)?' described it so neatly, the endless exposures of who bonked whom grew suddenly tiresome.

One day Vicki Hodge rang me to say she'd just had a fling with Prince Andrew while he was in the West Indies on leave from the navy. Her intimate account of their romance could be mine to publish for a not unreasonable sum. Vicki Hodge had been one of Felicity Green's favourite models in the sixties;

she was the daughter of a baronet, and, although married, had conducted a public affair with John Binden, a bit-part actor and a violent gangster.

John Binden had been photographed with Princess Margaret on Mustique, the island where she had a holiday home. Later, in a knife fight to the death with another gangster, Binden had triumphed over his opponent, although grievously wounded in the encounter.

Sometimes the Queen must have sighed when she heard of the company her family were keeping. With such notorious names involved, I thought the series would have some impact on the circulation, but it wasn't to be. There are always an impressive number of people who swing between newspapers, but they just weren't interested this time; five years earlier, it would have been a sellout.

Eventually, I returned from a September holiday to go straight to the political conferences in Blackpool, and, on my arrival, Maxwell took me into a private room and said Bob Edwards was leaving and he wanted me to be editor-in-chief with Richard Stott as editor of the *Daily Mirror*. I don't think I had felt such an overwhelming sense of relief since I was told at the age of eleven that my badly damaged left leg was not going to be amputated after all.

In the last months I'd found editing for Maxwell almost unendurable. He'd never harangued or bullied me, as I'd seen him do so often to others, but he was so infuriatingly crass and quixotic in his ways that for the first time in my life I began to find the job hard to take. Previously, I'd worked for men who understood newspapers. If I'd got things wrong, they would point out my shortcomings in no uncertain terms; and, if I'd got things right, they were generous in their praise.

Maxwell had no idea whether an edition of a paper was good or bad because he had no ability to judge how well the work had been done. Whatever the quality, it just looked like another newspaper to him. This meant there were no postmortems on poorly executed editions, but also there were no special days when the boss opened the champagne to celebrate a winner.

Soon after Stotty took over the editorship we met in my old office for a drink before taking our wives to dinner at the Savoy. My stuff had all been cleared out and Stotty had not yet put his own stamp on the room, so it looked a bit bleak.

As we were finishing dinner a call came from the newsdesk to say that the editor's office had been gutted by fire. It seemed a fitting ending to my tenancy.

In my new role I took up residency in a vast new office along the corridor from Maxwell and I had absolutely nothing to do, which suited me fine. I settled down to a new novel. With Maxwell as chairman there was no room for another editor-in-chief; it suddenly felt very strange and liberating to have no daily duties as far as the newspaper was concerned. Maxwell occasionally paraded me in front of visitors so I could field questions about the business that he didn't understand, and sometimes there were pleasant social obligations to perform, but in the main I got on with my writing.

Peter Thompson was having a bad time editing the *Sunday Mirror*. He'd come to the job with a plan to make changes, but the readers hadn't liked them much. The circulation started to drop and Peter fell into a deep despondency. Maxwell was genuinely fond of him, but eventually, Peter told Maxwell that he'd lost his nerve and Maxwell decided to remove him and asked me to take over the *Sunday Mirror* until we could find a new editor. It was a pleasant job for a year. I liked the staff – some of them had been there when I was an office boy – and I knew what to do with the paper. John Parker, my deputy, and I set about the job and we restored the fortunes of the title.

One of the highlights of the year was the day Dame Edna Everage (a.k.a. Barry Humphries) called in to see me. She'd been at the *Mirror* doing a photographic shoot. I heard her distinctive voice calling, 'Where's that dear little possum Mike Molloy?' I looked out of my door onto the newsroom to see the entire staff paying homage at her regal presence.

It is a peculiarity of Barry Humphries that he keeps the character of Dame Edna quite separate from his own. When he is dressed as the dame you address *her*, never Barry. I used to wonder who did the dreaming for the pair of them.

One of my favourites on the staff was Tony Smith, the sports editor, who knew how to relax after a hard day's work. One evening at about seven o'clock I saw him returning to his department.

'How's this for a record lunch, Michael?' he asked.

'Only seven o'clock, Smithy. I've known longer lunches than that,' I replied.

'I went out yesterday,' he retorted.

After a year at the *Sunday Mirror* I realised that I was making a terrible error: I was falling in love with the publication. It was clear to me from the day Maxwell bought the newspapers that he would eventually tire of anyone who worked for him. After all, he'd fired his son Kevin when he was set on marrying Pandora, a girl Maxwell disapproved of. For a time I'd believed he would keep to his claim and retire at sixty-five, but it gradually became clear that there was no chance of that.

I didn't want to devote myself to a newspaper that Maxwell would take from me on a whim. So I stepped back and let John Parker do the job, which he did splendidly. But finally Maxwell appointed Eve Pollard to the editorship. Eve stayed for three years until she went to the *Sunday Express*.

Chapter 43

NOT SEEING EYE TO EYE

Robert Maxwell always reserved his deepest hatred for *Private Eye*. Its constant lampooning drove him to incoherent rages. He launched several lawsuits against the publication and finally decided that he was going to attack it in print. So he asked me to produce a one-off publication in order to 'give them some of their own medicine'.

Like all the journalists of my generation, I liked *Private Eye*. It had given me a kicking from time to time, but nothing malicious. Bron Waugh had poked at me a bit, but in his younger years he'd worked for the *Sunday Mirror* and written quite a lot of longish captions for its glamour-girl pictures. The drooling prose and appalling puns were not among his best work, so I simply wrote to warn him that, if he continued to bully me in the *Eye*, I would reprint all the captions with his name prominently displayed.

He sent me a funny, grovelling apology by return of mail.

Not Seeing Eye to Eye

The first thing I did was deliver a secret message to the *Eye*'s editor Richard Ingrams, saying that all we were going to produce was vulgar abuse, no nasty stuff. I then seconded John Penrose to be my deputy. We knocked up some Soviet-style insults, copied the look of the *Eye* and called the publication *Not Private Eye*.

When he saw the proofs, Maxwell was delighted with our schoolboy efforts. He'd taken a huge shine to Penrose, whom he kept referring to as 'Johnny'. I was going on a brief holiday, so I left Penrose in my office with only the final proofs to dispatch to the printer.

When I returned I found chaos. It transpired that Peter Cook, accompanied by other *Private Eye* workers, had appeared at the *Mirror* front office with a case of whisky saying they had come to acknowledge a *Mirror* victory. Penrose had invited them up to my office and partaken too liberally of the drink they provided. With Penrose comatose on the sofa, Peter Cook had found Maxwell's private telephone number on my blotter and rang to say he was calling from the editor-in-chief's office, and then set about roundly insulting him.

Maxwell's rage was of epic proportions. He didn't want to believe that his new favourite, Penrose, could be responsible, so he blamed the security man at the door. The head of security defended his man and explained that Penrose had given instructions to let Cook and company into the building.

'Johnny betrayed me,' Maxwell lamented. 'He flung opened the gates of the moat and they swam the fortress. He must be fired.' And he was.

As soon as Maxwell had bought Mirror Group Newspapers, he'd ordered some new German state-of-the-art colour-printing machines. Then, suddenly, a famous Australian newspaper, the *Sydney Morning Herald*, came up for sale.

Maxwell told me that if he could buy the *Sydney Morning Herald* he was going to divert two of his new printing machines down there and send me to run the whole operation. For a brief time it made for a wonderful dream, being almost exactly on the other side of the world from Maxwellia.

Maxwell bought the building next door from Goldman Sachs, and, having refurbished the top floor and installed a helipad on the roof, he took up residence. The new home was a sprawling bachelor apartment (he had long abandoned Betty at Headington Hill Hall) with a twenty-four-hour kitchen staff. It was decorated like the home of a country gentleman. But the false Doric pillars in the living room rang hollow when you tapped them.

In making the move, he left Jean Baddeley, his long-time *consigliere*, and Debbie Dines, his faithful secretary, behind. In their place came a French-speaking blonde called Andrea, who was instructed to keep the world at bay.

The world needed keeping at bay, because Maxwell's empire was still in permanent chaos. He'd acquired a whole range of business, taken them to pieces, and then neglected to put them back together. Consequently, there was always a queue of senior managers from a variety of his companies who were grey with frustration awaiting decisions on the most trivial matters. But Maxwell refused to allow anyone the power to take them for him.

Finally, he announced that he was bringing in Peter Jay

as his chief of staff. It seemed to be a brilliant appointment. He'd been economics editor of *The Times* and served as British Ambassador to the United States. He was the perfect example of the British mandarin: son of a cabinet minister and educated to rule. No one could be better qualified to bring order and sanity to Maxwellia; at last, there was to be a wise man at the Emperor's side.

Jay's first act was a masterstroke. He instigated the Black Box system. As Maxwell hated any idea of a chain of command his outer office and desk were choked with vital papers that could be activated only by his signature. But Maxwell refused to delegate or to read them. The businesses of the empire were grinding to a halt.

Peter Jay took on the Herculean task of sorting through the piles of documents to get some order of priority. The most important papers would be placed in boxes that were black imitations of the red-leather boxes containing the papers of state received by cabinet ministers. Thus, the flow of documents would be brought down to manageable numbers and Maxwell could peruse them at his leisure.

The problem was that Maxwell wouldn't play. He liked the chaos, it was his natural element, and when there was utter confusion he could blame others for his own mistakes. It was a common sight to see him confronted with a document that explained a catastrophic decision and roaring at the presenter of the document, 'What fucking idiot decided to do this?'

When the presenter answered, 'You did, chairman,' Maxwell would shout even louder, 'And who was the halfwit who let me do it?'

Maxwell actually hated running companies. All he relished was making decisions on the most trivial level: about how much coffee should be served in a visitor's cup, or what kinds of pencils should be supplied.

Peter Jay, after his first exhausting weeks, got the measure of him. Over a drink he said to me, 'You know, he really only likes taking over companies. He and his sons gallop across the plains like Genghis Kan and his horde and they conquer a new city; but they don't actually know what to do with it. So they sit in a circle on their horses and they say let's leave someone incompetent in charge, and off they gallop to the next conquest.'

I saw the final demise of the Black Boxes when I entered Maxwell's office to find him actually kicking one across the room.

'That fucker Jay has put a vital document in there and gone off with the key. I'll sack him when I find him,' he shouted at me.

'Why don't you call one of the firemen?' I suggested. 'They may have a suitable key.'

He stopped kicking the box. 'Do we have firemen?' he asked, suddenly pleased by the idea.'

'Oh, yes,' I replied. 'Newspaper offices are full of flammable stuff.'

'Andrea,' he shouted, 'send for a fireman, and make sure he brings his fucking axe.'

Peter Jay managed to stand up under the battering he received from Maxwell, and I think it made him a nicer person in the long run. I'd met him only a couple of times before, once at a reception in Downing Street and another time in the arly

1980s, when he was launching TV-am, his disastrous franchise for breakfast television. On those occasions he'd struck me as being arrogant and rather pleased with himself, but Paul Foot liked him, and that was a fair recommendation.

It was Maxwell's pleasure to put another Cudlipp idea into practice and hold a lunch each Tuesday for the top executives. The original idea was to provide a forum for a 'free and frank' exchange of ideas, but it rapidly degenerated into a weekly monologue from Maxwell cataloguing his past triumphs, and victories to come. The lunches were painfully boring, but, when Jay first attended, the occasion was enlivened by Stotty, who, at the end of one of Maxwell's perorations about his role on the world stage, called out, 'Peter, you were once identified by *Time* magazine as one of the most brilliant men in Britain and a future world leader, were you not?'

'I did have that distinction, Richard,' Peter answered.

'And you got a double first at Oxford, didn't you?'

'I did.'

'Then tell me, Peter,' Stotty continued, 'why didn't you have the brains to wear a French letter when you got your au pair pregnant?'

Peter had the grace to laugh instead of punching Stotty, and answered. 'Actually, Richard, I was given to understand that she had taken the proper precautions.'

After that, the newspaper gang took to him, having previously been slightly daunted by his grandeur. I used to like dropping in to his office from time to time because his views on current affairs were always worth listening to. We were chatting one summer evening when we heard Maxwell approaching. The sound was unmistakable: there was much clearing of throat, slapping of feet and jiggling of loose change in pockets.

Peter's actions were well rehearsed. He opened a desk drawer and placed his smoking cigarette in a concealed ashtray. Maxwell entered the room and didn't notice the thin tendrils of smoke curling from the desk. Instead, he was gazing intently at Peter.

'What are you two talking about?' he asked.

'The building of Reagan's power base in Congress,' Peter answered.

'I know Reagan,' said Maxwell, staring intently at Jay. 'We were in hospital together during the war.' With that he spun round and stalked from the room. Peter retrieved his cigarette and we chatted on until we were interrupted by Maxwell's driver, Les.

'Yes, Les?' said Peter.

'Sorry to bother you, Peter,' he said, 'but the guv'nor says I'm to give you this.' He handed Peter a wad of fifty-pound notes that Peter stared at without comprehension.

'The guv'nor says you're to buy a new suit,' explained Les.

Peter looked down at his admittedly rather shabby apparel and shrugged resignedly.

I was puzzled by Maxwell saying he'd been in hospital with President Reagan, so I went to the library, where I confirmed my belief that Reagan had never left America during his war service. Still thinking about Maxwell's claim, I walked to my own office. Then I remembered a film I'd seen in my childhood. It was called *The Hasty Heart*, and was set in a military hospital. It starred both Ronald Reagan and Richard Todd.

Chapter 44

NOT *TODAY*

O ne problem that Maxwell created was even beyond the capability of Peter Jay's intellect. The *Mirror* building had an underground car park that was just about adequate for the newspapers, but Maxwell had crammed a lot of other businesses into the building and promised all their senior executives car-park spaces. This created more anguish than practically anything else Maxwell did – until he raided the pension funds.

Valuable employees threatened to resign and Maxwell ordered Peter Jay to sort out the problem. Peter assembled the thick bundle of memos promising spaces and, after a few minutes' study, realised there was absolutely no solution to the problem Maxwell had created. He pointed this out to Maxwell, who was not in the best of moods because he'd broken his ankle.

'Give the fucking papers to me,' he thundered. 'I've got to do everything in this fucking place.'

The Happy Hack

Peter handed over a fat file and Maxwell took it with him, as he was to take a helicopter from the roof to Headington Hill Hall. The helicopter pilot told us of the subsequent events. Maxwell, uncomfortable with his leg in plaster, opened a helicopter window to put his plaster-encased leg on the sill. The vortex created by the act sucked out all the paperwork relating the car-park problem and scattered the memos over Buckinghamshire.

The following day Maxwell returned and handed Peter the empty file.

'I've solved your car-park problem,' he said loftily.

Maxwell loved decorations. To see him in white tie and tails was an extraordinary sight because, in addition to his British wartime medals, he'd acquired a mass of sashes, stars, clusters and orders that gave him the look of a gaudily hung Christmas tree. But all of them had been presented by the dictators of Iron Curtain countries, where he was welcomed as 'a giant of the west who held the governments of the communist east in true fraternal friendship'.

His relationship with the Soviet bloc can best be summed up by the question he asked Romania's Nicolae Ceauşescu in the introduction of a book he published about the communist leader: 'How do you account for your enormous popularity with the Romanian people?' Just the kind of difficult question tyrants are forced to struggle with when they are confronted by critics.

I have heard it claimed that Maxwell was a British agent, a Soviet agent and an Israeli agent. Actually, I think he was all three. Not in the sense of betraying vital military secrets, but by supplying various governments with gossip they might find comforting. However, I'm convinced that, first and foremost, he was a genuine agent of Maxwellia.

I don't think he would have made much of a spy for the rest, because he didn't have the patience to absorb complicated information. Instead, he preferred to rely on his own instincts rather than bother with inconvenient facts. Early on he invited me to dinner on my own because he said he wanted to know the whole history of the *Daily Mirror*. But after a few sentences about Northcliffe's dream of a newspaper for women, he became bored and began to cram some large ripe pears into his mouth, at the same time telling me he was dieting. This was followed by a whole chicken. It was as if he wanted to swallow everything whole because he couldn't be bothered with bites – and that was the way he liked to assimilate information. He asked me why there was a plaque of Cassandra in the hallway.

'Because Huge Cudlipp and Cecil King regarded Cassandra as the jewel in the *Mirror*'s crown,' I ventured.

'I didn't know Cassandra was a Jew,' he said.

'Not Jew: *jewel*,' I corrected.

'Do you think anyone else deserves a plaque?' he asked.

'Harry Guy Bartholomew, Cecil King and Hugh Cudlipp,' I answered promptly.

'Who is Harry Guy Bartholomew?'

'He was the man who turned the *Mirror* into a popular Labour paper.'

'I shall have them so honoured,' he declared solemnly. And he did so – adding one of himself to complete his set of *Mirror* heroes.

In his never-ending search for publicity, Maxwell developed

the technique of hitching his personal cart to a passing bandwagon. The Ethiopian famine provided such a bandwagon. Maxwell set about garnering food supplies and medical equipment from charity contacts and persuaded Lord King of British Airways to lend him a jumbo jet. Always aware of his image, for the trip, which he was to lead himself, he wore a central European peasant's peaked cap that made him look like an extra from *Fiddler on the Roof.*

A team of journalists from Mirror Group Newspapers were also dispatched to take up residence in the Addis Ababa Hilton Hotel, where there was no sign of famine at all. Transporting Maxwellia with him, Maxwell directed operations from his hotel suite, but on one memorable occasion he demanded a room where he could brief his swelling team of reporters and photographers.

The harassed manager, whose life had been made unbearable by Maxwell's demands, agreed that he could have the early use of a large room for his briefing. Maxwell was running late when he finally got to the room where the journalists had assembled.

Maxwell began a military-style briefing outlining future operations for the hacks, but he was gradually having difficulty making himself heard above the shattering noise of rock records being played. Also, a large and staring crowd had materialised and were watching his performance.

'Send for the manager,' Maxwell stormed, outraged at this intrusion. The man arrived wringing his hands. 'Get rid of all these people, and stop that fucking music,' Maxwell shouted.

'But, sir,' wailed the manager. 'Your meeting is taking place in the disco.'

When he returned to Britain he sent for me. 'Mike, the Ethiopians are desperately short of light aircraft. I want to form a squadron to fly against the famine. What shall I do?'

'We do have a first-class pilot on the staff of the *Mirror*, Bob,' I told him.

'Who?'

'Peter Tory, our diary writer. His hobby is flying his own light aircraft. He used to be part of a stunt flying team; he was so good his nickname was Biggles.'

'Biggles, eh? Get him up here,' he instructed.

Peter Tory entered the room and Maxwell thrust a large whisky into his hand, saying, 'Boggles, I've got a special mission for you.'

'Yes, Bob,' said Peter, with the note of caution I had grown used to hearing when people spoke to Maxwell.

'I want you to form a special squadron of light aircraft to fly rescue and communication missions in Ethiopia. This is vital work. Hand-pick your men.'

Peter, who had trained at the Royal College of Dramatic Art, lived up to the moment. 'Bob, I'll find you chaps made of the right stuff,' he said, with a meaningful glance at me.

After a great deal of work, Tory produced a plan. But, when Maxwell saw that the aircraft would have to be hired, salaries paid to the pilots and support mechanics and fuel bought, his enthusiasm suddenly dimmed, and Peter's squadron was stood down.

The best job Maxwell ever gave me lasted only twenty-four hours. He called me to his office to have lunch and I found him sitting at a small dining table before his new toy. It was a computer screen that displayed market prices. It appeared also to have a two-way speaker connected to his broker – a bit like having a very special one-armed bandit. He was betting on the currency market when I took my place beside him.

'It's reached twenty-eight point five,' a disembodied voice said. 'Shall I sell?'

'No,' replied Maxwell. 'I'll hang on for a while.'

I could see he was in a very good mood. 'I have bought the *Today* newspaper from [businessman and Lonrho CEO] Tiny Rowland,' he said. 'I want you to go there on Monday and take over as chairman, managing director and editor. You can take one person from the *Mirror* with you.

As he spoke I could feel how much I wanted to do it, and the idea of being at Victoria, where the *Today* offices were located, filled me with joy. With Maxwell out of sight, he tended to be out of mind. I relished the idea of being even just a few miles from Holborn.

'Tomorrow we'll discuss the first moves. Dennis Hackett is coming in to give us a briefing. Do you know him?'

'A bit,' I said. I knew Dennis had been night-editing *Today* in recent months.

As I started to leave, Maxwell buzzed his broker. 'How high now?' he asked.

'Up another five points.'

'Sell. How much did I make?'

'Thirty-eight thousand pounds.'

'Not bad for a lunchtime's work,' said Maxwell.

The following day Maxwell was still in a bubbly mood.

'We'll get on with our plans when I've talked to Murdoch,' he said, and I remembered that some of the *Sun*'s Northern editions were contracted to print on satellite machines owned by *Today*. Dennis Hackett had arranged to come in after lunch, so I went to my own office and got on with my latest novel, but the planned call to Murdoch caused me a slight unease.

When I returned to Maxwell's office he looked at the time difference between New York and London and judged it was late enough in the morning to ring Murdoch.

'Rupert,' he purred. 'Bob here. I just thought you might like to be the first to know I've bought the *Today* newspaper from Tiny Rowland . . . Yes, thank you very much . . . Of course, you have my assurance that I will continue to print your editions on the machines . . . Excellent . . . Well, it's been good to talk to you.'

Despite the seeming cordiality of the call, what Maxwell was actually saying was, 'I've beaten you at last, you bastard.'

I don't think I'd ever seen him looking so happy. After hearing the conversation with Murdoch I was filled with foreboding.

Maxwell became diverted by other matters so I saw Dennis Hackett on my own. 'What does he want me here for?' asked Dennis.

'He wants you to tell him the secrets of *Today*,' I answered.

'There aren't any secrets. It's a bloody newspaper, not a Freemasons' lodge,' he said irritably.

'Just tell me the staff figures and if there's anyone there I don't know who's good. I'll make up the rest.'

Dennis gave me a brief rundown and, just as he was leaving, he said, 'You know, I don't think he's actually signed the deal yet.'

The Happy Hack

The following day was Sunday; I arrived in the afternoon and found a temporary secretary on duty. 'He's in ever so bad a mood,' she said, and I could hear shouting as I opened his door. Maxwell was bellowing in German into the telephone. I had never seen him in such a rage. Finally he slammed down the receiver and said, 'That bastard Rowland, he's double-crossed me and sold to Murdoch.'

It turned out that Murdoch had sensed Maxwell hadn't yet signed the deal. After Maxwell's call he'd contacted Tiny Rowland and offered him a better deal for *Today*. Maxwell never spoke of the episode again, and I missed the chance of an escape to Victoria.

Chapter 45

THE PRESIDENT AND THE PRINCE

'I want you to go and represent me with President Moi in Nairobi,' Robert Maxwell announced. 'You know I've bought newspapers there from him?'

'I did, Bob.'

'John Halloran will be signing the deal with the president. Keep your eyes open for opportunities: Nairobi will be the hub of our African communications empire. I already have feelers out to buy a television channel.'

I knew John Halloran, who ran the British Printing Corporation for Maxwell. Unusually for someone in the management part of Maxwellia, he had no fear of Maxwell at all.

On arriving in Nairobi, we managed a short night's sleep in a hotel festooned with animal heads and leather furniture; it hadn't changed much since the days of empire. In the morning we were driven to the headquarters of Maxwell's newly acquired newspapers. The offices were about the size of a suburban semi and they were located over an oriental carpet dealer's in downtown Nairobi. There was no air conditioning and the heat was brutal.

The handful of young staff were delighted to meet us, as they hoped we would fulfil the promises Maxwell had made them about supplying new equipment. John broke the news to them gently that Maxwell often promised more than he would deliver.

We then proceeded to President Daniel arap Moi's palace. It had once been the British High Commissioner's headquarters, but was now looking a trifle seedy.

Soldiers wearing camouflage uniforms and carrying sub-machine-guns lined the drive; their eyes, in their expressionless faces, looked dead. Most disturbing of all, a few of them had their fatigue pants stuffed into socks. It didn't seem much of a guard of honour. Luckily, the ceremony didn't take long. Moi, a man with eyes like poached eggs, seemed distant from the whole occasion, as he gently stirred the air with a fly whisk.

An official insisted on a photograph being taken and assured us we would receive prints later in the afternoon. Just before the signing, another official announced that there had to be a change in the contract.

John began a heated argument with him and the soldiers flanking the president, seeing discord, shifted their sub-machine-guns in a businesslike manner. But the moment passed and the official backed down.

We then departed for a country club that was, like the hotel, straight from the colonial past. John told me we were to have lunch with a minister. He was a charming man, and over our lamb chops John explained that the minister's fears for his daughter's future employment were groundless. John would see that she received an internship at the British Printing Corporation. In turn, the minister assured John that anything he required would be done in return.

While we lunched, photographs were delivered of our meeting with the president, and John stowed them in his briefcase. Our next call was to a small printing factory that was not fully operational. John asked some technical questions about offset printing and even I could tell the manager had no idea of how anything in the place worked.

'Let me meet your foreman,' John demanded, and a wiry, bearded American was finally produced. The man understood everything John asked him and he explained bluntly why the plant wasn't working.

'Can you fix it?' asked John.

'Sure,' said the American casually. 'If I ever get the parts I ordered.'

John fired the manager and made the American the new boss. We made for the airport to return home. At the baggage check-in, which took place at a tin-roofed hut, an official demanded to know if we had any foreign currency. When we said that we did, he insisted we place it in a collection tin that was supposed to be for the Red Cross.

John exploded in rage. As far as I was concerned he was welcome to the thirty-odd quid I had on me if it smoothed our journey, but John was made of sterner stuff. He dug into his briefcase and produced the pictures of us with President Moi taken earlier in the day and slapped them down on the counter.

The man looked at them and an expression of terror crossed his face. He actually turned a grey-greenish colour and began to stammer in Swahili; he was so terrified he'd forgotten what English he knew.

Seeing our blank faces, he pulled another man towards him and using him as an interpreter begged our forgiveness, saying it had all been a terrible misunderstanding. Relieved, we boarded the aircraft, having spent slightly less than twenty-four hours in Nairobi.

A few days after reaching home I was told why I had been chosen to represent Maxwell. The *Mirror*'s foreign editor, Nick Davies, encountered me a few days after my return from Nairobi. He asked, 'How did you get on with President Moi?'

'We didn't have a lot to say to each other,' I told him. 'I can't think why Maxwell sent me anyway.'

'I'm afraid that was my fault,' said Nick. 'I heard from a Mossad contact that Maxwell was going to be assassinated when he was in Nairobi, so he sent you instead.'

'Who would want to assassinate him?' I wondered later as I was recounting the tale in the Stab.

'Probably one of their print unions,' Stotty ventured.

Another example of Maxwell's ability to create illusions about himself was demonstrated when the editors and proprietors of Fleet Street were invited to attend a very grand cocktail party at the French Embassy. Dinner jackets were to be worn.

The Royal Family, the Cabinet and members of the House of Lords were attending a dinner and afterwards they were to join the rest of us in a vast marquee that covered the rear lawn of the embassy. The great tent was attached to the building above a row of French windows leading out onto a wide flight of steps.

We, the second division, arrived, having been carefully directed to enter at the rear of the garden on our invitations. Suddenly, we were confronted by a spectacular sight. Dinner had ended and now the whole of Britain's Establishment stood in splendour, filling the stairs descending from the French windows. Many were bedecked in white tie and tails, ball gowns, tiaras, others glittering uniforms, and magnificent decorations. And there in the middle of them all stood Maxwell in full dress regalia, Betty next to him. How on earth had they been invited to the dinner? we wondered.

Maxwell spotted me, and then Sandy. He gestured imperially for us to join him on the stairs, where he chatted to Prince Charles. We approached with the necessary deference and Maxwell caught the attention of Prince Charles to say, 'Your Royal Highness, do you know Mike Molloy?'

To my astonishment, Prince Charles smiled and said, 'Of course, Mr Molloy and I are old friends. Is this your wife? I'd like to meet her.'

I presented Sandy and Charles said, 'I'm so sorry you weren't able to join us when Mr Molloy came to lunch.'

Maxwell seemed disconcerted that I'd met Prince Charles, but he caught the elbow of Angus Ogilvy, husband of Princess Alexandra of Kent, and said, 'Angus, do you know Mike Molloy?'

'Why, yes,' he said. 'We sat together at the *Punch* lunch last week.'

Unable to introduce me to anybody else, Bob wandered away

and Prince Charles watched him go before saying to me, 'What an extraordinary man. What's he like to work for? Where does he get all his money from?'

A few days later one of the drivers told me how Maxwell had managed his appearance on the steps with Betty. They had been waiting outside the front door of the embassy until the dinner was over. Timing the event perfectly, they'd entered by the front door to mingle with the dinner guests as they made their way to the marquee. Thus he'd giving the impression he'd been selected as one of the greatest in the land.

Chapter 46

DOING THE CONTINENTAL

In 1985, to celebrate his fortieth wedding anniversary, Maxwell threw a party at Headington Hill Hall of which the Great Gatsby would have approved. Maxwell asked his editors and other contacts to recruit glamorous guests, and the dinner was conducted in a mighty marquee on the lawn of the house. Bands played, said glamorous guests decked in party finery drank champagne and dined in splendour. There were even lavish fireworks that spelled out Maxwell's name.

With his gift for the dramatic gesture, Maxwell took me aside on the night and we stood in the dark of the lawn while he revealed his plan to found a newspaper printed in English to be distributed in every country on the Continent. It was to be called the *European*. 'I want you to edit it,' he said. 'What do you think about that?'

'I'm really not the man for this job, Bob,' I said apprehensively.

'Why on earth not?' he asked.

The Happy Hack

'You need someone multilingual who's steeped in European history. I speak a few sentences of French. I'm an English journalist. I know a lot about the British, but I've no great grasp of European politics.'

Maxwell was bewildered by this attitude. He had the ego to take on any job, regardless of his lack of training. I had seen him argue with doctors, lawyers, scientists and engineers, blithely undaunted by his utter ignorance of the subject at hand.

'Well, you've got the job, mister,' he said stubbornly. 'Get yourself a team for the dummy.'

I was happy enough with that. I tried questioning Maxwell about the sort of paper he wanted it to be but he became irritable when I asked him to commit himself. 'Just go ahead and produce it,' he said. 'Then I'll tell you what I don't like about it.'

So I got on with it. First I put together a team and we spent a couple of days discussing content. I decided to make it a broadsheet, because at the time tabloid newspapers were still considered downmarket. I decided I'd designed enough newspapers so I gave the task to John Hill, who did a fine job. It looked powerful, punchy and, above all, sober. Then Maxwell dropped one of his bombshells.

'I've hired you a bunch of French journalists to help out,' he said. 'Their team are coming over tomorrow to meet your team.'

It transpired that a Frenchman called Jean Shalit, who had been preparing the dummy of a new paper that had been abandoned, had an exuberant nature. The French turned up, and with perfect symmetry the roles of their team exactly matched ours. We took over a large editorial space to work in and Jean

Shalit suggested a meeting to discuss the project. Three weeks later, the British team, numb with boredom, begged to be allowed to start. But the French wanted to go on defining the exact nature of the publication by debating every detail of the procedure with in excruciating detail.

'Why are they doing this?' I asked one Friday evening when the English team were drinking and the French had returned to Paris for the weekend.

'Cartesian logic,' answered David Bradbury.

'How does that apply?' I asked.

'It's the reason the British and the Americans find it so hard to work with the French. First they define what final result they want to achieve; once they've done this there's no deviation from the path they've constructed. The French despise American and British methods because we decide what we want to do but we're flexible and pragmatic about how we get there.'

'But if they decide on every step of the way once we've agreed to some French point there's no changing direction.'

'Exactly,' said Bradbury.

'We'd better win the argument, then,' I said.

Now we saw what the French were doing we soon reached an impasse, so it was suggested both teams take exactly the same material and process it in their own ways. Then we would test-market each team's printed dummy in every capital city in Europe. We called in a friend of mine, Mike Aalders, who would organise the research, as he ran an international public-relations company.

When the results came in the British version was decisively preferred over the French in every European capital, including

Paris. Jean Shalit was mortified. He couldn't understand how his meticulous plan had been defeated by British blundering. At last, I understood what the Allies had put up with when dealing with General de Gaulle.

The *European* was now proceeding towards the launch date, but Maxwell had another diversion for me. He was in a clandestine mood when he summoned me to his office. 'We're going on a mission to Moscow,' he confided. 'We leave from here at oh eight hundred hours on Thursday. Visas will be obtained.'

The Soviet Union was in turmoil because of the new policies of perestroika and glasnost. Maxwell had spent forty years cultivating key people behind the Iron Curtain, and he didn't want to see them all purged from his contact book.

As his own contribution to saving Soviet communism, he offered a team of us to go to Moscow and revitalise *Moscow News*, a propaganda publication that was translated into all known languages, but read by only a handful of people scattered across the globe.

Maxwell led the team, so we took his private jet to Moscow. On the flight, Maxwell slept in a single bunk and Kevin and I sat up drinking coffee. Suddenly he spoke frankly to me about what a burden it was to work for his father. He had no time to see his family and life seemed to be passing in a never-ending grind of work. I made some clichéd remarks about great success needing the kind of dedication he showed, but my homilies sounded pretty hollow, even to me.

The offices of *Moscow News* were housed in a rather comfortable, old-fashioned headquarters. There was a gentle, academic feel to the whole operation. Journalists had gone about their undemanding work for decades, explaining to a virtually nonexistent international readership the superiority of life under communism.

Our interpreter, Olga, was a charming girl who spoke excellent English. Olga was stunned by the hours we intended to keep and it became clear that no one in Russia worked very hard. They didn't get paid much, but they had a lot of leisure time. I remember vividly the time she said she was going home early because there was a new consignment of cheese due in the shops.

Maxwell took me around to meet a couple of his old cronies in the party and I was delighted to see how the atmosphere of the old Soviet system was still preserved in some quarters.

Heavily set men in offices crammed with framed awards and souvenirs would embrace Maxwell and pour us vast vodkas. Even though I couldn't understand the language, I could feel the almost wistful nostalgia that was in the air.

It later transpired that these men were part of the KGB class who seized the old wealth-producing industries. So they weren't too unhappy about the future prospects.

Eventually, I joined Maxwell on board his private jet to Paris. The possibility of buying the *Sydney Morning Herald* was still on the table and Maxwell was going to take over the negotiations himself.

Maxwell had somehow got the French government to provide him with a team of special police drivers whenever he was in Paris. These men could have given tips to James Bond on getting through bothersome traffic. In an entourage of cars, we hurtled along steeply sloped embankments, over pavements, down one-way streets and along pedestrian walkways until we arrived at the Ritz Hotel.

The Fairfax family, who owned the *Sydney Morning Herald*, had appointed a lawyer called Turnbull to act for them and he was reputed to be one of the most brilliant men in Australia. As they negotiated I sat, spellbound with boredom. Here I was in the most enchanting city in the world – beyond the room I sat in were magnificent museums, fabulous restaurants, inviting bars and some of the greatest paintings ever produced – and I was stuck in a room watching two men in shirtsleeves playing Monopoly for a newspaper.

The only time it became interesting was when Maxwell said, 'Why don't you put down the lowest figure you'll take for the business and I'll put down the highest figure I'll offer and we'll settle on halfway between the amounts?'

You could almost hear Turnbull's mind turning over the proposition, but, sensing some trap, he backed away. Finally the talks stalled and Maxwell wanted to return to London.

Pandora, Kevin's wife, was also staying at the Ritz and Maxwell, now as impatient as a child to get away to the airport, decided that Kevin, Pandora and I would take the second car. In the lobby, Kevin was still engaged in deep conversation with two men from one of Maxwell's French businesses. They were mortified that they didn't have more time with Kevin.

Finally, Kevin asked Pandora to go on with me to catch Maxwell's jet and he would take a later flight. Pandora looked devastated. Torrential rain began as we drove to the airport and Pandora spent the whole of the journey complaining bitterly about the dreadful life she and Kevin endured by being in Maxwell's thrall. We scrambled aboard the aircraft just in time for takeoff, and Pandora sat looking out of the window, gazing rather forlornly at the rain, and I wondered just how many wives Maxwell made miserable in life.

Chapter 47

WHAT'S IN A NAME?

'**W**ould you like to meet Mother Teresa?' Maxwell asked. Yes, I did want to meet someone who was clearly a candidate for sainthood; and I also wanted to observe her confrontation with Maxwell, a major representative of Mammon.

I have no religious beliefs, apart from an occasional vague feeling that there may well be a greater power in the universe. The rituals of any religion have never attracted me, apart from some of the Church of England hymns and the poetic passages of the King James Bible.

I once did meet someone in holy orders who impressed me: a young priest who gave a brief talk at the convent my daughters attended. He didn't say much, but he seemed to emanate goodness. I wanted to know if Mother Teresa was endowed with the same gift. She wasn't.

What's In a Name?

Maxwell and I waited in the living room of his apartment (this was in April 1988) listening to the chatter of his helicopter approaching the roof; then an entourage entered that consisted of some unidentified civilians, one of whom was an interpreter.

We were introduced and I looked closely at the little woman who stood before us. She appeared to be clothed in garments that had been made out of old tea towels. I shook her leathery hand and for a second she looked at me with a total lack of interest. I was slightly disappointed that there were no distant choirs or ethereal light.

For some unexplained reason she chose not to speak in English, a language she knew quite well, but instead conducted the interview in what I took to be her native Albanian. Maxwell kicked off with the customary platitudes he reserved for government representatives. Mother Teresa nodded her appreciation. Then she spoke in a language that sounded like someone cracking nuts with their teeth. The interpreter's translation was startling.

'Mr Maxwell, Mother Teresa has a message for you from God.'

Maxwell's beaming smile was a sight to behold. At last, I thought, in the hush that had descended on the room, the Almighty is about to reveal his plan for the future of Maxwellia.

'Yes,' said Maxwell, and we all leaned forward eagerly as the Albanian exchanges were made. The interpreter nodded and turned to Maxwell: 'God wants you to give Mother Teresa a million pounds to start a hospice in England.'

The smile remained on Maxwell's face, but he made no answering commitment. He simply thanked her for her visit and a few minutes later the helicopter chattered away and the usual chaos of the day returned.

In December 1988 the heads of state of the European Community were to hold a conference on Rhodes, and Maxwell seized the opportunity to give the forthcoming *European* a publicity boost. Maxwell's own yacht had been chartered by holidaymakers in the Caribbean, so he'd hired another one to impress the world's press with his status as a media tycoon. Unfortunately, all the best mooring had been booked and he could only find space to tie up on the unfashionable part of the island, in what appeared to be the car park of a trading estate.

European Community officials had organised the timetable and press releases with commendable efficiency. Coaches were supplied to take the world's press to various locations about the island in order to attend a rolling series of press conferences held by various heads of state.

There is always a festive air when politicians and journalists meet at conferences. At the bar I found friends from the Irish and American contingents and the usual gossip was exchanged. Our team had also found a pleasant restaurant a short stroll from the car park.

Someone also discovered a shop that sold bargain leather jackets and suddenly we all caught jacket fever. It was then that I realised Maxwell had become infatuated by his secretary, Andrea. He wouldn't let her leave his side and, when she wanted a brief time off to seek a leather jacket of her own, he refused to let her go, but had the trader spread his wares on the deck of the yacht so Andrea could make her choice.

One day she asked me rather wistfully where we were all going that evening. I told her about the restaurant and she said she wished she could come, but Maxwell made her have dinner with him every night.

The day dawned on which Maxwell had designated he would hold his own press conference and we were summoned to the yacht to have breakfast. He was in a foul mood and sat at the head of the table seeking victims to bully while he crammed astonishingly large amounts of food into himself.

The yacht was quite beautiful on the outside, but below it appeared to have been decorated by a new lottery winner. The table at which we ate was equipped with wrought-iron chairs, and, as he raved, his vast weight began to buckle his chair legs. Gradually, he sank lower and lower, until his chin was almost level with the table. He tried to get up but, it proved impossible to manage, so he ordered us all on deck. We never did find out how he extricated himself.

Alastair Campbell and Mike Aalders were with the team and between Maxwell's demands we began to enjoy ourselves. While we were at the bar discussing the paper, Mike Aalders, who had founded an advertising agency, told us it would be impossible for the *European* to make any money from advertising.

'Why not?' we asked.

'There are no pan-European advertising budgets. Clients just go to agencies in each country in Europe,' he explained.

'Does Maxwell know this?'

'Oh, yes, he just ignores the problem. I don't think I'd ever invest in any business Maxwell ran.'

The week over, a few of us flew to Athens for connecting

flights elsewhere. In the spirit of an end-of-term party we had dinner in a restaurant looking up at the Acropolis. We discussed life with Cap'n Bob in a general manner until Alastair made a startling claim: 'I bet I'm the only one who's seen Maxwell's prick,' he said. A silence followed.

'How did this come about?' asked Nick.

'At the Addis Ababa Hilton on the Ethiopian trip,' Alastair explained, 'he sent for me and I went to his suite. He was standing stark naked in the bathroom putting mascara on his eyebrows.'

'With his prick?' asked Nick.

It was a suitable remark on which to end the Rhodes venture.

Back in London, to my relief, Maxwell eventually appointed an editor for the *European*, Ian Watson from the *Daily Telegraph*, who set out with enthusiasm to tackle the task, but in time he blunted his vigour on Maxwell's intransigence. Maxwell fired him within a year of the launch.

Tom Bower was writing a book about Maxwell and Tony Delano and Peter Thompson had also produced a biography. Maxwell decided it was time for the authorised version. Joe Haines was detached from his editorial duties and set about the mammoth task of telling the tale. It was daunting. Part of the problem was, Maxwell had been so evasive, or had fantasised so much about his life over the years, that he'd often forgotten what the truth was about many of his escapades.

It had never been clearly explained how Maxwell, a penniless ex-officer, had acquired the initial money to start a business. What exactly were his financial arrangements in Lichtenstein? Why had he denied he was Jewish before the Arab–Israeli War?

What's In a Name?

Why did he speak all other languages like a native, but French like an Englishman?

I had to help with the pictures because Betty announced that she would trust no one but me with her archive. She had a huge safe at Headington Hill Hall where she stored every letter, photograph, cutting and other item of memorabilia concerning Maxwell. In the archive were five army pay books: one in the name of Ján Ludvík Hoch, the second Leslie Jones, the third Leslie Smith, the fourth Leslie Du Maurier and the fifth Ian Robert Maxwell. There was also a puzzling letter of authority allowing him to wear civilian clothes or any uniform, and assume any rank he wished.

No author of espionage thrillers would dare to invent such a baffling background for one of their characters. The final, wonderfully bizarre, twist to his past was supplied by his sister Sylvia. She visited his office one day when I happened to have a pile of photographs of their family that I was captioning. There was one of Maxwell in his days in the Czech army. I had just written Private Ján Ludvík Hoch on the back when Sylvia looked over my shoulder and Maxwell entered the room.

Having read my caption, she turned to Maxwell and said, 'Why do you always say your name was Ján Ludvik Hoch?'

'Because it is,' he replied.

'No, it's not,' said Sylvia. 'Your name is Ludvík. You were named after Uncle Ludvík, not Ján.'

'Was I?' said Maxwell, revealing that he didn't know exactly what his real name was.'

The photographs in Betty's archive of the young Robert Maxwell were fascinating. His transition from gaunt young

Czechoslovakian peasant to elegant, dashing British officer could have been equalled only by Hollywood.

In later years, when he wanted to recapture some of the romance of his past, Maxwell was invited to Poland to take part in the World War Two remembrance ceremony. He had a British uniform made in Savile Row for the occasion. He paraded before us and it had to be tactfully pointed out that he had his Sam Browne belt on the wrong way round.

Joe Haines, who was also attending the ceremony along with Field Marshal Lord Bramall, asked the field marshal if Maxwell was entitled to wear a uniform.

'Certainly, not,' he replied. 'The only people allowed to wear military uniforms in perpetuity are members of the Royal Family and field marshals. For anyone else it's an indictable offence.'

Later, I checked with Mike Maloney, the photographer who covered the ceremony, how it had all gone off.

'It was a bit of a nightmare,' Mike answered. 'No one had thought to provide Maxwell with a wreath to put on the memorial. You can imagine how he felt about that,'

'What happened?' I asked.

'He nicked the one belonging to the Americans,' said Mike.

Chapter 48

END OF AN ERA

M̲axwell decided he wanted yet another diversion, so he announced that he was going to start an evening paper. Then he announced that the *London Daily News* would be a twenty-four-hour publication, one that would appear first as a morning edition and then change edition by edition throughout the day and evening.

A management team were dispatched to various corners of the world where other twenty-four-hour papers had been produced. They returned and told Maxwell the idea had comprehensively failed wherever it had been attempted. Maxwell shrugged at the information and pressed on with his intention to produce a twenty-four-hour paper anyway. It was launched on 24 February 1987, but was very short-lived, for it was closed that July.

My own theory about the paper was that Maxwell wanted to have a project that never slept. He existed on cat naps, and endured long periods of boredom throughout the night. He could always eat, because he had a twenty-four-hour kitchen in operation; with a round-the-clock newspaper he would have something to play with it in the wee small hours.

Despite the staff producing a well-made newspaper, the project was doomed by the wasteful and pointless efforts of trying to keep a paper going over a twenty-four-hour cycle; and so it closed.

Meanwhile, Maxwell was becoming even more chaotic in his personal behaviour. He'd taken to sending for temporary secretarial help in the evenings and pressing his affections upon them. One complained that he had promised her a taxi home, but then told her she had to take a bus.

He was still infatuated with Andrea, and told her he would divorce Betty and build her a palace in Eastern Europe, but she was now living with the *Mirror*'s foreign editor, Nick Davies. Plagued with paranoia, he had Nick Davies followed by private detectives and the offices bugged of people about the building he considered disloyal.

The inevitable day arrived when Maxwell fired me. t came as no surprise. From any sensible business point of view, I should have gone years before, but somehow I lasted until 1990. The title I enjoyed, editor-in-chief, was as hollow as the false pillars in Maxwell's sitting room. Occasionally, he'd used me as a fireman, but by any measure I was a luxury he'd finally decided he could do without.

I felt no regret at the prospect of leaving the company for which I'd worked for most of my life; in fact, I looked forward to it. Maxwell had decided that he was going to sell the Mirror

End of an Era

Group site at Holborn Circus and relocate the newspapers' offices next to a sink estate south of the river.

The industry had changed so rapidly and so completely that I wanted a change myself. The leisure Maxwell had afforded me had allowed me to publish three thrillers, which had been well received, and I was in the process of completing a more ambitious novel. The payoff he'd offered was also what I'd hoped for.

As a boy I'd entered a trade that was wonderfully romantic. A village of newspapers scattered around Fleet Street, studded with pubs and steeped in history. All that had gone.

When I first came into that world, newsrooms were smoked-filled cockpits of energy, and sometimes high drama. Because of the new technology they had now become quiet, carpeted, halls of boredom, where people peered anxiously at computer screens, like any other office in the land.

My coming novel, *The Century*, was the saga of a newspaper dynasty that explored the lives of the successive owners of a newspaper and the journalists who worked for them. There was a villain in the book – a monstrous proprietor who traduced and bullied his staff and persisted with outlandish ideas that no one dared oppose. I did not have to invent anything about his character as he was wholly and truthfully modelled on my late employer.

Maxwell attended the publishing party for *The Century* and made a brief speech commanding the audience to buy the book. I had every confidence he would never read a word of it.

After a time I was invited to work as a consultant for the *Daily*

Telegraph and twice for the *Daily Express*, and I continued to write. When Tony Blair's New Labour was elected and he became prime minister I was truly happy. At last, I thought, the Labour Party had come to power with the coffers full and a commitment to encourage business and use the swelling tax revenues to build a decent society.

Well, we all know it didn't work out like that. In the end, Tony Blair turned out to be more interested in retaining power than reshaping Britain. Going to war in foreign countries was an easier option than tackling the problems at home.

Unable to control Gordon Brown, who was busy demonstrating his own idea of how the United Kingdom should be shaped, Blair came running every time George W Bush whistled. Meanwhile, millions of immigrants were drawn into Britain and everyone could see the unbearable pressure being put on housing, schools and hospitals; with no plan to tackle the problem, but the majority of the Labour Party remained in denial, trusting that their economic guru, Gordon Brown, would perform further 'miracles' and conjure up enough money to pay for his reckless excesses.

Out of the blue I got a brief call from Maxwell. He told me that he missed me and he wanted me to return to work for him. He said he was going away for a few days but he would ring me the following Thursday and he would tell me what he was going to offer me. The following week the news broke that he'd disappeared overboard from his yacht, *Lady Ghislaine*, so I never did find out what he had in mind.

People have often asked me what I thought had really happened to him. Geoffrey Goodman was convinced that he'd been assassinated by a hit squad from Mossad; some people argued that he'd committed suicide; and others angrily denied that he would ever contemplate such an act.

When I'd first met Betty Maxwell, she'd told me of their dreadful days when he'd first been disgraced, and pronounced unfit to run a public company by the Department of Trade and Industry.

'It was terrible, Mike,' she said. 'We couldn't afford the school fees, and our mantelpiece, that had always been crowded with invitations, was suddenly bare. But Bob fought his way back.'

Well, he'd finally reached the pinnacle of his ambitions: prime ministers and presidents took his calls, and claimed him as a friend. He received a hero's funeral in Israel and was buried on the Mount of Olives; world figures clamoured to send their tributes.

But then the news broke that the MGN pension fund had been plundered – something that caused saturated media coverage at the time, and has been revisited several times since, including in a 2006 BBC drama, *Maxwell*, starring David Suchet, who was quite brilliant in the eponymous role. The banks were circling his collapsing empire and he would have certainly gone to prison, with no hope of fighting his way back. Andrea, the woman he was infatuated with, had rejected his approaches and he was in poor health. The waters of the Mediterranean must have seemed suddenly inviting.

In my own life I'd gradually got the wind up with what Blair and Brown were doing to the country. I had not developed a sudden affection for the Conservatives, but they did seem to be part of the real world in comparison to the economic fantasies of 'ending boom and bust' cooked up by Brown, Balls and Milliband. Lunching with John Penrose one day, I met his friend Angie Bray, the prospective Member of Parliament for Ealing. After we'd discussed the appalling policies of Brown, she said, 'Why don't you do something about it?'

'What can I do?' I answered.

'Write a piece for my election pamphlet saying why you're going to vote Conservative.'

At that point I hadn't actually decided to vote for her. I never thought I could ever bring myself to vote Tory. I wrestled with it for a long time and finally decided that it would be dishonest not to stick with what I now believed: the Labour Party was not fit to govern.

The *Daily Mail* picked up on the pamphlet and asked me to write a longer piece for the paper. Still with a reluctant heart, I did so. The reaction was immediate: Tory leader David Cameron asked me if I would appear on a platform with him supporting his efforts to get people to switch from voting Labour to voting Conservative.

I did so, although it felt very odd to be greeted and made to feel welcome by people I'd always considered to be on the other side of the hill. After the election I received a handwritten letter from David Cameron, thanking me. I was flattered that he'd taken the time. I don't know how he'll finally end up, but he certainly has the best manners on any of the prime ministers I've met.